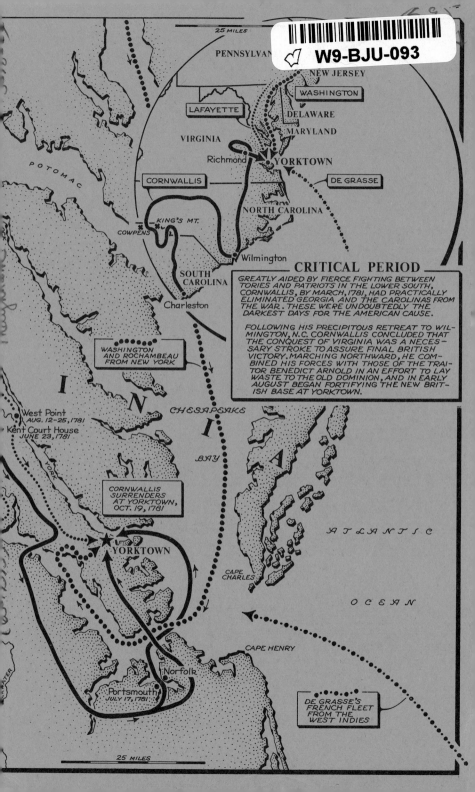

25 MILES

PENNSYLVAN

NEW JERSEY

WASHINGTON

LAFAYETTE

DELAWARE

MARYLAND

VIRGINIA

Richmond YORKTOWN

P O T O M A C

CORNWALLIS

DE GRASSE

NORTH CAROLINA

KING'S MT.

COWPENS

Wilmington

SOUTH
CAROLINA

Charleston

CRITICAL PERIOD

GREATLY AIDED BY FIERCE FIGHTING BETWEEN
TORIES AND PATRIOTS IN THE LOWER SOUTH,
CORNWALLIS, BY MARCH, 1781, HAD PRACTICALLY
ELIMINATED GEORGIA AND THE CAROLINAS FROM
THE WAR. THESE WERE UNDOUBTEDLY THE
DARKEST DAYS FOR THE AMERICAN CAUSE.

FOLLOWING HIS PRECIPITOUS RETREAT TO WIL-
MINGTON, N.C. CORNWALLIS CONCLUDED THAT
THE CONQUEST OF VIRGINIA WAS A NECES-
SARY STROKE TO ASSURE FINAL BRITISH
VICTORY. MARCHING NORTHWARD, HE COM-
BINED HIS FORCES WITH THOSE OF THE TRAI-
TOR BENEDICT ARNOLD IN AN EFFORT TO LAY
WASTE TO THE OLD DOMINION, AND IN EARLY
AUGUST BEGAN FORTIFYING THE NEW BRIT-
ISH BASE AT YORKTOWN.

WASHINGTON
AND ROCHAMBEAU
FROM NEW YORK

I

N

C H E S A P E A K E

West Point
AUG. 12-25, 1781

Kent Court House
JUNE 23, 1781

BAY

I

A

YORK

CORNWALLIS
SURRENDERS
AT YORKTOWN,
OCT. 19, 1781

A T L A N T I C

YORKTOWN

CAPE
CHARLES

O C E A N

CAPE HENRY

Norfolk

Portsmouth
JULY 17, 1781

DE GRASSE'S
FRENCH FLEET
FROM THE
WEST INDIES

25 MILES

✪ BEAT THE LAST DRUM

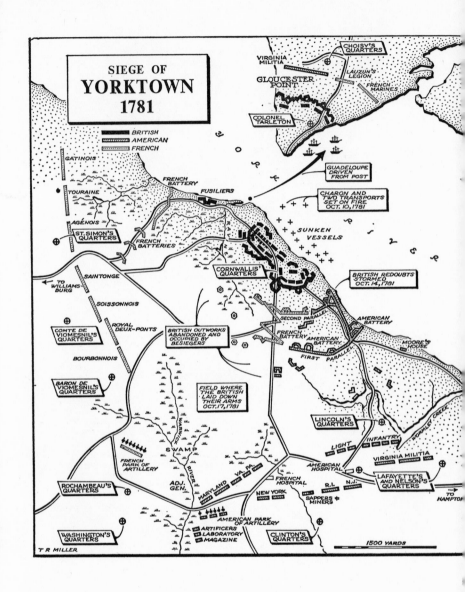

SIEGE OF
YORKTOWN
1781

BRITISH
AMERICAN
FRENCH

CHOISY'S QUARTERS

VIRGINIA MILITIA

GLOUCESTER POINT

LAUZUN'S LEGION

FRENCH MARINES

COLONEL TARLETON

GATINOIS

TOURAINE

FRENCH BATTERY

FUSILIERS

GUADELOUPE DRIVEN FROM POST

CHARON AND TWO TRANSPORTS SET ON FIRE OCT. 10, 1781

AGÉNOIS

ST. SIMON'S QUARTERS

FRENCH BATTERIES

SUNKEN VESSELS

SAINTONGE

CORNWALLIS' QUARTERS

BRITISH REDOUBTS STORMED OCT. 14, 1781

TO WILLIAMS-BURG

SOISSONNOIS

ROYAL DEUX-PONTS

COMTE DE VIOMESNIL'S QUARTERS

BRITISH OUTWORKS ABANDONED AND OCCUPIED BY BESIEGERS

SECOND PARALLEL

FRENCH BATTERY

AMERICAN BATTERY

AMERICAN BATTERY

MOORE'S HOUSE

BOURBONNOIS

FIRST PARALLEL

BARON DE VIOMESNIL'S QUARTERS

FIELD WHERE THE BRITISH LAID DOWN THEIR ARMS OCT. 17, 1781

WORMLEY CREEK

LINCOLN'S QUARTERS

SWAMP

FRENCH PARK OF ARTILLERY

WARWICK RIVER

LIGHT INFANTRY

VIRGINIA MILITIA

AMERICAN HOSPITAL

LAFAYETTE'S AND NELSON'S QUARTERS

ROCHAMBEAU'S QUARTERS

ADJ. GEN.

VA. PA.

MARYLAND

NEW YORK

FRENCH HOSPITAL

R.I.

N.J.

TO HAMPTON

WASHINGTON'S QUARTERS

AMERICAN PARK OF ARTILLERY

ARTIFICERS
LABORATORY
MAGAZINE

SAPPERS MINERS

CLINTON'S QUARTERS

1500 YARDS

T R MILLER

BEAT THE LAST DRUM

THE SIEGE OF YORKTOWN, 1781

BY THOMAS J. FLEMING

ST MARTIN'S PRESS ☆ NEW YORK

✪ CONTENTS

★ BEAT THE LAST DRUM

★✩✩✩✩✩✩✩✩✩✩✩✩✩✩✩✩

In the chill dawn of May 25, 1781, just outside the town of York, Pennsylvania, a bleary boy staggered from his tent and began beating a familiar tattoo on the big painted drum dangling from his left hip. Out of other tents on the sloping hillsides of the lovely valley stumbled soldiers by the dozens, then hundreds. Some cursed the drummer for a fool, swearing it was not dawn yet. Others cursed the sentry who had awakened the drummer. In the Continental Army of the United States of America, dawn was defined as the moment when a sentry could see a thousand yards—a judgment inevitably open to endless dispute. The cursing voices were an international mixture of American twang, German guttural and Irish brogue.

Five minutes of groping for shoes, kicking awake the slow

risers, and the sun peered redly over the low hills. Company cooks went to work; the men crowded around the fires, watching the day's bread being baked, complaining about the miserable food they had had yesterday. Officers passed among them warning everyone not to straggle. The brigade was to be paraded in an hour. When the drummer went to work again, beating the signal to fall in, the men seized their muskets, their cartridge boxes and knapsacks, and in a matter of seconds were ready for review by Brigadier General Anthony Wayne.

At thirty-six the stocky, handsome Wayne had a reputation as a fighting general which few could surpass. Called "Mad Anthony" by his men and "The Modern Hero" by his fellow officers, he was famous for the fury with which he led his troops to the charge. The capture of the British fort at Stony Point on the Hudson in a night assault, having attacked with bayonets only, was his best known exploit, but he had fought equally well in other battles. Discipline and courage were Wayne's two watchwords; at Stony Point officers had orders to execute any soldier who showed a sign of cowardice. At the same time, Wayne had a genuine affection for his men, and had been known to arrest and reprimand lieutenants who abused or struck a soldier needlessly.

For the troops confronting him now, Wayne had a special affection. These were the men of the Pennsylvania Line, soldiers of his own state, who had followed him into the thunderous fog at Germantown to rout some of the best regiments in the British army, and slugged these same haughty professionals to an exhausted draw at Monmouth. Their uniforms left something to be desired; most were patched, ripped, threadbare. Many were without shoes. But they handled their guns with the assurance and pride of veterans. Even the scattering of new recruits had profited from the weeks of drill and discipline which Wayne had given them while waiting for the equipment, ammunition and uniforms the Pennsylvania Assembly had promised but never delivered.

Now they could wait no longer. With or without shoes and new uniforms, they had to march. Grimly, knowing they would dislike the news, Wayne told them they were going south. Much as they hated the climate, they were needed there. In Virginia, a British army was looting and burning the richest of the united American states, practically unopposed. Eventually they might go even farther south, into the Carolinas and Georgia, where General Nathanael Greene commanded another tiny American army, which was struggling to regain these three colonies recently ripped from the American union by the soldiers of George III.

The war, which had begun as an impulsive, emotional revolt of a goaded people, had lasted a long time. Six years had worn away the first proud flush of nationhood, turned stale the high talk about freedom and rights, and made even honest men wonder about the wisdom of generals who won one battle and lost two. Not victory, but The Victory, was what every man panted after now. The leaders knew it; Wayne, who was always close to his men, probably knew it better than the other generals. But the leaders also knew something else, that the average soldier could not know. Never had The Victory been closer. The enemy was as tired as they were. Struggling to control an immense sweep of continent, he was even more vulnerable to a single decisive blow. Perhaps it could be struck in Virginia. It was easy enough for a general with Wayne's ability to study a map and see how this British army that was marauding through the state could be pinned against the coast by a swift concentration of American strength. But if these dreams of future glory were in Wayne's mind, they vanished in the appalling reaction of his men to the news that they were marching south.

Out of the packed companies came a barrage of shouts. "Don't march. We won't march until we get our money.

Where's the money you promised us? And the shoes? And the shirts? Don't march. We won't march. Not a man will march."

For a moment Wayne stood frozen with horror. It was happening again. Despite the May sunshine, his thoughts were catapulted back to the nightmare of the previous January when the Pennsylvania Line had erupted from their winter camp in Morristown, killed officers who resisted them, and had begun a march on Philadelphia, where they intended to settle their grievances with the Continental Congress at the points of their bayonets. It was an event which more than a few Americans had dreaded, and when it came, the Congress—and all of Philadelphia—was swept by wild panic. No one could deny that the men had grievances. For three years, they had bled on a dozen battlefields and starved in such winter quarters as Valley Forge, while their civilian compatriots ate well before their warm fires. For this they received $20 a month in collapsed Continental currency worth $1200 to one dollar of "hard money." Only Wayne's cool courage had saved the Revolutionary Army from turning into an armed rabble. At the risk of their lives, he and Colonels Richard Butler and Walter Stewart stayed with the enraged troops for six days, and finally persuaded them to camp outside Princeton. There the President of the Pennsylvania Assembly, Joseph Reed, negotiated with a committee of sergeants, and gave them almost everything they demanded, including back pay, provisions, and the right to discharge, if they had served three years or more. The disheartened Wayne had watched his beloved Line dissolve before his eyes. But he knew it was better than letting the soldiers dictate terms to the Congress itself—an example which every other unit in the American army might immediately have been tempted to follow.

A month later, Wayne had been ordered to York, there to recruit a new Pennsylvania Line. Amazingly, a large proportion of the discharged men responded to their general's call, while new recruits proved discouragingly scarce. But the old wounds were foolishly opened by Pennsylvania's state government, which casually promised the men that they would be paid in hard money—and then handed Wayne nothing but the worthless paper from the state's own printing presses, which had less backing than Continental dollars. Even the bounties paid to the men by the enlistment auditors had depreciated, by the time they received them, to one-seventh of their nominal value. "This was an alarming circumstance," Wayne admitted. "The soldiery too keenly felt the imposition."

The citizens of York were no help. They refused to part with even a cup of milk for paper money, and openly told the men that they were fools to take it, and greater fools if they marched before justice had been done to them. Having revolted once, and forced the civil authorities to humiliating surrender, the men saw no reason why they should not try it again. But this time Wayne was ready for them.

The moment the shouting began he ordered them to their tents. Not a man moved. But by now the general and his officers were able to detect the leading mutineers, all strategically placed on the right of each of the six regiments. Wayne snarled another order, and the officers, their sidearms drawn, rushed the men, knocked a few of them flat with the butts of their guns, and dragged a total of six ringleaders in front of the brigade. Wayne ordered a court martial on the spot.

While the appalled regiments watched, a board of officers was appointed, the charges were heard, and the men were condemned to death. Grimly, Wayne ordered the sentence to be executed immediately. "The particular messmates of the culprits were their executioners," the saturnine Wayne reported. "While the tears rolled down their cheeks in showers, they silently and faithfully obeyed their orders without a

moment's hesitation." One by one the men had handkerchiefs bound around their eyes, knelt on the spring earth,
and the platoons marched up on order and fired a volley into
their backs.

A fifer in one regiment, Samuel Dewees, remembered the
horror of the scene years later. "The distance that the platoons stood from them at the time they fired could not have
been more than ten feet. So near did they stand that the
handkerchiefs covering the eyes of some of them were set on
fire." One man's head was "literally blown in fragments from
his body. . . . The fence and even the heads of rye for some
distance within the field were covered with the blood and
brains." Wayne and his officers watched this horror with impassive faces. After the first four were killed, the general
ordered the executioners back into the ranks, and pardoned
the last two mutineers. Then he ordered the entire brigade
to march past the mangled, still bleeding bodies, single file.
The next morning Wayne marched south with 800 men, all,
in the words of one observer, "mute as fish."

Everything about the abortive mutiny was ominous—but it
was no more ominous than the dozen other signs of mounting
disintegration in the American ranks. Only a few days before,
at the headquarters of the Continental Army in Peekskill,
N.Y., George Washington had written in his diary a cry of
soldierly despair.

> Instead of having magazines filled with provisions, we
> have a scant pittance, scattered here and there in different
> states. Instead of having our arsenals filled with military
> stores, they are poorly provided, and the workmen are leav-
> ing them. . . . Instead of having the regiments completed,
> scarcely any state has an eighth part of its quota in the field,
> and there is little prospect of getting more than half. In a
> word, instead of having everything in readiness to take the
> field, we have nothing. And instead of having the prospect of
> a glorious offensive campaign before us, have a gloomy and

bewildered prospect of a defensive one. Chimney corner patriots abound; venality, corruption, prostitution of office for selfish ends, abuse of trust, perversion of funds from a national to a private use, and speculations upon the necessities of the times pervade all interests. . . .

Never, not even in the depths of the black winter of 1776 or the following year's travail at Valley Forge, had America's revolutionary spirit ebbed so low. The people were sick of the war. The Continental Congress was bankrupt. For a year and a half, British armies had rampaged through the South, subduing Georgia so totally that the colony now had a royal Governor once more, and annihilating two American armies totalling 12,000 men. The French alliance, which had promised so much in 1778, had proved to be only one more disappointment.

Everywhere there was talk of peace. The family quarrel over local taxation in British North America had become a world war with the entry of France and then Spain on the side of the rebellious colonies. French expeditions hounded the English in Africa and supported native uprisings in India, while Spain poured shot and shell on Gibraltar. But the global eruption of blood and death was ending in a dull stalemate. Minor French successes in India and the West Indies were cancelled by British successes in America, and by French and Spanish naval failures in European waters. More important, France, the treasurer for her side of the struggle, was close to bankruptcy.

No one knew all this better than an excitable young French nobleman, who sweated in a stifling tent on Virginia's South Anna River awaiting the arrival of Anthony Wayne and his Pennsylvanians. Marie Joseph Paul Yves Roch Gilbert du Motier, better known as the Marquis de Lafayette, was twenty-three and a major general in the Continental Army. Scion of one of France's wealthiest families (at four-

teen his income was 25,000 pounds a year), married at sixteen to the beautiful Adrienne de Noailles, daughter of one
of France's most powerful men, this headstrong reserve captain in the French army had defied the King of France himself, escaped a police search, and sailed to America in 1777
to offer his services to the struggling revolutionaries. His appointment as major general, when he was a mere nineteen,
appalled Washington. But the young nobleman's modesty,
wit and bravery (he was badly wounded at the Battle of
Brandywine) soon won the commander in chief's deepest
affection.

A combination of accidents had put Lafayette in charge
of defending Virginia against a British army which outnumbered him five to one. For a month he had marched and
countermarched, sending frantic demands to the Virginia
Assembly for militia, frenetic pleas to Congress for food, ammunition, clothing and frolicsome letters to his friends
in America and France describing his first adventure as a
commanding officer. To his friend Alexander Hamilton he
wrote: "To speak truth, I am afraid of myself as much as of
the enemy. Independence has rendered me the more cautious as I know my warmth." To his brother-in-law, the Vicomte de Noailles, stationed with the French at Newport, he
worried about the effect his campaign would have on his
military reputation. "I ask no better than to be blamed, and
shall plead guilty of lack of talent, lack of experience or even
of both; but as my numerical inferiority is immense, and our
difficulties indescribable, I hope that you will tell our friends
what you know about them, so that if condemned, I shall at
least be condemned only in so far as I deserve."

At the same time, he was not too busy to worry about the
current gossip in Paris. He fumed over a song some wit had
written about his erstwhile passion for the beautiful Madame de Hunolstein. In the next letter he was back to lament-
ing his deplorable military weakness. "I am not even strong

enough to get beaten," he moaned to General Nathanael Greene, whose army in Carolina was not much bigger than Lafayette's.

At a glance, a lad of twenty-three might seem to be the worst possible choice to defend Washington's home state against British invaders. Actually, no one was more strategically situated to understand the crucial condition of the Revolution and what was needed to salvage victory. Lafayette was keenly aware that appearances now counted almost as much as realities. A year and a half before, on a visit to France, he had urged on all his friends in the royal court at Versailles the need to act, to create at least the impression of a victory. He offered to lead an expedition against the English coasts and hold selected cities for ransom. "Every day that defers the news of a success which can be flaunted in America," he argued, "is a day which does us great harm in that country."

Now, in Virginia, he was still pursuing the same policy. "It appears to me," he wrote to the Duc de Luzerne, the French Ambassador to America, "that the enemy want to create the impression that the states of the South belong to them. Lord Cornwallis in one of his letters puts that idea forward as a matter quite well settled. My conduct in relation to him has been based upon the same political motives. When he changes his position, I try to give to his movements the appearance of a retreat. God grant that there be an opportunity to give to them the appearance of a defeat."

"My heart beats," he said in the same letter to the French ambassador, "when I think of the treaty of peace. On the one hand, I see America independent. I see the ambassador of England paying his respects to the ambassador of the United States. I see all the English biting their lips whenever by chance the name of America . . . is pronounced. I see Frenchmen and Americans marching arm in arm in foreign countries, passing by the English in attendance. In short, there are a thousand little pleasures that I promise myself exclusive of the great end of the revolution. But on the other hand, I feel that I would consent to an eternal silence rather than say 'the English colony of Georgia or of Carolina.' Even in writing it I experience the uneasiness of a man who blasphemes for the first time."

Unfortunately, not all of Lafayette's fellow Frenchmen felt the same tremulous enthusiasm for American independence. The lean, hollow-cheeked Comte de Vergennes, the French foreign minister, had brought France into the war for one reason, to redress the balance of power between France and England, which had swung overwhelmingly in Britain's favor after the Seven Years' War, in which France had lost Canada, most of her influence in India, and some of the choicest West Indian islands. But Vergennes knew from the start the parlous state of the French treasury, perniciously anemic from a century of warfare, and he had gambled on the success of a limited effort in America. It was now time to call in the bets, and see how much he was ahead.

In February of 1781, Vergennes had dictated and placed in his files a totally secret memorandum. It was his way of talking to himself. In it he outlined a way to end the war with what the twentieth century would call a summit conference of European powers. It would meet in Vienna, and the mediators would be the ministers of Austria-Hungary and Russia. To it might also be brought the ministers of the Netherlands, and perhaps Sweden, who depended almost totally on French financial and military support for their regimes. Then would come the belligerents, France, Spain, England—and the Americans.

The summit conference would then proceed to that horse-trading of islands, duchies, colonies and fishing rights which was the standard business of European diplomacy. Each belligerent, as well as each mediator, was prepared to lose a little and gain a little. But the Americans were the real reason for the conference, and they, with no interest in Europe's balance of power, only wanted one thing—independence. This was precisely what they were not going to get. According to Vergennes' plan, the conference would "arrange" a truce between colonies and mother country. It would be a truce which accepted the fortunes of war, as they stood at the beginning of 1781. This meant that British forces possessed the ports and much of the interior of North Carolina, South Carolina and Georgia. They possessed New York and Long Island and, occupying the mouth of the Penobscot River, could argue that they controlled almost all of Maine. Inland, they had garrisons in forts at Lake Champlain, Niagara, Detroit and elsewhere, enabling them to claim control of the area which now includes the states of Minnesota, Wisconsin, Northern Illinois, Northern Indiana, Michigan, Northern Ohio, Northwestern New York and Northern Vermont.

Coolly surveying the prospects of such an offer, Vergennes was honest enough to admit it would be a complete abdication of all the promises that France had made to America, when they signed their treaty of alliance in 1778. But this did not disturb the French foreign minister. Diplomacy would permit the desertion to be made in the most acceptable style. "One may presume to say that the King would be lacking in delicacy, that he would be somewhat violating his engagements, that he would be giving the Americans just cause for complaint or at least distrust, if he should propose to Congress to sign a truce leaving the English what they possess on the continent. Therefore only the mediators, bound by no such ties, could make a proposition so painful to the United States."

Would the Americans ever assent to such an offer, even when made by mediators, with all the panoply of Europe's power arrayed around them? The American minister plenipotentiary in charge of negotiating a treaty of peace was John Adams—a truculent Yankee with a healthy suspicion of

Vergennes' intentions. But this too was easily fixed. The suave Duc de Luzerne, French Ambassador to the Continental Congress had, thanks to his superb diplomatic skills, something very close to total control of this assembly. "Vergennes simply ordered Luzerne to get Adams' instructions changed, so that he would go to the Vienna summit conference with his hands tied, dressed for the slaughter. By June 15, 1781, a new peace commission, selected and instructed with more than a little attention to Vergennes' specifications, was en route to France.

Bankruptcy was not England's problem. Her fleets still ruled the seas more or less unchallenged, and this meant she remained the commercial mistress of Europe and the world. But she was no less hungry for peace for another reason. The American rebellion had created more political bitterness inside Great Britain than the nation had known since the sanguinary civil war of the previous century. Talented admirals and generals resigned rather than fight their "American brethren" and even the generals willing to serve against the contentious colonists were dubious servants, who had often voted down the government's aggressive policies in Parliament, and who led the King's armies with something less than all-out enthusiasm.

Moreover, arrayed against the government in Parliament were some of the best minds and sharpest tongues in British politics. Edmund Burke, the sonorous Irishman who had pleaded magnificently with Britain to conciliate America before it was too late; Charles James Fox, the erratic but gifted rake who could skewer blimpish Prime Minister Lord North with a sentence, and was not above wearing what looked very much like an American military uniform to Parliament to celebrate the British surrender at Saratoga in 1778; Colonel Isaac Barré, another thunderous Irishman, who had lost an eye fighting the French in America; Lord Shelburne, the most respected legal mind in the realm: all these were part of a ferociously vocal minority who never ceased crying out that England was fighting a fundamentally unjust war and could expect nothing from it but ruin.

Lord North himself had absolutely no faith in the war, and had already offered the Americans every concession short of independence, in a too little and too late attempt to stave off the French alliance. He regularly tried to resign, but was kept to his task at the helm by the one man in England who devoutly and wholeheartedly believed in the sanctity of the fight: George III. Thanks to the immense personal resources of the Crown, and an electoral system which cried out for democratic reform, George III was able to buy, cajole and threaten his way to complete control of Parliament, and to ignore the denunciations of his policies. But by 1781, there were ominous signs that the country was becoming restive.

Twice London city, repository of pro-American sentiment, had been swept by appalling riots, which sent the King's ministers fleeing for their lives, and left their houses, coaches and clubs in smouldering ruins. British troops had killed hundreds of Londoners in suppressing the riot of 1780 which began as an anti-Catholic demonstration and exploded into an orgy of all-out hostility against the Establishment. The financial impact of the war was serious, if not disastrous. All over the nation, merchants were being ruined by the savage inroads of American and French privateers. The staggering expense of maintaining armies and fleets in India, the West Indies, the Channel, the Mediterranean, and in America was beginning to make those tax-conscious country squires who constituted Parliament's independent bloc think twice about battling their American cousins over a threepence duty on tea.

Finally, the brilliant, intense Vergennes had scored a tremendous diplomatic coup in 1780, when he engineered the "League of Armed Neutrality"—a union of theoretically neutral European states including Russia—in what amounted to total defiance of Britain's policy of blockading all ships from the ports of her enemies. In earlier wars, London had rallied the rest of Europe against the threats of French domination. Englishmen found it an unnerving experience to be on the other end of the diplomatic gun, with most of the civilized world glowering at their riches and power with unconcealed envy.

So George III's ministers were more than willing to consider attending a peace conference which suggested an end to the war without conceding American independence. They would never be permitted by their royal master to so much as mention this hated word, independence. In this almost all Englishmen were strangely united—even the most extreme oppositionists saw independence as the dismemberment of the British Empire, and the death knell of England's greatness. But peace without independence, based on the current *status quo* in America, yes, the whispered word went out from Whitehall along the cordon of agents and spies linking France and England, yes, His Majesty's Government might be very willing to consider such an idea.

For his part, Washington knew some sort of peace conference was close, although he had no idea that independence was to be for sale at it. Peace was evidently much discussed at American headquarters. In June the general's aide, Tench Tilghman, wrote to his brother, assuring him that "the mediating princes will not find much difficulty in bringing the contending parties to terms." But Washington left diplomacy to the politicians. He was still fighting a war, and to remind France of this vital fact he had sent a special emissary to the court of Versailles with a warning that the Revolution might well collapse before any sort of peace was achieved, if the American Army did not get an immediate injection of money and equipment.

In choosing twenty-six-year-old John Laurens of South Carolina to bear this message, Washington might have seemed to have sent a boy on a man's errand. But this tall, almost too handsome cavalier had been educated in Geneva, Switzerland, by his wealthy father, and spoke fluent French. He had also spent a year studying law at London's Inner Temple. Most important, six years of defeat and frustration had failed to quench his revolutionary fervor. He was uniquely suited to shock the discouraged and weary French into one last effort to win the war.

Only a few days after he arrived in France on March 11, 1781, Laurens received a letter from Washington, which underscored the desperate necessity of his mission:

> Day does not follow night more certainly than it brings with it some additional proof of the impracticability of carrying on the war without the aids you were directed to solicit. As an honest and candid man, as a man whose all depends on the final and happy determination of the present contest, I assert this, while I give it decisively as my opinion that without a foreign loan our present force (which is but the remnant of an army) cannot be kept together this campaign, much less will it be increased and in readiness for another . . . We cannot transport the provisions from the States in which they are assessed to the army because we cannot pay the teamsters . . . Our troops are approaching fast to nakedness and . . . we have nothing to cloathe them with; our hospitals are without medicines and our sick without nutriment except such as well men eat . . . all our public works are at a stand and the artificers disbanding. But why need I run into detail, when it may be declared in a word, that we are at the end of our tether and that now or never our deliverance must come.

Small wonder that Laurens threw protocol aside and stormed Paris as if he were leading a bayonet charge. He was scarcely off the boat when he encountered the Marquis de Castries, the French Minister of Marine, on the road to the capital. Buttonholing the astonished nobleman in his carriage, Laurens made a fervent plea for a strong French fleet in American waters. De Castries haughtily informed him that the dispositions of the fleet were already made—and they were exclusively directed to the West Indies.

Laurens went on to Paris, where he coolly asked Vergennes for an immediate loan of twenty-five million livres, cash, plus immediate supplies of arms, ammunition, materials and clothing, equipment and tents. Vergennes tried to squelch him with the same wet blanket de Castries had used. "It is impossible for His Majesty to favor a loan in this kingdom," said the Count. "But in order to give proof of his friendship for the United States, he grants them as a donation a sum of six million livres tournois." This would seem to be generous, but Laurens knew Vergennes was reiterating a gift already promised to Ambassador Benjamin Franklin. The French government had by now advanced the Americans, in the form of loans, gifts and supplies, well over 100 million livres —about $25 million. Still Laurens told the Count "in the strongest terms the insufficiency of the above mentioned succor." He warned Vergennes that France was "in danger of losing all her past efforts in favor of America unless the requests were complied with."

Vergennes took a very dim view of this high-pressure diplomacy, and let Benjamin Franklin know it. The aging Ambassador totally agreed with the French minister. "I believe," he wrote agitatedly from Passy, "there is hardly another instance in the world of people risking their credit so much who unfortunately have so little and who must by this proceeding, if continued, soon have none at all. This Court is our firm friend, but the best friends may be wearied by too frequent & unexpected demands."

Franklin was undoubtedly right. Vergennes was certainly justified in his pique at Laurens' insistent demands. But desperate men are entitled to do almost anything—and neither the minister in the vast palace at Versailles nor the American sage in his comfortable house in Passy could share the images which haunted Laurens' mind: sick soldiers begging in the streets, maddened men murdering each other in the January snow. He had to get the money!

For six weeks, Laurens ran from Vergennes to Franklin, always insisting, finally pleading, and getting nothing but words for his efforts. His secretary, William Jackson, recounted the climax—when Laurens finally exploded. Vergennes, after hearing the young southerner one more time, "in a manner at once smiling and sarcastic, observed: 'Colonel Laurens, you are so recently from Headquarters of the American Army that you forget that you are no longer delivering the orders of the Commander in Chief, but you are addressing the minister of a monarch who has every disposition to favor your country."

Laurens leaped to his feet. "Favor, sir! The respect which I owe my country will not admit the term—say that the aid is mutual, and I cheerfully subscribe to the obligation. But as the last argument which I shall use with your Excellency; the sword which I now wear in defense of France as well as my own country, unless the succor I solicit is immediately accorded, I may be compelled to draw against France as a British subject."

Vergennes was so shocked by this threat he could hardly speak. Laurens then informed him that his next petition would be presented to the King in person, and departed.

Franklin was as horrified as Vergennes by Laurens' declaration. He declined to have anything to do with petitioning the King. But Laurens went ahead anyway. At a levee the following day, Laurens stepped forward to meet His Most Christian Majesty Louis XVI, surrounded by his glittering ministers and courtiers. Laurens in his simple uniform of buff and blue bowed to the young king, and then handed him a small scroll containing his special plea. The King stared at it, startled, then handed it to his Minister of War, the Comte de Ségur, who was standing nearby, and went on to greet other guests. Laurens probably thought he had failed again.

But the next morning, Laurens received a note from M. Necker, the Minister of Finance, requesting an interview at noon. With one bold stroke, the young American had broken through the Franklin-Vergennes impasse. The Finance Minister promised him liberal supplies and an immediate delivery of at least part of the cash he insisted on having. Vergennes of course was outraged that anyone should approach the King at a social gathering and attempt to open a business discussion with him. He wrote to Lafayette, telling him in very strong terms what he thought of his American friend's gaucherie. But having achieved his objective, Laurens was more than willing to apologize. He admitted he was "a soldier, little acquainted with the usages of courts, but warmly attached to his country."

He then went to work, and in a month of furious activity rounded up 2,289,109 livres worth of supplies and 2,300,224 livres in cash. He also negotiated a loan of 10 million livres from Holland, which France agreed to guarantee. Franklin, finally impressed, admitted to Congress: "His indefatigable endeavors have brought the good dispositions of this court to a more speedy addition than could well have been expected so soon after the former grant."

Laurens found time in the midst of his feverish diplomacy for a touching personal interlude. During his year in London, he had married "Patty" Manning, the daughter of his father's English partner. A daughter had been born after he sailed to join Washington's army. Mrs. Laurens had made countless plans to join her husband in America, but her delicate health made the journey impossible. Laurens must have smuggled her a letter about his coming to France, and she and her daughter in turn smuggled themselves across the English Channel and joined the young colonel in Paris. It was a long, difficult journey, made at considerable risk. John

Laurens' father, the former President of the Continental Congress, was a prisoner in the Tower of London. (He had been captured en route to negotiate a Dutch loan, and only American threats of reprisal saved him from being hanged, drawn and quartered.) Young Laurens himself was engaged in fundamental sabotage of His Majesty's hopes of victory; yet in the finest traditions of romance, Patty Laurens ignored the English spies and informers swarming in Paris and in the channel ports, and rushed to her soldier.

They did not have much time together. On May 28, while Lafayette was sweating out the fortunes of war in Virginia, Laurens sailed from Brest with his desperately needed cash and supplies. Even more important, he had had word from the French ministry that the West Indies fleet had been ordered to proceed to the American coast sometime during the summer months. Perfectionist that he was, Laurens was probably discouraged by the things he had not accomplished. He had nowhere near the 25 million livres he had been sent to get. Nor could he claim full credit for the naval decision; Lafayette, Washington and others had written letters begging for ships, and the naval order as it now stood was vague. But he no doubt consoled himself with the thought that small favors were better than none at all.

This distant diplomacy was totally remote to Lafayette's little army of 1,000 weary American light infantrymen in Virginia. All they knew was the humiliating experience of marching south to fight and deciding to run when they got a good look at the size of their opponent. Such activity was especially painful to veteran troops, which is what they were, almost to a man. Mostly New Englanders, they had marched to Virginia reluctantly. Near Baltimore, Lafayette had had to hang one deserter and dismiss another from the service. When desertions continued, he announced that anyone who wanted to return north had only to apply for a pass. As for himself, he was going to Virginia to fight. Thereafter, Lafayette recalled proudly in his memoirs, "all desertions ceased." But the first weeks of the campaign were inglorious. By the end of May the Yankees had retreated over 100 miles in a winding twisting trail from Williamsburg all the way to Fredericksburg, Maryland, while the British harassed and burned and raided as far as Richmond and beyond, as if an American army did not even exist.

The Virginia legislature had been sent scurrying into the woods by the unexpected appearance of British cavalry on the outskirts of Charlottesville, whence the lawmakers had retreated for security. Governor Thomas Jefferson had joined them in ignominious flight a half-hour later, as the dragoons thundered up to Monticello. The sky over Richmond was the color of ink for days, as 2,000 hogsheads of precious tobacco, needed to finance the war, went up in smoke. Stores of clothing, harness, salt and other provisions destined for the American army in the Carolinas were seized and destroyed, along with 5,000 muskets and 600 barrels of powder. The state was almost totally demoralized, its citizens cowed, its militia afraid to show their faces. Criticism of Lafayette was heard everywhere, as if the Marquis had thousands of men he was deliberately holding back to let the British win. The old animosity for the French even reappeared. A Virginia militia officer wrote, "I fear the Marquis may lose his credit. Deserters, British, cringing Dutchmen and busy little Frenchmen swarm about HdQuarters. The people do not love Frenchmen; every person they can't understand they take for a Frenchman."

To the disgruntled Virginians, foreigners seemed to have taken over their revolution and were botching the job. Before Lafayette arrived, the state had been in the hands of Baron Friedrich von Steuben, and he too had won nothing but obloquy and condemnations from the natives. The truth was that the Baron and the Marquis were both trying to fight a war, while the Virginians seemed intent on doing everything but that one supreme task. Thomas Jefferson, brilliant theorist of the Declaration of Independence, was a disaster as the state's wartime governor. Instead of organizing the Old Dominion's resources on an emergency basis, he had concentrated on building an ideal government where nothing was done without the consent of the governed. As a result, Virginia, with 50,000 militia on her rolls, was unable to repulse 900 British under traitor Benedict Arnold, when they came to raid in late 1780.

Steuben, a veteran of twenty-seven years of warfare on the continent, had been driven almost to distraction by the chaos Jefferson created. While the Governor bemoaned the people's "lack of virtue," the Baron had frantically tried to raise recruits, and organize some sort of defense against the British. Nobody paid the slightest attention to his instructions to build forts on the James River to prevent its use as a British highway; he could get neither recruits nor equipment. He rode to one barracks where he was told 500 men would be waiting and instead found five, three of whom deserted the next day. By March 30, 1781, he was writing to Nathanael Greene in Carolina: "I am not less tired of this state than they are of me."

The Baron finally managed to scrape together 450 men, "more ragamuffins than soldiers," and began training them in the classic discipline he had imparted to the whole American army at Valley Forge. By this time his temper, for which he was justly famous, had become volcanic. When the British made a lunge in his direction, the old Prussian wisely decided to retreat into Carolina and join forces with Nathanael Greene. As they were moving down the road from Point of Fork where the Rivanna River met the James, a good-looking man rode up and introduced himself to the Baron. He said he had brought him a recruit.

"I thank you, sir," the Baron said, "with all my heart. He has arrived in a happy moment. Where is he?"

Whereupon the man, who was a colonel of the local militia, presented a boy who could not have been more than twelve years old. If the Baron accepted him, this meant under Virginia law, that the colonel would be exempt from military duty. The Baron got off his horse, and examined the lad. He told him to step out of his shoes, and found them stuffed with paper to make him look taller.

The veteran of Europe's battlefields patted the boy on the head and looked up at the militia colonel. "Sir," said the Baron, "you think me a rascal?"

"Oh, no, Baron, I don't," the man replied.

"Then, Sir, I think you are one, an infamous scoundrel thus to attempt to cheat your country!" He whirled to the officers around him. "Take off this fellow's spurs. Place him in the ranks and tell General Greene from me that I have sent him a man able to serve instead of an infant whom he would basely have made his substitute. Go, my boy, carry the colonel's horses and spurs to his wife. Make my respects to her and tell her that her husband has gone to fight as an honest citizen should for the liberty of his country."

The Virginians, seething over such treatment, accused the Baron of cowardice because of his retreat from Point of Fork, condemned him in the State Assembly, and sent a delegation to Lafayette, demanding an investigation. Lafayette accepted their version of the story, and wrote a "private" letter to Washington, attacking the Prussian drillmaster for military ineptitude. Only when Steuben marched his 450 recruits into Lafayette's camp, and explained his conduct personally did the young Marquis realize that he had accused the Baron wrongly.

But relations between the boyish Frenchman and the Prussian veteran did not improve with the removal of this misunderstanding. Both were acutely aware that the Baron had been fighting battles when Lafayette was yet unborn, and it was more than a little difficult for the Marquis to be the ranking major general. A few days after he arrived in camp, Steuben asked permission to retire to a country house to regain his health; a severe skin infection and an attack of the gout were incapacitating him. Lafayette instantly gave him permission to depart. "The hatred of Virginians toward him was truly hurtful of the cause," he wrote to his friend Alexander Hamilton.

Not many weeks after he arrived in Virginia, Lafayette's own personal stock had sunk almost as low as Steuben's. He too was hamstrung by the state's revolutionary laws, which guaranteed the citizens so many rights no one could force them to contribute as much as an ear of corn to the war effort. By now Thomas Jefferson had resigned in favor of energetic militia general Thomas Nelson, but not even Nelson could make up for four years of inertia and disorganization. He and Lafayette were soon quarreling bitterly over the Marquis' habit of commandeering state supplies for his Continentals.

It was a mad way to fight a war, and Lafayette soon gave up on the Virginians and began sending frantic appeals to Wayne to come quickly with his Pennsylvanians. "On their arrival we shall be in a position to be beaten more decently," he said.

He did not realize this was a prophecy. When Wayne finally joined him on June 10, bringing the Marquis' force of regular troops to over 1,900 plus about 2,000 militia, Lafayette was already confronted by the puzzle of what, to his eyes, looked like a British retreat. Abandoning their previous interest in bringing the Americans to battle, the 5,000 man British army was falling back toward the Virginia coast. Had the junction with Wayne frightened the enemy with rumors of potent reinforcements? It was hard to say, but Wayne and Lafayette decided to follow the redcoats, both to find out what they were planning, and to make it look as if the valiant Americans were pursuing the foe with the ardor and confidence of victors.

To keep up with the British and to avoid showing their weakness, Lafayette and Wayne marched by night. Sleep became a rarity for the weary men, and their diaries began to record their disgust with the seemingly aimless tramping. On the fourteenth of June, Lieutenant William Feltman of the Pennsylvania Line noted grimly: "Marched through a d——— poor country, the water being very scarce. This day see a number of Negroes, the greater part of them being naked."

The Northerners were fascinated by Virginians and their folkways. Lieutenant Feltman noted that "a person can scarcely discern any part of them but the nose and eyes, as they have themselves muffled up with linens, etc., in order to prevent the sun from burning their faces—I mean the female sex. At the same time they will have a number of black around them, all naked, nothing to hide their nakedness. You can easily distinguish their sex, I mean the blacks." Less pleasant was the British habit of leaving Negroes dying of smallpox on the roads in order, Lieutenant Feltman was convinced, "to prevent the Virginia militia from pursuing them; left numbers in that condition, starving and helpless, begging of us as we passed them for God's sake to kill them, as they were in great pain and misery."

For others in Lafayette's little army, the march began to take on all the reality of a pursuit. On June 17, Lieutenant Colonel Francis Barber wrote his wife: "We have as yet had no action with the enemy. They have made a third tack, and are now at Richmond. Their behavior wears the appearance of a retreat. Since my last we are re-enforced very considerably—Wayne has come with three battalions. We now begin to imagine ourselves a match for the enemy, and unless they receive re-enforcements they must undoubtedly retire to Portsmouth. From the most accurate intelligence the enemy are about 4000 strong, and we expect within three or four days to have that number of militia."

Lafayette and Wayne soon became as convinced as Barber that the enemy was running away from them, and all the Marquis' resolutions about caution began to evaporate. Dr. James McHenry, one of Washington's ex-aides who was now serving Lafayette in the same capacity, began to worry. He wrote an anxious letter to Nathanael Greene, pointing out that "Wayne was impetuous, and the Marquis loved glory." McHenry begged Greene to confirm his warning to avoid a battle "with as much expedition as possible . . . lest military ardor should be too powerful for reason." Greene advised McHenry to keep to his task of reining in Lafayette. "You are useful to him in moderating his military ardor, which no doubt is heated by the fire of the Modern Hero [Wayne] who by the by is an excellent officer."

Lafayette, meanwhile, was stewing because he had not heard a word from Washington in weeks. The friendship between the boyish French nobleman and the reserved middle-aged Virginia planter seems improbable at first. Many think Lafayette was the son Washington wanted so badly but never had. And the Marquis, orphaned at ten, found in Washington a unique father. Whatever the explanation, the emotion between the two men was deep and true, and Lafayette was justly puzzled by his general's long silence. Finally, on June 18, a weary messenger came pounding into camp with duplicates of two letters Washington had mailed over a month before.

Both had been intercepted by the British. It was another small but painful reminder of the sinking cause. With their superiority in cavalry and money, the British had no trouble capturing American military dispatches and letters. A year before, Washington had set up a series of expresses, which would have been guarded by armed escorts, but had soon had to abandon them because of the shortage of money. This meant that the army had to rely on the regular postal service, never knowing when a rider had been bribed by the British to make duplicates of military mail, or when the mail was intercepted and sold to the British by loyalists.

The first of the intercepted letters was a routine official message, complimenting the Marquis on his widsom in fighting a purely defensive, supercautious war. There was nothing in it to excite British eyes. But the second letter was personal and Lafayette saw at a glance that its interception was nothing short of disaster. In it, Washington had outlined his plans for the coming campaign. He told of meeting the French generals at Wethersfield, Connecticut, on May 21, and discussing the prospects for striking a strong blow at the British during the coming summer months.

> Upon a full consideration of our affairs in every point of view, an attempt upon New York with its present garrison (which by estimation is reduced to 4500 regular troops and 3,000 irregulars) was deemed preferable to a Southern operation as we had not the command of the water. The reasons which induced this determination were, the danger to be apprehended from the approaching heats, the inevitable dissipation and loss of Men by so long a March and the difficulty of transportation; but above all, it was thought that we had a tolerable prospect of expelling the enemy or obliging them to withdraw part of their force from the Southward, which last would give the most effectual relief to those States. The French troops are to march this way as soon as certain circumstances will admit, leaving about 200 Men at Providence with the heavy stores and 500 Militia upon Rhode Island to secure the works.

The entire plan of battle was in British hands! In one stroke, the British had what they needed to frustrate American victory for another campaign—and Lafayette knew enough to suspect that there would be no more campaigns after this one. His desire to force the British to a battle on his own terms became even more intense. Victory, any kind of victory, even a newspaper victory, was what the Americans needed.

But the British had 800 cavalry to screen their flanks and rear. Lafayette could muster barely sixty horsemen. He tried the desperate maneuver of augmenting these by mounting light infantry behind his dragoons, though the double load, in the Virginia heat, was almost certain to exhaust the horses. But on June 26 it worked well enough to catch part of the British rear guard, commanded by Lieutenant Colonel John Graves Simcoe, on a raiding and foraging expedition some miles from the main army. A fierce skirmish erupted, and the Pennsylvanians, supported by Virginia militia, rushed to support the American horsemen.

Simcoe commanded a regiment known as the Queen's Rangers. More than half the men and a considerable portion of the officers were American born and had chosen the loyalist side of the Revolution. They were every bit as tough as their rebellious opponents, and for half an hour, a small and bloody civil war raged in the fields around the tavern known as Spencer's Ordinary, about six miles from Williamsburg. Simcoe had about 400 men, including 100 cavalry. He had been expecting an attack and had disposed his troops with considerable care.

When the American cavalry, led by Major William McPherson, appeared, Simcoe's trumpeter instantly sounded the alarm, and then shrewdly led the attackers in the direction of some infantry who were busy collecting local cattle. The Americans charged in, assuming they had caught the enemy totally unprepared. Before they reached the cattle drivers, the British cavalry hit them in the flank, and in Simcoe's words, "Broke them entirely." Major McPherson was flung from his horse by a saber stroke from a British sergeant, and crawled into a swamp, where he hid until the fight was over. The rest of the horsemen took to the woods, leaving nine men dead, fourteen wounded and fifteen prisoners on the field.

What was left of the cavalry was saved from the inevitable British pursuit by the arrival of the Amercan advance corps under Colonel Richard Butler. Both sides sent messengers rushing back to the main armies. Simcoe got about a hundred cattle and some wagons of forage moving down the road to British headquarters at Williamsburg. He then turned and ordered a frontal assault on the Americans, who had taken possession of a wood and a series of wooden fences facing the British position. The spirit with which the British fought is conveyed by Simcoe's words, in which he describes himself in the third person: "Lt. Col. Simcoe did not expect victory, but he was determined to try for it; his best hopes were to obtain and line the wood, checking the enemy's advance, till such times as the convoy was in security, and then to retreat. He had the most general and particular confidence in the officers and soldiers of his corps, who were disciplined enthusiasts in the cause of their country, and who having been ever victorious, thought it impossible to suffer defeat."

Simcoe had drawn off his cavalry behind a hill, out of American sight, and he now used them with crushing effect. As his infantry moved forward across the plowed fields, he saw a "considerable body" of American troops climbing over high fences into the road in order to get into the fields beyond it and flank the British advance. The colonel sent his horsemen thundering down the road, scattering the hapless infantrymen like leaves. The British footsoldiers gave a shout of victory, and charged in a body, driving the Americans helter-skelter from the woods and fences. Simcoe's second in command, Captain Ewald, turned the American left flank and his soldiers poured in a destructive volley "as they fled in the utmost confusion." So cool was the British advance that one officer, Lieutenant Charles Dunlop, who was a mere seventeen years of age, "led on his division on horseback without suffering a man to fire, watching the enemy, and giving a signal to his men to lay down whenever a party of theirs was about to fire; he arrived at the fence where the enemy had been posted with his arms loaded."

Knowing he might soon be opposed by the entire American army, Simcoe hastily drew off his attacking men and with thirty-two prisoners in his bag, retreated down the road to Williamsburg. Two miles back he met General Cornwallis and the bulk of the British army; they about-faced and returned to the field of battle, which Simcoe describes as littered with arms flung away by fleeing Americans. It was hardly a victory, but Lafayette decided to call it one. He wrote to Greene in the Carolinas, and to newly-elected Governor Thomas Nelson of Virginia, telling him that they had killed sixty of Simcoe's Rangers and wounded a hundred. Simcoe's version gives his casualties as ten killed, twenty-three wounded.

From the prisoners Cornwallis learned for the first time that Lafayette and Wayne had followed him from Richmond. The information astonished all the British officers. Cornwallis remarked to Simcoe that if any word of it had reached them, they could have cut the Marquis to pieces en route. They now decided to do what they should have done days before: trap the boyish general and his little army.

For a week Lafayette hovered about Williamsburg, shifting his camp almost daily. Once more the diaries reflect the growing weariness of the men. On July 3, William Feltman wrote: "Maneuvers retrograde and many; the troops almost worn out; very hot weather." On the fourth of July Lafayette celebrated the Declaration of Independence by entertaining his officers at a dinner. The troops were issued extra rations of rum, and celebrated with a camp parade and the firing of salutes. The next day found them on the march again. Cornwallis had evacuated Williamsburg and was moving toward the coast once more.

Lafayette, still eager for battle, pushed Wayne forward with 500 troops. The Marquis was paying ten guineas for information about the British plans. He had a Negro spy working as Cornwallis' own servant, and on another occasion sent an enterprising private, one Charley Morgan, into the British camp pretending he was a deserter. The Marquis soon learned that Cornwallis planned to cross the James River and join forces with another body of British troops under General Alexander Leslie, stationed at Portsmouth. Here, it seemed, was the ideal moment to strike an effective blow at the British army, with a minimum of risk. He would wait until the rear guard alone held the river bank, and then attack with everything he had. If he could drive them into the river, it would be a simple matter to trumpet the news through Virginia that they had crushed the better half of the British army.

Unfortunately, Cornwallis was thinking one step ahead of his young opponent. He foresaw that this was exactly what Lafayette hoped to do. Early on the sixth of July he ferried Simcoe's rangers across the river, with orders to light fires along the shore and otherwise give the appearance of a large encampment. The main body of the army he held out of sight, behind some woods along the river's edge. Meanwhile, he paid some not-so-loyal Virginians to carry stories into Lafayette's camp, confirming that the better part of the British would be across the James by afternoon.

Although his men had marched all night and had had nothing to eat since the previous noon, Wayne drove them forward again and around two o'clock reached Green Spring Farm, a mile or two above Jamestown Island, where Cornwallis was crossing the river. It is hard to imagine a better place to construct a military trap than Green Spring Farm. Bounded by marshes and the river, the Americans had only one narrow causeway across a swamp for entrance and exit. But Wayne and Lafayette, hot for battle, noticed none of this, and ordered their riflemen into a lively skirmish with patrolling British dragoons. The enemy cavalry immediately fell back, convincing the Americans that there was indeed only a rear guard left to oppose them. When British infantry picketed in the woods along the river made a more determined stand, this only convinced the Americans all the more. Actually, the infantrymen were under orders to hold the Americans on their side of the woods, so that they would not discover the main British army immediately behind the trees.

Virginia gentlemen who were serving as mounted scouts assured Lafayette that the main British army had crossed the river. He decided to call up the rest of his Continentals, whom he had been holding at Norrell's Mills, six miles to the rear. At the same time, he was a little uneasy about the stiff resistance from the British pickets in the woods. It seemed to him evidence of more than a rear guard. He decided to reconnoiter the field for himself, and galloped off, leaving Wayne in command.

A few minutes later, with the fire growing hotter on both sides, the British brought up a three pounder and opened on the Americans. Major William de Galvan, a French officer in command of a small party of light horsemen, asked Wayne's permission to attack and capture the gun. Wayne told him to go ahead. At almost the same moment, Lafayette had gained a point of land higher up the river from which he could see the whole battlefield. He watched Galvan's detachment moving toward the British field piece, gallant and determined in their assault. But his admiration vanished when he saw behind the woods the entire British army in motion, portions of it moving through the trees to meet Galvan's attack, and more regiments filing off to the right, where they could easily get between Wayne and his retreat to Williamsburg. Aghast, Lafayette spurred his horse madly back to the battlefield to warn Wayne that he must withdraw immediately.

He was too late. Wayne, watching the numbers of men pouring out of the woods, had realized long before Lafayette reached him that he was confronted by the entire British army. He had two choices. One would be to abandon Galvan and his men, who were already in the middle of a heavy exchange of fire. But a retreat in the face of an enemy who had more than enough men to execute the ominous flanking movement now in process could easily turn into a disastrous rout. It might be wiser to charge the enemy before they were set to pursue, hoping to check and disorder their lead units and then withdraw.

Wayne and his eight hundred men filed out into the open, forming a thin line across the marshy ground of Green Spring Farm. With three small cannons barking in support, they flung themselves at the British with bayonets leveled. Like all magnificent heroics, the gesture proved expensive. The British did drop their plans for pursuit, but they were much too well disciplined to let a bayonet charge fluster them. Crisp commands were quickly issued, and the Scots of the Seventy-sixth and Eightieth Regiments, the immediate recipients of the attack, opened ranks and answered it with a withering fire from their muskets and cannon.

The Pennsylvanians came on, returning the fire, but the charge began to melt, first on the right, then on the left. The British artillery swept the whole line with grapeshot, while the infantrymen, in Major Galvan's words, "kept up a devil of a noize of firing and huzzahing." In fifteen minutes the Pennsylvanians were in full retreat, which rapidly became a rout as the British moved after them. Lafayette frantically tried to rally them around the cannon, but the British storm of bullets was too heavy. The men were not going to stop running until they got off Green Spring Farm.

The Marquis was utterly indifferent to his own safety. His groom, riding directly behind him, had his master's favorite horse killed under him. The animal Lafayette was riding had its jaw fractured by a musket ball. Almost all the other field officers lost their horses, and every artillery horse was also killed on the spot. To Lafayette's mortification, this meant they had to abandon the two cannon, one of which had been captured from the British at the battle of Bennington in 1777.

By now it was growing dark. The general action had not begun until four-thirty. The British abruptly called off their pursuit and retired beyond the woods. Lafayette regrouped his battered Continentals around a brick house, about a mile beyond Green Spring Farm, and assessed the damages. He had lost almost two hundred men, killed and wounded, and had come very close to losing his whole army. Wayne's Pennsylvanians had no illusions about their narrow escape. One, Dr. Robert Wherry, wrote home: *"Madness!* Mad A——y, by G——, I never knew such a piece of work heard of—about eight hundred troops opposed to five or six thousand veterans upon their own ground."

The following morning the British dragoons were out once more scouring the roads, but found only a horse troop of American riflemen lurking near Green Spring. They fled at the sight of the vaunted British cavalrymen. Lafayette, who had retreated six miles during the night, fully expected the British army to be on his heels. But instead, Cornwallis proceeded to ferry the rest of his men across the James River, and continued his retreat toward the sea.

The delighted Lafayette immediately leaped to his pen and began writing letters in all directions describing the miraculous victory of his little army, which had forced Cornwallis to evacuate all of Virginia north of the James River. To his close friend General Greene, he did admit: "There were serious blunders on both sides," but since the enemy had chosen to retreat, "it will look well in a gazette." More than a few historians were to read only Lafayette's version of the affair and choose to see Green Spring as a superb example of American military prowess.

The exact opposite was true, and no one knew it better than the Marquis. He clearly understood that he was operating as a combination general and publicity man. No one was better fitted for such an incongruous combination of jobs. To most of the world he miraculously managed to convey the impression that he had driven Cornwallis out of Virginia. Even his cautious aide, McHenry, called Lafayette's achievement "a kind of sorcery and magic."

"Legerdemain is a very necessary science for an American general at this moment," McHenry added wryly.

There were times when Lafayette, with Wayne's help, may have actually convinced himself that the British were retreating from Virginia because of some extravagant misinformation about the strength of the American army. But in his more sober moments, the dashing Marquis knew that this could not possibly be true, and he was soon bombarding his friends with letters speculating on the possible intentions and motivations of the British general. Although Charley Morgan, and the Negro servant and all the other spies the Marquis was paying did their best, no one ever told him the real reason why the enemy was retreating. Not until this century, when historians at last had a chance to study the headquarters papers of the British army, did the truth emerge. Behind the proud bearing and confident manner of the commander of the British Army in Virginia, a gifted, even brilliant general was being slowly reduced to an angry muddle of resentment and indifference.

Few British soldiers had experienced more acutely the frustrations of war in America than Charles Cornwallis, Sixth Earl of Eyre. Since 1776 he had been in the forefront of almost all England's victories, though always as second or third in command. He had seen the soldiers of George III win battle after battle, only to have the final prize slip away like a wraith across the swollen rivers and through the trackless forests of this impossible continent. It was a war designed to drive European soldiers mad; fought one moment by rebels in battle array, the next by snipers who shot officers and men while they sat around their campfires; fought by armies who were beaten again and again on the battlefield, yet refused to surrender; a war fought by a people, rather than an army. Confronting such a war, other British generals soon felt both helpless and hopeless. As a subordinate, Cornwallis had been forced to watch in silence while the fruits of brave men's sacrifices dwindled away. What irony that now, when final victory was so close, he should find himself once more saddled with a commanding officer who seemed to personify all the incompetence, indifference and timidity which had oppressed him for so long. From his comfortable citadel on Manhattan Island, the shadow of Sir Henry Clinton, Commander in Chief of His Majesty's Armies in North America, was a large dead weight on Charles Cornwallis' weary shoulders.

At forty-three Cornwallis was in his physical and military prime. With a fine fierce nose, imperious lips and bold, almost arrogant eyes, he was every inch the nobleman. He was also a first-rate soldier. Though he was an oldest son, and hence under no necessity to choose a military life, he entered the army at eighteen, studied tactics on the continent, and was lieutenant colonel of the Twelfth Regiment

at the age of twenty-three. In 1760 and 1761 he had fought
with distinction against the French in Germany, and when
his father died in 1762 returned home to take his seat in the
House of Lords. Like almost every other British general who
commanded in America, he had voted against George III's
taxation policies, even joining with a handful of other peers
in voting against the resolution which affirmed Parliament's
right to tax the colonies at all. But unlike other Englishmen,
Cornwallis never let this theoretical sympathy for the Americans interfere with his eagerness to fight them. Six genera-
tions of noble blood made armed rebellion against his lawful
sovereign a repugnant thing to him, and he believed in stren-
uous efforts to repress it. As subordinate to Sir William Howe
in 1776 and 1777, he had played a key role in defeating the
Americans at Long Island, had hounded Washington across
New Jersey, and had led the flank attack which crushed Washington once more at Brandywine and gave the British Philadelphia.

Though he had no personal grudge against the Americans,
there was a deep personal reason for his fierce desire to win
this quasi-civil war. It had cost him the love, and finally the
life, of his wife. Unlike many other couples of that adultery-
prone age, Cornwallis and his wife were extremely devoted
to each other, and she was horrified when he was ordered to
America. She even persuaded the Archbishop of Canterbury
to intercede with the King to rescind the order. The Archbishop was successful, but Cornwallis angrily refused to take
advantage of the royal offer. At the end of the campaign of
1776, he sailed back to England in the middle of the winter—
the worst possible passage—to see his wife, and returned
in time for the next campaign, once again despite her pleas
and protestations. Then in 1778 Lady Cornwallis' health
began to decline alarmingly, and her soldier rushed home
once more, reaching England in December. She died three

months later, and ordered her lady-in-waiting to plant a thorn tree over her grave, to let the world know that she had been slain by a broken heart.

It all sounds impossibly quaint to the twentieth century, but Cornwallis was so griefstricken he retired from public life for six months. When he had seen how ill his wife was, he had resigned his commission in America and informed the King he would not return. But after his period of mourning, his friends persuaded him that there was a desperate need for his services in America, and like many men of action, he himself undoubtedly decided that work was the best way to purge his sorrow.

So Cornwallis had returned to the war, and throughout the year 1780 he had been the bright star of a new British strategy: to split the revolution by capturing the thinly populated southern states, where loyalist support was plentiful. Originated in 1778 after the stunning defeat and capture of General John Burgoyne's army at Saratoga had convinced England that the northern colonies were hopelessly disaffected, the strategy had proved extraordinarily successful. In 1779 Georgia had fallen with barely a struggle to British armies moving up from Florida, and in 1780 the capture of Charleston, South Carolina, and its 5,000 defenders had been a crushing blow to American hopes and strength.

The Americans had retaliated by sending southward Horatio Gates, the conqueror of Burgoyne, with an army of 7,000 men. Cornwallis had met him at Camden, South Carolina, and though he was outnumbered two to one, promptly attacked. Inside of an hour, the fighting Earl had annihilated the entire American army, and Gates, on the fastest horse he could find, did not stop running until he was sixty miles away.

From there, Cornwallis marched into North Carolina, and did battle with a shrewder and more cautious American general, Rhode Island's Nathanael Greene. Scraping together the remnants of Gates's army and what militia he could find,

Greene fought a war of maneuver against Cornwallis, who with typical pugnacity, literally marched the shoes off his soldiers, with one purpose in mind: to seek out the American army and destroy it. Twice he and Greene met and their armies slugged it out, hand to hand, bayonet to bayonet. Each time the battered Greene was forced to quit the field, abandoning wounded men and cannon but with his army still more or less intact.

Both men knew they were fighting not only for a battle-field but for the thousands of fence sitters in the South who were loyal to neither side and would pledge allegiance to the winner. That is why Green never stood his ground to the point where the fate of his entire army hung on victory or defeat in a particular spot; and Cornwallis, though he was the acknowledged winner, ended each battle more frustrated than he began it. He knew that only the destruction of the American army would win the South; and Greene knew that the preservation of an army, no matter how tattered and battered, would keep the hope of independence alive.

Moreover, Greene had the advantage of operating along interior lines of supply. Men and munitions flowed down to him from Virginia along the numerous rivers, while Cornwallis saw his army steadily dwindle away from wounds and the multiple diseases of the local climate, which was especially unhealthy for British soldiers. After the Battle of Guilford Court House, on March 15, 1780, Cornwallis sat the night out on the field, listening to the screams of wounded men dying in the rainy darkness, brooding about the problems of conquering America. Morning found him with little more than 700 fighting men, and a hospital train of twice that number, prostrated by wounds or fever. The neighboring countryside had turned out to be almost totally hostile. His men had fought and died on empty stomachs—not a bite of food had been issued to them in forty-eight hours. From the supply wagons that finally reached them on the morning after the victory, only half rations could be issued to both the sick and the well.

Pondering his map not long after that unhappy morning, Cornwallis studied the geography of southern America. Suddenly he saw the source of his woes plainly outlined by the cartographer. The whole South depended on Virginia as a child depends on its mother. She was the richest and one of the most populous colonies. Virginia's tobacco and cotton had long been almost the only sources of fresh money for the feeble American economy. From Virginia Greene had been drawing his fresh men and his meager supplies. There was no money or stores in the rest of the South capable of supporting war. As his crippled army began a humiliating 200-mile retreat through North Carolina to the sea, the conviction fastened itself more and more upon Cornwallis that Virginia was the key to the South and might well be the key to the war. When he reached the port of Wilmington, where there were ample supplies of ammunition, food and medicine for his weary men, he was ready to stake his military reputation on the conquest of Virginia. It was, therefore, to his extreme satisfaction that Lord Cornwallis discovered that there was already a British expeditionary force in Virginia, commanded by none other than his old friend, Major General William Phillips. Cornwallis immediately sat down and wrote him a letter.

April 10, 1781

Dear Phillips:

I have had a most difficult and dangerous campaign, and was obliged to fight a battle 200 miles from any communication, against an enemy seven times my number. The fate of it was long doubtful. We had not a regiment or corps which did not at some time give way; it ended however happily, in our completely routing the enemy and taking their cannon. I last night heard of your arrival in the Chesapeak. Now my dear friend, what is our plan? Without one we cannot succeed, and I assure you that I am quite tired of marching about the country in quest of adventures. If we mean an offensive war in America, we must abandon New York, and bring our whole force into Virginia; we then have a stake to fight for and a successful battle may give us America. If our plan is defensive, mixed with desultory expeditions, let us quit the Carolinas (which cannot be held defensively while Virgina can be so easily armed against us) and stick to our salt pork at New York, sending now and then a detachment to steal tobacco, &c. I daily expect three regiments from Ireland; leaving one of them at Charlestown, with the addition of the other two and the flank companies I can come by land to you . . . I have as yet received no orders. . . .

The same day, Cornwallis wrote another letter to Sir Henry Clinton, his commander in chief in New York, expressing his eagerness to learn the orders for the summer campaign, and suggesting in more guarded terms the idea of operating in Virginia.

Eight days later Cornwallis wrote another letter, this one to Lord George Germain, the secretary for the American colonies and the man in charge of prosecuting the British side of the war. Lord George fancied himself a general, although twenty years before he had been cashiered from the army for cowardice against the French in Germany and forbidden ever to hold military rank in Great Britain. He had won the favour and the appointment of George III because he was one of the few British statesmen who were enthusiastically in favor of all-out war against the colonies.

Aside from having limited gifts as a strategist, Lord George made the mistake of sending specific orders to his generals in America, which often reached them four months later, when the situation had totally changed. Nevertheless, he was the man in charge, and Cornwallis felt obligated to give him his views. In emphatic terms, the Earl reiterated that the conquest of Virginia was the key to the South, and he deprecated as a waste of time the sending of small expeditions such as the Virginia raid which Benedict Arnold had led on Britain's behalf the preceding winter. "The great reinforcements sent by Virginia to General Greene, whilst General Arnold was in the Chesapeak," he said, "are convincing proofs that small expeditions do not frighten that powerful province."

Then, on April 23, thirteen days after he had written Phillips, and five days after he had written the Secretary of State, Lord Cornwallis sat down and wrote again to his commander in chief, Sir Henry Clinton, in New York. It was a friendly note, enclosing copies of his letters to the Secretary of State, and telling him that he must begin his march into Virginia the following day.

> It is very disagreeable to me to decide upon measures so important, and of such consequence to the general conduct of the war, without an opportunity of procuring your Excellency's direction or approbation. But the delay and difficulty of conveying letters and the impossibility of waiting for answers, render it indispensably necessary. My present undertaking sits heavily on my mind. . . . The situation in which I leave South Carolina adds much to my anxiety, yet I am under the necessity of adopting this hazardous enterprise hastily, and with the appearance of precipitation, as I find there is no prospect of speedy reinforcements from Europe, and that the return of General Greene to North Carolina . . . would put a junction with General Phillips out of my power.

This was a very deferential letter, but it was a trifle misleading. If Cornwallis had been truly anxious to learn what Sir Henry was thinking, he might have insisted that the commander in chief's recent dispatches be forwarded to him from Charleston, where he knew they had been sent. Instead the Earl had been satisfied with a vague summary of these documents, sent to him by the city's British commander,

Lieutenant Colonel Nisbet Balfour. Actually, orders were the last thing the Earl wanted to receive from his commander in chief. As far as Charles Cornwallis was concerned, Sir Henry Clinton was everything a general should not be.

It would be difficult to imagine two more opposite personalities than the fiery, pugnacious Earl and the fussy, cautious Clinton. Cornwallis was always ready to risk everything on the chance of destroying his enemy. Nothing ventured, nothing lost, was the motto of Clinton's military career. For his part, Sir Henry was an excellent planner. He was the type of general who makes a first-rate chief of staff—if the commander in chief is willing to put up with his constant carping about details. He handed Sir William Howe the British battle plan for Long Island and the American rout showed just how good it was. But before the next year was over Howe had learned to close his ears to Sir Henry's plans. There were too many of them, and when one was turned down Sir Henry went into a decline and moaned for weeks about no one appreciating his talents.

When Howe resigned and the King appointed Clinton in his place, a kind of panic seized Sir Henry. Now there was no one to turn down the plans which teemed in his brain, but if one of them failed, his neck, not Billy Howe's, would be in the Parliamentary noose. So Sir Henry hastily invented an invisible commander in chief to turn down his plans. His name was Perfection, and without him Sir Henry refused to go anywhere or do anything. His letters to London were one long wail about lack of troops, lack of supplies, lack of wagons, lack of horses, lack of ships. The navy would not cooperate, the loyalists would not cooperate, the Secretary of State would not cooperate.

There was a certain amount of truth in Sir Henry's cries of woe. By the time he took command in North America, the American rebellion had become a world war, and Great Britain was being pressed by the French all around the

globe—in the West Indies, in India and on the coasts of England herself, where there was a serious plan afoot for an invasion. Muddling along in a peace-happy languor, the government had let the navy decay and the army decline, and found
itself totally unprepared for such a tremendous conflict. Reinforcements promised to Sir Henry went to the West Indies,
or to rebellious Ireland, while ships he needed were rushed
to India.

When he had first taken command, Sir Henry had been
forced to dispatch over 5,000 men to the West Indies, and
would-be-General Lord George Germain had ordered him
to retreat to New York, and rest upon a "strict defensive"
except for minor expeditions. Lord George soon found himself regretting that order. Except for the foray to Charleston,
it proved impossible to get Sir Henry into motion again, no
matter how many men he had. Later Germain remarked
sourly in a letter to an associate: "I expect little exertion
from that quarter. . . . When we are to act with such a man
as Clinton we must be cautious not to give him an opportunity of doing a rash action under the sanction of what he may
call a positive order." By thus boxing in his immediate superior, Sir Henry was able to remain happily inert inside his
Manhattan bastion.

The living was easy for Sir Henry in old Manhattan. He
had, according to one account, four houses, including a comfortable mansion in town, a country manor on Long Island,
plus a somewhat rotund mistress to enliven them. Around
him collected some of the worst characters in the history
of the British army, and Clinton did nothing to stop their
depredations and grafting. His second in command was
Major General James Robertson, an aging Shylock who
had a large interest in McAdams, Rhinelander & Co., a
firm which sold goods to the British army. He was also
in complete control of a lottery which purportedly raised

money to help needy loyalists, and meanwhile drew two salaries, one as general, the other as military governor of the state. Not satisfied with this take, he also occupied two large Manhattan farms with mansions, outhouses and offices, and had another at Jamaica, a fourth in Kings County and a fifth on Staten Island, paying a total rent of 2000 pounds a year. Robertson was a Germain appointee, and his graft was a payoff for the hatchet job he had done on Sir William Howe, when that frustrated general went home to denounce Germain's mismanagement of the war. In testimony before a parliamentary committee, Robertson had made Howe seem a gross incompetent.

The military commander of New York was Brigadier General Samuel Birch, a rascal who plundered rebels and loyalists indiscriminately. Judge Thomas Jones, a right wing royalist himself, tells of one loyalist, Samuel Pintard, who lost all his property in Westchester for his faithfulness to the cause, and retired to a small house on Long Island. Birch, who was commander of a regiment of dragoons, quartered some of his brawling horsemen nearby; Pintard shut his house and moved in with a relative some miles away for a little quiet. Birch promptly broke into the house and took possession of it. When the hapless victim tried to regain it, Birch damned him for a rebel and threw him out on his head.

From December 31, 1775, to May 16, 1778, the British army under the command of Sir William Howe spent 1,079,412 pounds. Under Sir Henry Clinton's regime, a somewhat smaller army spent, between May 26, 1778 and December 31, 1780, 3,278,429 pounds—three times as much in approximately the same length of time. A board of inquiry was appointed by Sir Henry to find out why, but did not even manage to turn up a decent explanation, much less any evidence of chicanery. This was hardly surprising, since the members of the board were all army officers, most of whom were probably up to their elbows in the very graft they were investigating.

No one ever directly accused Clinton of participating in this graft, but he certainly participated in the general air of indolence and corruption which permeated the city. For his chief personal advisor, Clinton preferred William Smith, a man who was on equally good terms with rebel Governor George Clinton in Poughkeepsie. (Smith used to sign his letters to the Governor, "I am, dear George, affectionately . . .") His brother, Joshua Hett Smith, was thick in Benedict Arnold's plot to betray West Point, but talked fast and was acquitted by the Americans. Small and bony, with a gaunt face and sunken eyes, Smith was described by Thomas Jones, who hated him cordially, as "an artful close designing man with an unbounded deal of ambition, hypocrisy and craft." Certainly he was a peculiar loyalist, who maintained that "the violent on both sides" had brought on the war. As late as 1780 he wrote a pamphlet condemning "the pride and avarice of Great Britain."

Smith's favorite theme was "the debility of the Independents, the number of the loyalists, and the discords of the Confederacy." He ran an intelligence service in New York which perpetually forwarded facts supporting this thesis to Sir Henry. Smith's conclusion from these facts was simple enough: one solid blow by the British army and the starving rebellion would be over. But Sir Henry drew an opposite conclusion. He decided that the best way to win was to sit tight behind his fortifications and let the rebels wither away outside. In mid-1781, Clinton was firmly in favor of "the policy of avoiding all risks as much as possible, because it was now manifest that, if we could only persevere in escaping affront, time alone would soon bring about every success we could wish."

Smith frequently despaired of getting Sir Henry moving.

At one point he calls him a "trifler, jealous and domineering." On May 24, Smith noted that "Clinton confesses he hates business—that he thinks himself fit for a small Army but not for the complicated work assigned him. He wishes a Viceroy above both him and the Admiral." Elsewhere, in a slightly better mood, he avows Sir Henry "is only timid when he thinks ill, brave when he perceives hope of success." Yet Clinton consulted Smith constantly on military and civilian policy.

The sight of the commander in chief on his island citadel, surrounded by this melange of characters, plunged more than one loyal Briton into gloom. A distinguished admiral who visited the city late in 1780 wrote back to London that Benedict Arnold, who had just switched sides, was "worth all the British Generals put together." But no one in the War Office would have been caught dead taking advice from an admiral, so Clinton was allowed to bumble onward. All this was especially repugnant to Cornwallis, who thought a soldier's place was in the field. Relations between him and Clinton had been bad from the first. The Earl had returned to active duty in America just a few weeks after Sir Henry had received the supreme command. Cornwallis was so disgusted by the prospect of total inaction that he promptly wrote to Lord George Germain and requested permission to go home again, because "no offensive measures can be taken against the enemy in this part of the world." He was undoubtedly worried about his wife, yet Clinton could hardly have considered it a compliment to have his gifted subordinate resign when he was scarcely off the boat. The King refused Cornwallis' request, and he spent the summer and fall in leading the several "desultory expeditions" of which he speaks so harshly to General Phillips, little raids which accomplished little more than the destruction of stores and ammunition.

After the fall of Charleston, which was achieved under Sir Henry's direction, Clinton had returned to New York, leaving Cornwallis in charge of the war in the South. Because Cornwallis was operating at such a distance from headquarters, Clinton gave him permission to correspond directly with Germain in London. Sir Henry thus in effect created a semi-independent command for Cornwallis. It was an arrangement very much to Sir Henry's liking. If anything went wrong in the South, Cornwallis would get the blame. If he succeeded, Clinton was still the commander in chief, and could at least claim a share of the laurels.

But the victories which Cornwallis proceeded to ring up soon began to stick in Clinton's craw. Because the Earl wrote directly to London, Sir Henry did not even have the pleasure of composing victory dispatches. Yet he could hardly call Cornwallis unsuccessful, and so he was forced to dispatch more and more troops to him, leaving himself well short of the force his commander in chief, old Perfection, deemed necessary for venturing beyond the city limits of New York.

But Sir Henry never complained to Cornwallis. The Earl was simply too formidable. His family had represented Suffolk in Parliament since the thirteenth century, and his political connections were far superior to Sir Henry's. While Cornwallis was at Wilmington, for instance, he had the pleasure of receiving a letter from the Rt. Hon. H. C. Cornwall, speaker of the House of Commons and representative from the Cornwallis home borough of Eyre, informing Cornwallis that the House had recently voted him its thanks. In fact, Sir Henry felt himself so beneath Cornwallis in status that the moment the Earl returned to America for the third time, Clinton had written a long whining letter home, offering to resign in his favor. The King refused the offer. It was one of the worst of George III's many blunders.

One of the difficulties in giving orders to a prestigious subordinate who was operating at a distance was the time it took for letters to travel. Clinton did not get Cornwallis' let-

ter of April 10, in which he first broached the idea of a campaign in Virginia, until May 22. Sir Henry's answer was a
masterpiece of negative thinking:

My Lord,

I make no doubt that you will think it right to communicate to Major General Phillips without delay the plan of
your future operations in that quarter, together with your
opinion how the Chesapeak army can best exert theirs to assist them. . . . General Phillips is directed by his instructions to act in favour of your Lordship to the best of his
judgement, until he receives your orders, and afterwards in
such manner as you may please to command him. But I
should be sorry to hear your Lordship continue in the opinion that our hold of the Carolinas must be difficult . . . until Virginia is in a manner subdued, as that is an event which
I fear would require a considerable time to accomplish; and
as far as I can judge, it might not be quite so expedient at
this advanced season of the year to enter into a long operation in that climate. This, however, will depend upon circumstances, of which your Lordship and General Phillips may
probably be better judges hereafter.

With regard to operations of the summer, which your Lordship is anxious to receive my directions about, you cannot
but be sensible that they must in great measure depend on
your Lordship's successes in Carolina, the certainty and numbers of the expected reinforcement from Europe, and likewise on your Lordship sending back to me the corps under
Major General Leslie . . . for until I am informed of the
particulars of your Lordship's march through North Carolina, the effective strength of your moving army, your plan
of operations for carrying those objects you had or may have
in view into execution, as well by the corps acting under your
own immediate orders, as those acting in cooperation under
Major General Phillips, it must be obviously impossible for
me to determine finally upon a plan of operations for the
campaign. . . .

All the most maddening aspects of Clinton's personality are in this letter. He was the commander in chief, and Cornwallis had asked him for orders, a plan of campaign. The answer was a question about Cornwallis' own plans, as if he were operating a totally independent command on the moon. Then there were the pecking little asides—the remark that the campaign depended on the "successes" in North Carolina, the veiled request to send back troops he had detached to Cornwallis, the disagreement with Cornwallis' thinking on Virginia—couched in a language that was about as commanding as a valet talking to his employer.

But this was mild compared to the missive Sir Henry sent when he learned from Cornwallis' letter of April 23 that the Earl was marching into Virginia. Sir Henry reacted to this news with the pique of a husband who discovers his business partner has designs on his wife. From where he sat, Virginia was not part of Cornwallis' share of the continent. Not satisfied with running half the war, the Earl was now about to take over the whole show. It was more than Sir Henry's persecution complex could tolerate, and his reply of April 30 pulsates with vexation in almost every line. Disregarding all the things he had said about Phillips being under Cornwallis' command, he wrote:

> I cannot . . . conceal from Your Lordship the apprehensions I felt on reading your letter to me of the 24th ult wherein you inform me of the critical situation you supposed the Carolinas to be in, and that you should probably attempt to effect a junction with Major General Phillips. . . . In the disordered state of Carolina and Georgia, I shall dread what may be the consequences of your Lordship's move. . . . Had it been possible for your Lordship in your letter to me of the 10th ult to have intimated the probability of your intention to form a junction with General Phillips, I should certainly have endeavoured to have stopped you, as I did then, as well

as now, consider such a move as likely to be dangerous to our interests in the Southern Colonies. . . . I am persuaded your Lordship will have the goodness to excuse my saying thus much; but what is done cannot now be altered; and as your Lordship has thought proper to make this decision, I shall most gladly avail myself of your very able assistance in carrying on such operations as you shall judge best in Virginia, until we are compelled, as I fear we must be, by the climate, to bring them more northward. Your Lordship will have been informed of my ideas respecting operations to the northward of the Carolinas by my instructions to the different General officers detached to the Chesapeak. . . . By these your Lordship will observe that my first object has ever been a cooperation with your measures. . . . They were originally directed to assist your Lordship's operation in securing South and recovering North Carolina; their attention was afterwards pointed to saving South Carolina; and now your Lordship may possibly think it necessary to employ your force in recovering both or either of these provinces, by either a direct or indirect operation. With respect to the first, your Lordship must be the sole judge; with respect to the last, you have my opinions, which may however probably give way to yours, should they differ from them, as they will have the advantage of being formed on the spot and upon circumstances, which at this distance I cannot of course judge of: I shall therefore leave them totally to your Lordship to decide upon, until you either hear from me or we meet.

Thus Sir Henry managed in his usual tortuous prose, to disapprove of Cornwallis' decision to march into Virginia, to remind him that the Carolinas were shaky and it would be Cornwallis' fault if they fell, and simultaneously to divest himself of all responsibility for what was happening. No one could pass the buck quite so expertly as Clinton. He wrote this letter on May 29. By then Cornwallis had arrived in Petersburg, Virginia, the junction he and Phillips had agreed upon. There he was greeted with the doleful news that Phillips was dead, struck down by a "bilious fever"—probably malaria.

Phillips' death rarely receives even a line in the history books. Yet if we see history not merely as a bloodless play of forces but as a drama which depends heavily on the motivations of its human actors, the death of this genial, relatively obscure artilleryman is an event of world-shattering importance. Phillips was the one man in North America, and possibly in the entire world, to whom Sir Henry Clinton could speak with absolute sincerity. Somewhere in his papers, Clinton characterizes himself as "a shy bitch." He was an emotional cripple, forever cut off from direct and open communication with other men, even in the best of circumstances. But if Phillips had lived to act as intermediary between Clinton and Cornwallis, the older man might have done much to bridge the already considerable gap between the commander in chief and his brilliant subordinate. Cornwallis too had a deep affection for Phillips, who had been captured with Burgoyne and only recently exchanged. In two letters he remarked at his "distress" and "affliction" at the death of his good friend. But beyond this, the other realities were neither realized nor expressed by the principal actors. Death was accepted quite matter-of-factly by eighteenth century soldiers, and once his regret at losing Phillips passed, Cornwallis undoubtedly felt that it was fortunate indeed that he had marched into Virginia. Otherwise, the very substantial army Phillips commanded would have been left inactive for weeks while Sir Henry Clinton sent it another commander.

Cornwallis promptly took command of the combined army, and opened all of Phillips' letters from Clinton which were marked "On His Majesty's Service." He found more than the orders for which he was searching. Reporting on his latest news from Cornwallis, Clinton had written to his one close friend:

His Lordship tells me that he wants reinforcements—with nine British battalions, and detachments from seven more, five Hessian battalions and a detachment of Yagers, and eleven provincial battalions exclusive of the cavalry and infantry of the Legion— How can that be possible? And if it is, what hopes can I have of a force sufficient to undertake any solid operation?

If Cornwallis had any lingering doubts about Sir Henry's feelings toward him, this letter undoubtedly ended them. Still the Earl restrained any irritation on his side. He wrote a cool, professional letter to Clinton, explaining his plans for operating in Virginia. The best thing he felt he could do was raid on an extensive scale. The news from South Carolina was good. Lord Rawdon, a raw lieutenant when he had distinguished himself at Bunker Hill five years before, had now proven himself a general at twenty-six by defeating Nathaniel Greene at Hobkirk's Hill in the Carolina back country. By devastating Virginia, Cornwallis felt he could give decisive support to the men he had left behind in Carolina.

But when Clinton pointedly noted that he would now "avail myself of your very able assistance" in the operations in Virginia, he meant it. Cornwallis was now in Henry's yard, and he had to do what Henry said.

On June 8 Clinton wrote, in his usual style: "I am persuaded that I need not say to your Lordship how necessary it is that I should be informed without delay of every change of position in your Lordship's army. . . ." Then as an additional barb, he added: "As your Lordship is now so near, it will be unnecessary for you to send your dispatches immediately to the Minister; you will therefore be good enough to send them to me in the future."

He was soon sending the Earl letters by the volley, through a variety of messengers, so that they arrived at wildly different dates, to Cornwallis' further dismay and confusion. The one he wrote on May 29, for instance, disapproving of Cornwallis' march to Virginia, did not reach his lieutenant until July 12.

Meanwhile Cornwallis, reading Phillips' extensive series of dispatches and orders from Clinton, including notes Clinton wrote on a series of conversations they had had about the expedition to Virginia, could not make any sense out of them. As usual, Sir Henry was juggling three or four different plans at once, committing himself to none of them, and telling his subordinate to make up his own mind. He meditated operations in the "upper Chesapeake" around Baltimore, he thought a "descent" upon Philadelphia might be a good idea, he reiterated that the main object of the trip was to establish a small station for British ships to use during the stormy winter months, possibly at Portsmouth, possibly at Old Point Comfort, possibly at the small, almost defunct seaport of York, at the mouth of the river of the same name. Cornwallis wrote, asking for more explicit instructions, and with due respect opined that the operation against Philadelphia would be dangerous, impractical and a waste of time. They had captured the city once and had had to abandon it. Any hope of surprising a city which is 150 miles up a river controlled by enemy forts was specious. Virginia, Cornwallis repeated, was the prize they should fight for now. To do it right, a "considerable army" was needed. With a small force the business "would probably terminate unfavourably, though the beginning might be successful." Following his personal doctrine of winning the war by fighting battles, he added: "From the experience I have had, and the dangers I have undergone, one maxim appears to me to be absolutely necessary for the safe conduct of this war, which is—that we should have as few posts as possible, and that wherever the King's troops are, they should be in respectable force."

The implication, of course, was that Sir Henry was not supporting him with the proper reinforcements, but was follow-

ing his own preference for nibbling raids, which seemed to
Cornwallis a complete waste of time. Cornwallis also in-
directly rebuked Clinton for forcing him to erect a series of
forts along the borders of South Carolina, which were now
in danger of being destroyed one by one. At this point in
the mounting acrimony there arrived in Sir Henry's hands the
letter Washington had written to Lafayette, telling him
about their plans for a summer assault on New York. It was
all Sir Henry needed.

He leaped to his pen, and proceeded to tell Cornwallis
exactly how many men he had in his command. With regard
to the stations in the James and York rivers, he referred
Cornwallis to his correspondence with Phillips, which the
Earl had already said he did not understand, then added his
inevitable hedge against taking responsibility: "I shall . . .
of course, approve of any alteration your Lordship may
think proper to make in those stations." Returning to Cornwallis' strength, he told him the army he had was "quite
sufficient to carry on any operation in Virginia; should that
have been advisable at this advanced season."

Then he noted the intercepted letters, revealing Washington's plan.

> You will observe I am threatened with a siege in this post.
> My present effective force is only ten thousand, nine hundred
> and thirty one. With respect to what the enemy may collect
> for such an object, it is probable that they may amount to at
> least twenty thousand. . . . Therefore, unless your Lordship
> . . . should incline to agree with me in opinion and judge it
> right to adopt my ideas respecting the move to Baltimore or
> the Delaware Neck, I beg leave to recommend it to you as
> soon as you have finished the active operations you may be
> now engaged in, to take a defensive station in any healthy
> situation you choose (be it at Williamsburg or York-town).
> And I would wish in that case, that after reserving to your-
> self such troops as you may judge necessary for an ample de-

fensive, and desultory movements by water for the purpose of annoying the enemy's communications, destroying magazines, &c, the following corps may be sent to me in succession as you spare them:

    Two battalions of Light Infantry
    Forty third regiment
    Seventy sixth or eightieth regiment
    Two battalions of Anspach
    Queens Rangers, Cavalry and infantry
    Remains of the detachment of 17th Light
    Dragoons and such proportion of Artillery as can be spared, particularly men.

This amounted to some 2,000 men, almost half Cornwallis' army. If he had any hope of doing something substantial in Virginia, it evaporated with this letter. Not satisfied with thus crippling his most gifted general, Clinton proceeded to salt the wound by again arguing against Virginia in words that let Cornwallis know exactly what he thought of the latter's so-called successes in the Carolinas: "Experience ought to convince us that there is no possibility of re-establishing order in any rebellious province on this continent without the hearty assistance of numerous friends. These, my Lord, are not, I think to be found in Virginia . . . but I believe there is a greater probability of finding them in Pennsylvania than in any, except the southern provinces. In these your Lordship has already made the experiment; it has there failed—they are gone from us, and I fear not to be recovered. . . ."

This letter reached Cornwallis on June 26 at Williamsburg to which he had returned after his raid beyond Richmond, with Lafayette in pseudo-pursuit. With it were three other letters each demanding reinforcements in a more peremptory tone. The very same day, in New York, Clinton received eleven letters from Lord George Germain, dating from January 31 to May 2. One of them, written on March

7, casually pointed out to Sir Henry that he ought to be doing something in the North at least equal to what Cornwallis was doing in the South. The loyalist provincial regiments alone, Lord George declared, outnumbered Washington's collapsing army. But the May 2 missive was the one which undoubtedly turned Sir Henry slightly green. It totally approved Cornwallis' ideas about Virginia, and all but denounced Clinton's plans.

> It was a great mortification to me to find by your instructions to Major General Phillips that it appeared to be your intention that only a part of the troops he carried with him should remain in the Chesapeake. . . . Your ideas, therefore, of the importance of recovering that province appearing to be so different from mine, I thought it proper to ask the advice of his Majesty's other servants upon the subject, and their opinions concurring entirely with mine, it has been submitted to the King. And I am commanded by his Majesty to acquaint you that the recovery of the southern provinces and the prosecution of the war by pushing our conquests from south to north is to be considered as the chief and principal object for the employment of all the forces under your command which can be spared from the defense of the places in his Majesty's possession until it is accomplished.

Lord George was of course writing from the assumption that South and North Carolina were totally subjugated. How wrong he was can be glimpsed from a concurrent dispatch sent to Clinton by Lieutenant Colonel Balfour in Charleston. "I must inform Your Excellency that the general state of the country is most distressing and that the enemy's parties are everywhere. The communication by land with Savannah no longer exists. Colonel Brown is invested at Augusta, and Colonel Cruger in the most critical situation at Ninety Six. Indeed, I should betray the duty I owe your Excellency did I not represent the defection of this province

as so universal that I know of no mode short of depopula-
tion to retain it."

This information of course only made Clinton all the more
enraged over Cornwallis' success in selling his plans in London. Here was the so-called conqueror, with all his conquests
going up in smoke behind him, telling his commander in
chief how to run the war. A more rational man might have
resigned on the spot and sailed home. He did not need permission from the King to do this. Lord Cornwallis had a
dormant commission to succeed Clinton, whenever he abdi-
cated. Instead, Sir Henry decided, in an anguish of neurotic
pride, to launch his cherished plan to raid Philadelphia,
ignoring all the things Cornwallis had said against the idea.
His letter was the sort a captain might send to a second
lieutenant, ordering him to bring a squad of men over to
mow his lawn.

> My Lord:
>   Having for very essential reasons come to a resolution of
> endeavoring by a rapid move to seize the stores &c collected
> at Philadelphia, and afterwards to bring the troops employed
> on that service to reinforce this post, I am to request that if
> your Lordship has not already embarked the reinforcement
> I called for in my letters of the 8th, 11th, 15th and 19th in-
> stants, and should not be engaged in some very important
> move, either of your own, or in consequence of my ideas re-
> specting operation in the Upper Chesapeak, you will be
> pleased as soon as possible to order an embarkation of the
> troops . . . in as full a manner as your Lordship can with
> propriety comply. . . .

This letter did not reach Cornwallis until July 8. On June
30, he wrote a letter of his own, acknowledging the letters
demanding the reinforcements for New York, and arguing
once more, in a most pointed way, against the folly of any
attempt on Philadelphia. He also enclosed intercepted let-

ters from General Greene to Lafayette, in which Greene meditated the possibility of moving north to help the Marquis. To Cornwallis this clearly vindicated his policy of invading Virginia to take the pressure off South Carolina.

The Earl then made the following report on the town of York, which Clinton in his correspondence with Phillips had inclined to favor as his "defensive post" on the Chesapeake. "Upon viewing York, I was clearly of the opinion that it far exceeds our power, consistent with your plans, to make safe defensive posts there and at Gloucester, both of which would be necessary for the protection of shipping. . . ." He then went on to argue against the idea of a small post. "Magazines &c may be destroyed by occasional expeditions from New York, and there is little chance of being able to establish a post capable of giving effectual protection to ships of war. I submit it to your Excellency's consideration whether it is worth while to hold a sickly defensive post in this bay which will always be exposed to a sudden French attack, and which experience has shown makes no diversion in favour of the southern army. . . ."

On the eighth of July, when Clinton's orders for the Philadelphia expedition came in, Cornwallis wrote again, protesting the idea of a small post: "I must again take the liberty of calling to your Excellency's serious attention the question of the utility of a defensive post in this country, which cannot have the smallest influence on the war in Carolina, and which only gives us some acres of an unhealthy swamp, and is forever liable to become a prey to a foreign enemy with a temporary superiority at sea. . . ."

Meanwhile, Cornwallis was retiring toward the coast, to embark the troops Clinton had requested. This was the reason for the movement which Lafayette hopefully styled a "retreat." In fact, if he were not under what he regarded as positive orders to rush the troops to New York, there is no doubt that Cornwallis would have followed up the jolt he gave Lafayette at Green Spring Farm, and the Marquis would have had to run very fast indeed to save his army.

To embark the troops Clinton wanted, Cornwallis had to retire to Portsmouth, then the only local harbor held by British forces. To reach Portsmouth he had to cross the James River, which bisects Virginia, and give Lafayette a chance to boast that he had cleared the state of British troops, north of the James. But to Cornwallis, it was all part of the distasteful chore he was performing for Clinton. Then, on the twelfth of July, came another bolt from the commander in chief:

> I cannot be more explicit by this opportunity than to desire that if you have not already passed the James River, you will continue on the Williamsburg Neck. If you have passed, and find it expedient to recover that station, you will please do it, and keep possession until you hear further from me. Whatever troops may have been embarked by you for this place are likewise to remain until further orders.

With this same telegraphic message came the old letter of May 29, disapproving of Cornwallis' march into Virginia in the first place. It was almost more than Cornwallis could take. He ordered the troops, most of which had already embarked, to stay aboard the transports and await further orders. A few days later, he wrote a letter to his young friend, Lord Rawdon, which amply demonstrated his feelings:

> My Dear Lord:
> I dare not be so sanguine as to hope that you can or ought to stay in Carolina. I have not time to explain to you my situation. Suffice it to say that Clinton is determined to throw all blame on me, and to disapprove of all I have done, and that nothing but the consciousness that my going home in apparent disgust, would essentially hurt our affairs in this country could possibly induce me to remain. . . .

The day after he wrote this, Cornwallis exploded in Clinton's direction. He wrote a long letter, detailing all the problems he faced and the risks he had taken while Clinton sat snugly in New York. The ink was scarcely dry when in came two letters which Clinton had written on the eighth and eleventh of July. When he learned that Cornwallis thought Yorktown was a most unsuitable position, Clinton had rushed to a conference with the admiral in command in New York and without much difficulty persuaded him to agree that Great Britain needed a port on the Chesapeake for line-of-battle ships, as well as for frigates and other smaller vessels. He was obviously determined to keep Cornwallis in a defensive position all summer, by selecting for him the unpalatable job of fortifying a hitherto undefended town. The admiral must have been a little startled by Clinton's sudden concern for the welfare of the navy; until then, Clinton had spent half his letters home denouncing all the sailors in sight for incompetence. The admiral undoubtedly was delighted that the army was going to immobilize one of its best generals to build a port for the navy. So the letter went out to Cornwallis, telling him that the admiral and Clinton agreed: "it is absolutely necessary that we should hold a station in Chesapeake for ships of the line, as well as frigates." This eliminated Portsmouth, which was already fortified, but not suitable for battle ships. It meant Cornwallis would have to choose and fortify some other town. Which one? Here is a literal transcription of Sir Henry's instructions:

> The Admiral seems to think that should the enemy possess themselves of Old Point Comfort, Elizabeth River would no longer be of any use to us as a station for the frigates, therefore judges that Hampton-road is the fittest station for all ships, in which your Lordship will see by the papers in your possession I likewise agree with him. It was moreover my opinion that the possession of York-town even though we did not possess Gloucester, might give security to the works we might have at Old Point Comfort, which I understand secures Hampton-road.

At this rate, Clinton had Cornwallis fortifying half the Virginia coast. The Earl was not by nature a patient man, and this was too much for him. On July 27 he wrote Sir Henry a letter which gave him as good as he was dishing out. "I was honored with your dispatches of the 8th and 11th instants," it began, "the contents of which I will confess, were to me as unexpected as, I trust, they are undeserved." He then recapitulated their correspondence, with its barrage of contradictory orders mixed with oblique criticism. Then he delivered his counterstroke to Sir Henry's machinations: he told him he had detached engineers to survey Point Comfort and the channels adjoining it. Both they and the naval captains on duty in Hampton Road agreed that it was totally unsuitable for line of battle ships.

> This being the case, I shall, in obedience to the spirit of Your Excellency's orders, take measures with as much despatch as possible to seize and fortify York and Gloucester, being the only harbour in which we can hope to be able to give effectual protection to line of battle ships. I shall likewise use all the expedition in my power to evacuate Portsmouth and the posts belonging to it, but until that is accomplished it will be impossible for me to spare troops; for York and Gloucester from their situation command no country, and a superiority in the field will not only be necessary to enable us to draw forage and other supplies from the country, but likewise to carry on our works without interruption. . . .

Cornwallis must have permitted himself a smile when he finished that letter. He could picture Sir Henry sputtering in New York over his lost reinforcement. Then with weary disgust, Cornwallis went to work. He put the Eightieth Regiment on board transports in Portsmouth Harbour, and himself embarked with them. Uncooperative winds kept them at sea four days, but on August 2, he saw the town of York, dozing in the humid morning, a cluster of about sixty houses down on the riverside and another 250 residences on the bluffs above. Here is how one German soldier described it in a letter home:

> This Yorktown, or Little-York, is a small city of approximately 300 houses; it has, moreover, considerable circumference. It is located on the bank of the York River, somewhat high on a sandy but level ground. It has 3 churches, 2 reformed English and 1 German Lutheran, but without steeples, and 2 Quaker meeting houses, and a beautiful court or meeting house, which building, like the majority of the houses, is built of bricks. Here stood many houses which were destroyed and abandoned by their occupants. There was a garrison of 300 militia men here, but upon our arrival they marched away without firing a shot back to Williamsburg, which is 16 English miles from here. We found few inhabitants here, as they had mostly gone with bag and baggage into the country beyond.

Cornwallis could hardly have been surprised to find Yorktown deserted. Its citizens had been supporters of American resistance long before the first shots of outright revolution had been fired at Lexington. In December, 1774, they had staged a miniature "tea party" in Yorktown harbor and later they had sent one of their native sons, Thomas Nelson, Jr., to the Continental Congress, where he became a signer of the Declaration of Independence. A number of other Yorktowners were prominent in Virginia's revolutionary government.

Founded in 1691 on land owned by Nicholas Martiau, the earliest known American ancestor of George Washington, Yorktown had been until about 1750 the busiest port on the Chesapeake. Tobacco from the Virginia plantations streamed out, and manufactures from England poured in across its wharves. An English visitor who stopped there in 1736 reported: "You perceive a great air of opulence among the Inhabitants, who have some of them built themselves Houses equal in Magnificence to many of our superb ones at St. James. . . ." Though the rich houses remained, in the next twenty years Yorktown began to decline. The center of the tobacco-growing industry moved southwest, and other ports began to dominate Virginia's basic trade. The fortunes of war did nothing to improve the situation. Its strategic location made Yorktown the target for British raids, and American troops who sporadically occupied the town for purposes of defense were almost as destructive. By 1781, most of the merchants had moved inland for safety, and the place was almost entirely depopulated.

A half-mile away across the York River was the smaller village of Gloucester. Cornwallis ordered a detachment to occupy it also, and debarked at Yorktown. The houses along the water's edge were mostly taverns, warehouses and business offices. The Earl led his men up the steep road to the residential section on the bluffs. There he demonstrated his good taste by selecting for his headquarters the finest house in sight; it was owned by Thomas Nelson, former secretary of the Virginia legislature in loyalist days and cousin of the man who had just succeeded Jefferson as rebel Governor of Virginia. "It was a handsome house," one visitor tells us, "from which neither European taste nor luxury was excluded. The chimney piece and some bas reliefs of very fine marble were particularly admired." Nelson, now in his seventies, was still living there. The old man had not taken sides in the Revolution, and having sat out the war in Yorktown could see no reason for running away now. Cornwallis respected his neutrality and treated him with the utmost courtesy.

The basic preliminaries of bivouacking the troops and selecting houses for the officers settled, the Earl sat down and wrote a weary note to his close friend and second in command,

Brigadier General Charles O'Hara, who was still at Portsmouth:

> Dear Charles:
> After a passage of four days we landed here and at Gloucester without opposition. The position is bad, and of course we want more troops. . . .

The rest was sarcasm about the ways of commanding generals.

While Cornwallis sweated out the dog days of August on the banks of the York River, complaining about the heat and the lack of Negroes to build fortifications and assuring Clinton that he still needed every man in his army to carry out Sir Henry's "orders," George Washington sweated over problems of his own in his headquarters at New Windsor, New York. Nothing was right. Almost all his energy was being consumed in a struggle to procure bread and meat for his army. The figures on new recruits were appalling; by August 2 he had only 5,835 men fit for duty, less than half the number Congress had promised him for the preceding January.

To make his suffering more acute, he had had to sit idle outside New York while first Benedict Arnold and then

Lord Cornwallis ravaged his home state. Not even his personal representative at Mount Vernon, his nephew Lund Washington, seemed capable of conducting himself properly. When a British raider sailed up the Potomac, Lund had obsequiously gone on board, obeyed British demands for food, and asked them to return a number of the plantation's Negroes who had run away to the enemy. Other neighbors who defied the British had their houses burnt. The general wrote Lund a stern rebuke for not showing a proper spirit of independence.

Lund was not the only American who needed an injection of independence. Each month officers resigned by the dozen, and many more enlisted men took the deserter's path to obscurity. Only one thing held the rest of the American army together: Washington's leadership. This leadership remains a mystery that still puzzles us; it was almost abstract, somehow larger than the man's personality. On his own staff there were men who disliked him personally, men who even considered him an inferior general. But they took his orders, they stayed in his ranks, enduring long years without victory. Not since Princeton in 1777 had Washington won a battle. But only a tiny minority ever thought of replacing Washington with one of the men who had won battles. They recognized the strange, obscure force in this tall Virginian—call it will, perseverance, magnetism—as the heartbeat of the revolution.

If there was mystery in Washington's leadership, there was also something more understandable: steady, unremitting toil. The papers of his war years stretch volume after volume, each one packed with a seemingly endless stream of letters and orders. Looking through them communicates a vision of the man at work, day after long day, plowing through the details of court martials, dealing with ignorant and interfering Congressmen, soothing officers in search of promotion, begging state governors for money and supplies, coolly manipulating a half-dozen interlocking intelligence networks. And through it all he never lost his faith in ultimate victory. "We must not despair," he wrote to John Mathews of South Carolina in June. "The game is yet in our hands; to play it well is all we have to do. . . . A cloud may yet pass over us; individuals may be ruined; and the country at large, or particular states, undergo temporary distress; but certain I am that it is in our power to bring the war to a happy conclusion."

When men failed him he found other men, or simply took over their jobs himself. More than once he had been his own quartermaster. He was always his own chief of staff. He spent six long years of constant toil, of unwavering refusal to admit final defeat even when to other men it seemed close enough to touch. After such a purgatory, could failure still be the final answer of the providence to which he often referred in his letters? Working away at his headquarters in New Windsor, the tired man from Mount Vernon could only admit that this was possible; without a major victory the revolution could well expire at the end of this campaign.

To Washington, there was only one major victory that mattered: the capture of New York, the heart of British power in America. But Sir Henry Clinton sat on Manhattan Island behind a bristling network of forts and redoubts, with twice as many men as his would-be attacker. New York could never be captured without the help of the French army and the French fleet. But how, where, when, would this help materialize?

A year before, 4,000 French troops had arrived in Newport, shepherded by a French naval squadron of eight ships. Great had been the fanfare and excitement in the American camp. After two years of waiting for something more than promises from the French alliance, help had arrived. But to the chagrin of Washington and his generals, the French had done nothing for a full year but enjoy the hospitality of Rhode

Island. It had been another thorny reminder of the accusa-
tion the British perpetually tried to pound into American
ears: the French were giving the Americans only enough aid
to keep their feeble revolution alive and pin down British
troops while France carved out conquests in more important
parts of the world.

Now the French had left their Newport base, and marched
south to join Washington's army at White Plains. The plan,
agreed upon at the Wethersfield meeting in May, was for an
assault on New York. Washington had promised to have at
least 10,000 regular troops ready, and all the militia he
could gather. Instead he had 5,000 regulars, and not a single militiaman. And by now it was well known, of course,
that the British had intercepted Washington's letter to Lafayette which revealed the campaign's plan. It was enough
to make even an American dubious about Washington's
promises and abilities, let alone foreigners who had been led
to expect a military genius at the head of an armed, enthusiastic host of free citizens.

Fortunately for Washington and America, the general in
command of the French expeditionary force was no ordinary
man. Jean Baptiste Donatien de Vimeur, Comte de Rochambeau, was fifty-five years old, and a thoroughly professional
soldier. Yet he had none of the rigidity which often marked
the military men of the period. A veteran of innumerable
battles and sieges against the English and the Prussians, he
had risen in the French army almost entirely on the strength
of his military deeds. He detested "court soldiers" and had
always avoided the intrigues and superficialities of Versailles,
preferring to spend his time with his troops in the field.
Soldiering was in his blood; he was of a line which had
sent men into battle for France since the Crusades. In an age
which blandly accepted the most brutal discipline in armies,
he followed a completely different maxim, given him by an
old French marshal: "I do not say to you: Try to deserve

the respect of the men whom you command, but I say to you: Try to deserve their love. . . ."

Proof of his success was the nickname his troops gave him: "Papa Rochambeau." He looked the part; he was a well-padded man of middle height, with full cheeks and a mouth which was firm as well as friendly; in his eyes there was almost always the hint of a smile. But the best qualities of Rochambeau the man are to be seen in his relations with Lafayette. A few days after the French landed in Newport, Washington sent Lafayette to greet the visitors. The volatile Marquis promptly handed Rochambeau an impromptu plan of campaign. He gave a vivid description of the sufferings of the American army, and warned that if the French did not launch an immediate offensive to take New York before winter, the revolution might well collapse. Rochambeau graciously declined to do so. He did not see how New York could be taken without a superior fleet; moreover, there was a second French division on the docks of Brest, waiting for transport to America. It seemed wiser to remain on a safe defensive in Newport until it arrived, hopefully with a covering fleet.

Lafayette withdrew in a sulk and a few days later forwarded to Rochambeau a twelve page despatch which proposed even more extravagant plans and declared without equivocation that America's fate depended upon the activity or inactivity of the French during the rest of the summer. Rochambeau wrote the Marquis a rather sharp reply, declaring his intention to stay in Newport and requesting an interview with Washington. A lesser man would have been by now in a towering rage; Lafayette was not much older than Rochambeau's own son and was still a reserve captain in the French army. However marvelous his American commission as a major general might seem to him, it meant nothing to Rochambeau and "Papa" firmly but politely pointed out to him that he was not running the war.

Lafayette, with that candor which made him so irresistibly likeable, cheerfully admitted he was wrong. "If I have offended you," he replied, "I beg your pardon for two reasons: first because I am earnestly attached to you; and secondly because my purpose is to do everything here that I can to please you."

Rochambeau proved himself more than equal to an answer in the same spirit:

> My dear Marquis, allow an old father to reply to you as a dear son whom he loves and infinitely esteems. You know me well enough to believe I have no need to be spurred, that at my age when a decision is founded on military reasons and upon reasons of State brought about by circumstances, all the incitements possible cannot make me change without a positive order from my general. . . . It is always good to think the French invincible; but I am going to tell you a great secret learned from the experience of forty years: There are no easier men to defeat when they have lost confidence in their leaders and they lose it at once when they have been endangered through personal and selfish ambition. If I have been fortunate enough to maintain their confidence in me until now, I owe it to the most scrupulous examination of my conscience; it is because out of about fifteen thousand men who have been killed or wounded under my orders in different ranks and in the most murderous engagements, I do not have to reproach myself for having caused one of them to be killed on my own account. . . .

This was no small statement. In the battle of Klostercamp in the Seven Years' War (where one of his opponents was Charles Cornwallis), Rochambeau's famous Auvergne Regiment lost fifty-eight officers and eight hundred men killed and wounded. Such experiences made him acutely aware of his precarious situation in America. Before he had left Paris, he had made repeated protests over the size of his expeditionary force. "The four thousand men I have with me is really nothing," he wrote in one letter. "You do not have to be very tenacious in holding your ground to lose one-third of your force in an infantry action. I repeat and I repeat," he insisted, "that I need twelve battalions, six thousand men, at least, and a detachment of cavalry." The Minister of War put him off with a promise of a second division, which was to sail a few weeks later.

The following spring (March, 1781), Washington himself learned much about Rochambeau's remarkable geniality when he made the mistake of criticizing the French in a private letter to Lund Washington. He had asked Rochambeau and his naval commander, Commodore Charles Destouches, to make an attack on the Chesapeake, where at that time Benedict Arnold was raiding with ferocious effect. After much hesitation the French had detached a small squadron, and the British had met it with a squadron of their own. Though the French had slightly the better of the sea battle, they decided it was too risky to attempt to land troops and returned to Newport. Washington's letter telling Lund all this was captured by the British and published in New York. They arranged for Rochambeau to get a copy of the paper. Washington ruefully admitted the letter was authentic and pleaded weakly: "Whatever construction it may bear, I beg your Excellency will consider the letter as to a private friend, a gentleman who has the directions of my concerns at home, totally unconnected with public affairs, and on whose discretion I could absolutely rely. . . . No idea of the same kind has ever gone to any public body. . . ."

This might hardly have satisfied a less generous man. But Rochambeau replied: "I did what I thought was most consistent with a sincere heart; I wrote about it to your Excellency with candor, being fully persuaded your Excellency's answer would be wrote in the same style, and I wrote only to have the means of smothering up that trifle at its birth."

Now, with the American army in such a deplorable state, Rochambeau continued to display his forbearance. He was under orders to regard Washington as his commander in chief, and he did so with consummate tact, even after he marched into the American camp at White Plains and saw the skeleton army Washington had to offer. After six years of war, they still had no uniforms, except for the officers who wore the blue uniform with buff facings prescribed by Washington the year before. Abbé Claude Robin, the French chaplain, describes several regiments which had fringed hunting tunics and linen pantaloons, an effect which he finds "quite agreeable." But young Baron Ludwig von Closen, a Bavarian who had come over with the Royal Deux-Ponts Regiment and won a position on Rochambeau's staff, was anything but impressed. "It is really painful to see these brave men, almost naked, with only some trousers and linen jackets, most of them without stockings, but, would you believe it? very cheerful and healthy in appearance." A few days later, Von Closen went with Rochambeau to see the Americans "present arms" for him. Here Von Closen thought "the whole effect was rather good. Their arms were in good condition; some regiments had white cotton uniforms. Their clothing consisted of a coat, jacket, vest, trousers of white cloth, buttoned from the bottom to the calves, like gaiters." He was particularly impressed by the Rhode Island Regiment, which was three-quarters Negro. It was "the most neatly dressed, the best under arms, and the most precise in its maneuvers."

Washington reviewed the French army the same day Rochambeau reviewed the Americans. He had already seen the French on parade in their magnificent uniforms when he had visited them at Newport, so he was prepared for the display. But Von Closen noted that the other American officers "seemed to be ecstatic."

The French loved color in their troops. The infantry wore

white coats and long waistcoats. The coat lapels and collar bands of the different regiments and units varied; some were crimson, some pink, sky blue, green, yellow. The sergeants sported white plumes in their hats; the grenadiers had red and the chasseurs, the French light infantrymen, had green. The artillerists wore long iron gray coats with red velvet lapels. It was a dazzling array, and the American officers, used to their drab, all-but-uniformless Continentals, could be excused for their wide-eyed pleasure. Moreover, it was evident at a glance that these Frenchmen were good for something more than parade-ground brillance. If they were few in number, Rochambeau's regiments were also among the best in the French army.

The Bourbonnais Regiment had a tradition which went back to 1600, and a proud motto, "en avant sur les Canons." The Soissonais, in which Lafayette's brother-in-law, Vicomte de Noailles, was second colonel, went back to 1598, and for its motto had the words of a sergeant who was killed at the moment of victory: "What does it matter? We have won the battle." The Saintonge regiment was commanded by Rochambeau's son, and it too was over 200 years old, tracing its lineage back to an ancient regiment of Navarre. Finally there was the Royal Deux-Ponts Regiment, whose men came from the Saar Basin and spoke German. It was a "proprietary" regiment, under the command of the ruler of the Duchy of Deux-Ponts. The colonel was Count Christian Forbach de Deux-Ponts and the lieutenant colonel, Count William Forbach de Deux-Ponts. While the rulers of other German principalities sold their men to the British as mercenaries, the Dukes of Deux-Ponts remained fiercely loyal to the throne of France.

Abbé Robin was astonished to find in the American tents, where three or four men lived, "not over 40 pounds of baggage." Hardly a man, the Abbé noted, had a mattress. Compared to the Americans, the French were prodigals. When they marched from Newport, Baron von Closen tells us, "the army left its heavy equipment." This meant that the general "allotted 14 wagons to a regiment." This was in addition to what each soldier carried. Abbé Robin describes them as "bent under the weight." Von Closen, who was only an aide, had four horses and several servants.

As glittering as the regiments were the retinues of many of the young French nobles who had come over with Rochambeau. The expedition was enormously popular among the liberal thinkers of the French court, who leaped at the chance to strike a blow against England and at the same time see if the theories of Rousseau and the other *philosophes* about the origins of society and the virtues and nobility of natural man, unspoiled by overcivilization, were really true. Besides the Vicomte de Noailles, there were the Prince de Broglie, son of Marshal de Broglie, one of France's greatest generals; Comte de Charlus, whose father was the former French Minister of Marine; the Chevalier Charles de Lameth and Comtes Mathieu Dumas and Charles de Damas, also from influential court families. Then there were two wellborn young captains, Louis Alexander and Charles Jean Berthier, who stowed away with the expedition, were sternly put ashore by Rochambeau, and wangled their way to America aboard the next ship out. Louis, showing a genius for paperwork that was to make him Napoleon's chief of staff, quickly won a place as one of Rochambeau's aides. Most glittering of these musketeers, in reputation at least, was Count Axel Fersen of Sweden, who was Marie Antoinette's favorite courtier. *Le beau Fersen,* as he was called, went to America to dispel ugly rumors about himself and the Queen. Everyone knew the story of his last night in Paris, when the Queen, seated at the clavicord, sang the romance from the opera *Didon.* When she came to the verse, "Blessed is the memory of the day I first welcomed you to my court," she looked directly at Fersen, "her cheeks flushed, her eyes filled with sad tenderness."

Within a few days of the allied junction the generosity of the wealthy young French officers became an embarrassment to the Americans. One general sent Washington an entire keg of claret. American field officers and junior officers were being continually invited to dinners in the French camp, though they had not the least hope of repaying the hospitality with their starvation rations and bankrupt currency.

If the Americans were embarrassed, the French were enjoying themselves immensely. For the younger soldiers, the whole expedition was a marvelous adventure, a unique exploration of a new world. Ragged and poor though the Americans might be, they were nature's noblemen in French eyes, and no one fulfilled this theory better than Washington.

Cromot du Bourg describes Washington's visit to the French camp on July 5, 1781. "He is a very fine looking man. His bearing is noble in the highest degree and his manners are those of one perfectly accustomed to society, quite a rare thing certainly in America. . . ."

Aide Mathieu Dumas declared: "His dignified address, the simplicity of his manners and mild gravity, surpassed our expectation and won every heart. . . ."

Count Axel Fersen described Washington in a letter to his father: "His face is handsome and majestic but at the same time kind and gentle, corresponding completely with his moral qualities. He looks like a hero; he is very bold and says little but is frank and polite. There is a sadness in his countenance which does not misbecome him and indeed renders his face more interesting."

The French commissary, M. Blanchard, found Washington's physiognomy "something grave and serious, but is never stern, and on the contrary, becomes softened by the most gracious and amiable smiles. He is affable and converses with his officers familiarly and gaily."

Major General François Jean de Chastellux, member of the French academy and one of Europe's leading men of letters, was almost enraptured by Washington: "The continent of North America, from Boston to Charleston, is a great volume, every page of which presents his eulogium. Brave without temerity, laborious without ambition, generous without prodigality, noble without pride, virtuous without severity, it will be said of him at the end of a long civil war, he had nothing with which he could reproach himself."

All this was very fine. But mutual admiration was not enough to win the war. The problem which confronted Washington and Rochambeau was: what to do now? On the eighth of May they had received doleful news from France, borne by Rochambeau's own son. There was to be no second French division, and Washington's request for another 10,-000 men was dismissed as sheer fantasy. However, the much requested "superior naval forces" were on the way, and could be expected to arrive in the latter part of July or August. In a personal letter to Rochambeau, the Minister of Marine, Marquis de Castries, was more explicit. "That fleet," he said, "is under the command of Admiral de Grasse. He has twenty ships, and he will find ten in the islands. You have eight more to give him; thus, master of his movements, I hope that for quite a long while he will be master of the coasts of America and will be able to act with you if you wish to undertake some engagement."

Washington and Rochambeau had to decide on possible moves, should this "superior naval force" actually materialize. A letter from the French admiral had already warned them that his stay upon the American coast would be short, and everything should be ready for instant military cooperation the moment he arrived. It was up to the generals to signify the point of arrival.

There were two possibilities—Virginia or New York. Thanks to Lafayette's assiduous letter writing, Rochambeau was keenly aware of the desperate situation in Virginia, and expressed a desire to do something substantial in that area to help "the poor Marquis." He even offered to lead an expeditionary force southward. But Washington disagreed. Barras, the French naval commander in Newport, had already refused to consider transporting troops to Virginia by sea. The English fleet guarding the sea lanes off New York was simply too strong. This meant a march south to Virginia, in the heat of the summer, with the expense and difficulty of procuring wagons and the very real danger that as much as half the American army might evaporate through sickness and desertion. As Lafayette had already discovered, Americans from the North regarded southern climes with sullen suspicion, convinced that the sulphurous air had a destructive effect on their constitutions. To Washington, it seemed obvious that the best way of relieving the pressure on Lafayette was to mount a determined attack on New York. The jittery Clinton was sure to recall troops from the South, leaving Cornwallis on the defensive.

Rochambeau yielded, but with considerable reluctance. In fact, General de Chastellux, who served as Rochambeau's interpreter at the conference and was ardently pro-Washington, wrote an outraged, even scurrilous letter to the French minister in Philadelphia, telling how poorly Rochambeau had treated Washington and accusing his superior of "incredible ignorance" and aversion to the United States. Chastellux, incidentally, took the credit for persuading Rochambeau to attack New York—something which makes one suspect his account is a little overdrawn. "It is not easy to make a man give way who has always been accustomed to do as he pleases," Chastellux wrote. To the academician's horror, this letter was captured by Clinton who immediately sent it to Rochambeau under a flag of truce, warning him "that he ought to be on guard against his associates."

Rochambeau could have court-martialed Chastellux on the spot. Instead, he summoned him to his headquarters and asked him, "Do you recognize this letter?"

Chastellux blushed furiously. He lamely explained that the letter had been written in a fit of bad temper because Rochambeau had been sharp with him the day before.

Rochambeau angrily rebuked him, saying he would never have expected such conduct from him. There was total silence for a moment. "Here is the letter," Chastellux finally said, handing it back.

"Yes," Rochambeau said, "I want to put it where it belongs."

"I threw it in the fire," he tells us in his *Memoirs,* "and left him a prey to all his regrets."

Rochambeau may have verbally submitted to the wishes of his American commander in chief. But he was a stubborn man, and a clever one. Washington did not have any control over Admiral de Grasse and his fleet. All he could do was urge Luzerne, the French Minister in Philadelphia, and Rochambeau, in turn to urge the admiral to come to New York forthwith. In his letter to Luzerne, Washington also reveals how aware he was of the approaching peace, and the touch-and-go status of American independence. He begs the Minister to advise Admiral de Grasse to add "a body of land forces" to his "Naval Armament," so that by "one great, decisive stroke, the enemy might be expelled from the Continent, and the Independence of America established at the approaching Negociations." Rochambeau proceeded to take advantage of his position as correspondent with De Grasse to give the admiral instructions which made it practically inevitable that he would sail not to New York, but to the Chesapeake.

> The enemy is making his strongest efforts in Virginia. Cornwallis marched from Wilmington near Cape Fear to unite on the Roanoke at Halifax with the troops of Phillips and Benedict Arnold. With this army of 6,000 men he proceeded to Portsmouth and fortified a position at the mouth of the Elizabeth River, whence he ravages in small armed

boats all the rivers of Virginia. Washington assures me that he has no more than 8,500 regulars and 3,000 militia for carrying on the campaign against New York. . . . That is the state of affairs and the very grave crisis in which America, and especially the states of the South, finds herself at this particular time. . . . There are two points at which an offiensive may be made against the enemy: Chesapeake Bay and New York. The southwesterly winds and the state of distress in Virginia will probably make you prefer Chesapeake Bay, and it will be there where we think you may be able to render the greatest service, whereas you will need only two days to come from there to New York. In any case, it is essential that you send, well in advance, a frigate to inform [Admiral] Barras where you are to come and also General Washington. . . .

In a second letter, Rochambeau urged De Grasse to bring troops and money. The French military chest was close to empty, and experience had proved to them that no one in Newport was going to supply them with food out of patriotic generosity. Rochambeau too was aware of how close to disaster the war was tending:

I must not conceal from you, Monsieur, that the Americans are at the end of their resources, that Washington will not have half of the troops he is reckoned to have, and that I believe, though he is silent on that, that at present he does not have 6,000 men; that M. de la Fayette does not have 1,000 regulars with militia to defend Virginia. . . .

Washington disagreed emphatically with the idea that De Grasse should make the Chesapeake his first port of call. He wanted the French fleet to make for Sandy Hook, where, considering the short time the admiral could stay on the coast, he would almost certainly join them for an attack on New York. Around the time Rochambeau was writing to De Grasse, Washington was writing to Ambassador Luzerne, "The Count de Rochambeau and the Chevr. Chastellux agree perfectly in sentiment with me, that will affrs remain as they now are, the West India Fleet should run immediately to Sandy Hook, where it may be met with all the information requisite, and where, most likely, it will shut in, or cut off, Adml. Arbuthnot. . . ."

While this jockeying for control of the French fleet was going on between the two commanders, they did not delay their plans for joining the French and American armies. On June 10, to the inexpressible grief of more than one New England damsel who had fallen in love with a dashing French chevalier, Rochambeau left Newport. On the second of July, Washington, anxious to probe the defenses of New York, had Rochambeau hurry ahead the French cavalry, to support him in a night attack on the British outposts north of Manhattan Island.

At the head of the cavalry, there rode into American history the one, the only, the incredible Armand Louis de Gontaux Biron, Duc de Lauzun. This thirty-four-year-old *Beau Sabreur* extraordinary had been Marie Antoinette's lover, and had been forced on Rochambeau at the Queen's express insistence. To the French veteran, Lauzun combined all the worst characteristics of the court soldier. Actually he concealed under his aristocratic flamboyance a keen and serious mind. In 1777, the playboy had amazed the French court by producing a penetrating pamphlet on the state of defense of England and her possessions. The King was so impressed that Lauzun won permission to raise a legion and assault the British in Senegal, which he did with outstanding success. In the eighteenth century a legion was a mixed unit of cavalry and infantry (Lauzun had two companies of foot soldiers and about 400 horsemen), often composed of foreign adventurers. Most of Lauzun's legionnaires were Poles, with a sprinkling of Germans. They were a swaggering, hard-drinking bunch, and during the year in Newport Rochambeau exiled them to Lebanon, Connecticut, on the pretext that fodder for their horses was cheaper there. Lauzun ended up charming the local citizens, as he eventually charmed Rochambeau. A story survives of him drinking at the tavern with one of the Lebanon farmers, who asked him what business his father was in. "My father is not in business," Lauzun replied, "but I have an uncle who is a *maréchal*." He was speaking of the Duc de Biron, one of France's best known field marshals.

"Indeed," replied the villager, "not so bad. There are worse trades than that."

Lauzun rode into battle with a black heron feather quivering in his cap. This was the parting gift of his latest passion, Madame de Coigny. He had met her at a banquet only a few days before he sailed for America. "She appeared wonderfully attired and with a great black heron feather on the right side of her robe," he explained. He won the feather, among other things, in the few hours he had left, and his lady fair wrote him regularly while he languished in the "forests of Connecticut." By now he had a packet of her letters which he carried over his heart, and his hussars were under orders that should he fall in battle, they were to bury him on the spot "but not disrobe him."

At Lauzun's side rode an almost equally fabulous character, Baron Robert Guillaume Dillon, one of a famous family of Irish soldiers in the service of France. After the battle of the Boyne in 1689, over 18,000 Irish officers and men had gone into exile rather than live in an Ireland conquered by Britain. The Dillons had been among the most prominent, and for almost a century now the King of France had maintained an Irish regiment under a contract which stipulated that a Dillon must be in command. The regiment led by Comte Arthur Dillon had fought at the siege of Savannah and had captured the island of Grenada against fierce British resistance in the current war. Baron Robert, known as "Billy," was a fighter in the family's wildest tradition. He was a famous duellist, and while the expedition had been waiting to sail, he had slipped away one night and returned in the morning with two sword wounds which he refused to explain. Rochambeau had put him under arrest until they sailed.

In spite of these two fire-eaters, the Anglo-American attack on the British outposts was a complete failure. Alert British patrols spotted the advancing column and Clinton hastily pulled his men back from their exposed positions to the more formidable forts on the Manhattan side of the Harlem River. Discouraged, Washington retreated to White Plains, where the two armies finally joined.

The French obviously regarded the performance of the American army on the night of July 2 as inauspicious, at the very least. In his memoirs, the Duc de Lauzun gives the impression that the American division he was supporting came close to being cut off and wiped out by their British opponents, and that only the intervention of his cavalry saved them. But the Duke always saw himself as the center of a heroic drama. In his diary, Washington wearily maintained that the reason for failure was that "The length of Duke Lauzun's March & the fatigue of his Corps prevented his coming to the point of Action at the hour appointed."

For a month the allied army made repeated reconnaissances in force around New York. Usually the generals accompanied them, and the British never failed to let them know they were watching. Rochambeau tells in his *Memoirs* how one day he and Washington ventured upon a "small island," probably in the East River. "While our engineers were making . . . [a] calculation we went to sleep, overcome with weariness, beneath a hedge, under the fire of enemy ships which wished to interfere with this work. Awakened first, I awoke General Washington, and called his attention to the fact that we had forgotten the time of high tide. We quickly returned to the millbank upon which we had crossed this little arm of the sea that separated us from the main-

land. We found it covered with water. They brought two little boats to us, into which we got with the saddles and the
harness of the horses."

The reconnaissances and reconnoiterings may have been
fruitless and frustrating to the generals, but they were lively
enough for the enlisted men. Joseph Plumb Martin, a Connecticut soldier who had joined the army in 1776 and was
now a sergeant in the sappers and miners, tells how the bolder
of the Americans considered it good sport to snipe at the
British in their Manhattan redoubts, "disturbing their tranquility." Martin soon found out that this could be dangerous
business.

He and two other noncommissioned officers went down
near the bank of the Bronx River. His two friends stopped
under an apple tree which was growing in a nearby gulley,
but Martin strode boldly out on the bank, and in a few
minutes four or five British horsemen came riding along the
opposite shore.

"When they saw me," Martin says, "they hallooed to me,
calling me a 'white livered son of a b——h.' We then became quite sociable," Martin continues dryly. "They advised
me to come over to their side and they would give me roast
turkeys. I told them that they must wait till we left the
coast clear, ere they could get into the country to steal them
as they used to do. They then . . . inquired what execution
some cannon had done, just before fired from the island, if
they had not killed and wounded some of our men, and if we
did not want help, as our surgeons were a pack of ignora-
muses. I told them in reply, that they had done no other execution with their guns than wounding a dog (which was the
case) and as they and their surgeons were of the same spe-
cies of animal, I supposed the poor wounded dog would account it a particular favor to have some of his own kind to assist him."

Martin became so fascinated by his "very polite conversation" that he forgot he was a perfect target there on the riverbank in his white undershirt. "I observed at a house on the island, in a different direction from the horsemen, a large number of men, but as they appeared to be a motley group, I did not pay them much attention," he says. "Just as I was finishing the last sentence of my conversation with the horsemen, happening to cast my eyes toward the house I saw the flash of a gun. I instinctively dropped as quick as a loon could dive, when the ball passed directly over me and lodged in the tree under which my comrades were standing.

"The people at the house set up a shouting, thinking they had done the job for one poor Yankee, but . . . I immediately rose up, and slapping my backsides to them, slowly moved off. They sent another shot at me, and I again dropped, but that did not come so near me as the other."

Martin decided "it is poor business to stand thus a single mark." But his perils were by no means over. That same afternoon he was idling in a narrow gateway, talking with a friend, when a redcoat crept out of his redoubt and fired at them. "The ball passed between our noses which were not more than a foot apart. The fellow walked off and we sent him something to quicken his pace, but our shots did as little execution as his had done."

The French opinion of American troops improved somewhat during these days of reconnoitering. Cromot du Bourg, Rochambeau's aide, tells of his impression after one particularly lively trip across Morrisania, the great estate of Gouverneur Morris, at the gateway to Westchester. "We made it most carefully, although we were harrassed by six or seven hundred cannon. The Americans lost two men and we captured about twenty or thirty of the English and killed four or five. I cannot insist too strongly how I was surprised by the American Army. It is truly incredible that troops almost naked, poorly paid, and composed of old men and children and Negroes should behave so well on the march and under fire . . ."

Of Washington's coolness under fire, the young Frenchman wrote with even more enthusiasm: "I do not have to speak of [his] *sang-froid*. . . . It is known. But this great man is a thousand times more magnificent and more noble at the head of his army than in any other situation. . . ."

If mutual admiration increased during the month they spent before New York, hope of a successful assault decreased at a much more rapid rate. Washington's diary is crowded with reports of his personal reconnaissances and his thoughts about capturing New York. But the details of what he saw were invariably discouraging. "Forts Tryon, Knyphausen and Ft. George appear to be well friezed, ditched and abbatised. In a word to be strong and in good repair. . . . The island [Manhattan] is totally stripped of trees and wood of every kind. . . ." By July 21 it is evident that Washington had abandoned all thought of a general attack. Now it is a "crossing place most favorable to a partisan stroke" which is carefully noted. But partisan strokes were not going to win the "decisive victory" so desperately needed for the coming peace negotiations.

As late as August 1, Washington still clung forlornly to the ghost of his wish to attack Clinton's citadel. He noted how "ordnance (heavy) has been brought to East River." Then he adds: "Everything would have been in perfect readiness to commence the operations against New York if the States had furnished their quotas of Men . . . of 6,200 . . . pointedly and continually called for to be with the army by the 15th of last month, only 176 had arrived from Connecticut and two companies of York levies—about 80 men."

On August 2, Washington was cautiously writing to financier Robert Morris in Philadelphia, asking him if he would discreetly explore the amount of shipping available for transporting a detachment southward. But the allied army still lay in their Westchester camps and persisted in its probes of New York's defenses. Washington's state of mind at this point is an enigma which has puzzled more than one historian. The strength of New York's defenses slowly turned his thoughts south, but the news he got from there— Lafayette's reports of Cornwallis' putting men on board ships—only made him convinced that Clinton was bringing men from the south to reinforce New York, and that a march to the Chesapeake would only decimate the American army and gain nothing but a handful of enemy troops in a garrison at Portsmouth. Rochambeau repeatedly pressed him for a definite plan of operations to be presented to De Grasse the moment he arrived, but Washington evaded making such a commitment.

By the end of July, the most pressing reason for avoiding the march south was finances. Since May, the American army had been able to get food only by "impressment"—taking it by force from farmers in New York and New Jersey. Elsewhere, Quartermaster General Timothy Pickering informed Washington, "without money in hand it is impossible to do business in the States at a distance from the Army." At the same time, Washington was still convinced that Admiral de Grasse would come directly to Sandy Hook, and might possibly sail away or be mauled by a British fleet if there were no land force on hand to cooperate with his attempt to force New York harbor.

Then on August 12 came a blow from an unexpected direction: a fleet of twenty vessels stood into New York harbor. At last, the reinforcements from Virginia! Proof that the attack on New York could take pressure off the South. But no, Washington's efficient spies on Manhattan soon informed him that the ships carried German reinforcements from Europe, at first believed to be 2,880, later found to be 1,500. It was enough to bring Clinton's numbers above those of his would-be attackers, without any help from Cornwallis.

Then on August 14 a messenger came panting into the allied camp from Newport with a letter from Admiral Barras. He had just received word from Admiral de Grasse that he was coming to the Chesapeake, not to New York, and that he was bringing with him twenty-nine warships and 3,000 soldiers under the Marquis de Saint-Simon. Now, or never, was the moment of decision. Which would it be? A battle for New York, the prize of Washington's heart? Or a possibly ruinous march south?

Rochambeau plumped for an immediate march to the Chesapeake. For a moment, Washington wavered. Only when he was on the point of being forced to abandon it, did he realize how acutely he wanted to capture New York and wipe out forever the stain of the humiliating defeat he had suffered there in 1776. He was no man of marble, this Washington of 1781. He was an intensely emotional human being who had learned to keep his emotions under the rein of an extraordinary will. He *wanted* New York—and here was this Frenchman advising him to march to Virginia. It was natural for Washington to see nothing at first but bad advice in the idea. Only a seer with an authentic crystal ball could have foreseen that here, on the conference table before them, was the crucial card, the play that was to change the game from stalemate to triumph.

M. Desandrouins, a colonel of the Engineers who had fought with Montcalm at Quebec, noted in his haphazard journal the lively exchange between Washington and Rochambeau over De Grasse's message. According to the colonel, Washington wanted to send the French engineer, Duportail, to Virginia and tell De Grasse to come to New York.

> The French General pointed out to him that the English, having just received reinforcements . . . were impregnable at that point; that the French and American armies did not exceed eight thousand men; that Monsieur de Saint Simon was bringing only three thousand men, all of which brought us only to an equality in numbers with the enemy who were entrenched and surrounded by rivers and coves. . . . Washington replied that Cornwallis would not wait to meet us and would get away from us. Monsieur de Rochambeau answered that we still would not have wasted our time in delivering Virginia. Finally he was obliged to tell him that it was true that he was under his orders but that Monsieur De Grasse was not; and that he could not abandon his admiral who had come at his own request nor cause him to change his plans; and that, for this reason, he could not keep from setting out at once with the French troops. But he did not, however, wish this to seem that he was withdrawing from his command; on the contrary he invited him to place himself at our head with as large a following of his army as he felt able to withdraw from before New York. Washington stated that his troops had so great a repugnance to going into the South toward Virginia that they might possibly revolt rather than go there.
>
> Monsieur de Rochambeau answered that . . . the greater part of the Congressional troops would follow the French; and he added that if it was necessary to share our army's money to set his in motion he was willing to do this. . . . I have all these details from him (Rochambeau) himself and I am writing them the moment after I have heard them from his own mouth. . . .

The general's son, Vicomte de Rochambeau, went even farther than this in his journal. Among the French difficulties, he mentions "the determination which General Washington showed in wishing to make an attack upon New York. This was impracticable, because the entrenched garrison greatly outnumbered the besiegers. It was therefore necessary to fool him and to seem to adopt his plans but to form others."

Some writers have used this French evidence to argue that Washington was all but dragged to Yorktown as an unwilling captive. Others, citing the evidence of his preparations to move south long before he heard where De Grasse was headed, maintain the whole idea was engineered by Washington. The answer lies in Washington's diary. On the twentieth of July he specifically stated that he was unable to make a decision "from the uncertainty with respect to the time of the arrival of the French Fleet and whether Land Troops would come in it or not as had been earnestly requested by me and inforced by the Minister of France."

"Troops" is the key word. Washington hesitated to attack New York only because he lacked men. Now De Grasse was bringing the men from the West Indies. Why not go ahead? It undoubtedly took some vigorous arguing on the part of Rochambeau to persuade Washington that the West Indian reinforcement was not decisive. What probably convinced him was the time limit on De Grasse's stay in American waters. It might take two weeks to get a messenger to De Grasse in Virginia and at least another week for him to bring his fleet into action against New York. Washington puts time at the head of the list in his diary when on August 14 he reports the decision to march south:

> Matters having now come to a crisis and a decisive plan to be determined upon I was obliged, from the shortness of Count De Grasse's promised stay on this coast, the apparent

disinclination in their naval officers to force the harbor of New York, and the feeble compliance of the States to my requisitions for men, hitherto, and little prospect of greater exertion in the future, to give up all idea of attacking New York, and instead thereof to remove the French troops and a detachment from the American Army to the Head of Elk, to be transported to Virginia for the purpose of cooperating with the army from the West Indies against troops in that state.

It is interesting to note that he does not even mention Lord Cornwallis. At this point, Washington frankly did not believe Cornwallis would be there when the French and Americans arrived. There might be "troops" but there would not be an army. He expressed this pessimism even more forcefully in a letter to his stepson, Jacky Custis, on July 25: "I am of opinion that Lord Cornwallis will establish a strong post at Portsmouth, detach part of his force to New York and go with the residue to South Carolina." Writing to Lafayette on August 15, after the decision to march had been made, he tells him De Grasse is coming to the Chesapeake, and adds: "Whether the enemy remain in full force, or whether they have only a detachment left, you will immediately take such a position as will best enable you to prevent their retreat through North Carolina, which I presume they will attempt the instant they perceive so formidable an armament."

The decision made, Washington immediately began preparations for the march south. There were two large problems facing the allies: money and Sir Henry Clinton. He wrote to Robert Morris, the Superintendent of America's collapsed finances, and begged him to get some "hard money" for his troops:

> I must entreat you, if possible, to procure one month's pay in specie for the detachment under my command. Part of the

troops have not been paid anything for a long time past and have upon several occasions shown marks of great discontent. The service they are going upon is disagreeable to the Northern regiments; but I make no doubt that a *douceur* of a little hard money would put them in proper temper. . . .

He then went to Rochambeau and accepted his promise of a loan. The Count's war chest was by no means full; all he had left was forty thousand gold dollars. He generously gave Washington half.

On the seventeenth of August, Washington's spirits were lifted somewhat by another dispatch from Lafayette, telling him that Cornwallis had gone to Yorktown and was using his entire army to fortify the peninsula. This inspired everyone to redouble his efforts. Letters were sent winging to Artillery General Henry Knox in Philadelphia, ordering him to get the precious American cannon ready to move. Circulars were sent out once more to the recalcitrant state governors, begging them for recruits to fill up the regiments that would be left to guard the Hudson. Finally, general orders were issued sternly forbidding women to go with the troops on the march south. "No women will be suffered to ride in waggons or walk in the ranks this campaign unless there are very particular reasons for it of which the general officer or the officer commanding the division or brigade is to be the judge. A written permission only will avail," the order read. During two years of inactivity on the Hudson the Americans had built up a formidable corps of camp followers, some of whom lived with the soldiers in the wedded state, others without benefit of clergy. This was standard procedure for eighteenth century armies; it was customary for women to draw food from the army commissary and to accompany the men right up to the edge of the battlefield. Washington's strict declaration that no women would be issued rations on the march was a grim sign that the trip was serious business.

But much more pressing was a plan for decoying Henry Clinton into believing that the Americans were still going to attack New York. Fortunately, this was not hard to do, because until August 14, every American movement had been with this plan in mind.

After six years of war, Washington had come a long way from the amateur general who had sent Nathan Hale on his almost foredoomed mission into New York to find out something about the size and strength of the British army. There were at least a half-dozen espionage networks toiling for the American army now, and within these wheels were more than a few double-agents, who were also on Sir Henry Clinton's payroll, feeding him carefully concocted false information. Washington was never under the least illusion that he could maintain any secrecy about his movements. His only hope was to outfake Sir Henry long enough to give the allies a substantial headstart on the dash to the Chesapeake.

A glance at Clinton's extant secret service papers reveals just how thorough the British agents were. When Washington was maneuvering about New York, Sir Henry knew exactly what he did at almost every minute of every day. On July 13, for instance, the spies reported Washington's headquarters before he set them up: on the fourteenth, an agent declared, the general would be "at Edward Brown's, two miles above Phillips's, on the North River Road." Without a variation, all through the month of July, the British spies reported plans for a siege of New York. On July 24, a report signed "F" declared: "If there is any attempt made you may depend on it will be made on the island that will be the first place of the attackt." On August 10, another secret agent rode coolly through the entire allied camp, and reported that the attack on New York was still definitely in the works. All this, of course, only confirmed Clinton's belief that the letter Washington had sent to Lafayette was genuine.

Washington proceeded to play shrewdly on this by now

hardened British presumption. He had selected for the march south 2,500 of his own Americans and all of the French division. Screening these with the 3,500 men he was leaving behind under Major General William Heath to protect the vital Hudson River, he sent both detachments across the river at Kings Ferry on August 20. The Americans, practically destitute of supplies and equipment, crossed the river in a day. It took the French four days to get their elaborate supply train, their heavy artillery and their cavalry horses across. All this time, they were in a sweat of anxiety that Clinton would attack them.

It was an unbelievably opportune moment for Sir Henry. Even the pretense of an attack could have thrown the American plans into chaos, and an aggressive commander might easily have destroyed the French as they struggled across the wide river, only a day's march from the British forts in Manhattan. One French regimental commander, Lieutenant Colonel William de Deux-Ponts, noted in his journal: "An enemy a little bold and able would have seized the moment of our crossing the Hudson, so favorable for him, so embarrasing for us, for an attack. His indifference and lethargy at this moment is an enigma that cannot be solved by me."

It was also an enigma that could not be solved by any of the loyalists inside New York. William Franklin, who had ignored his famous father's advice and thrown in his lot with the forces of the Crown, commented wryly: "Every measure of Sir Henry Clinton since he came to the command has been so far beyond the view of vulgar capacity that this in particular strikes with less force and is in some degree buried amidst a multiplicity of more unaccountable actions. And we have only to lament that we have not penetration to fathom the policy of his deep laid schemes. For deep laid they must be because unintelligible."

If Franklin affected wry hopelessness with Clinton, Benedict Arnold was a volcano of frustration and impatience. From entries in William Smith's diary, it is obvious that the fiery turncoat was constantly bombarding Clinton with requests to let him at Washington and Rochambeau. When the French and American armies were about to join, Arnold vowed he could defeat them piecemeal with no more than 6,000 men. On July 23 he came to see Smith "disgusted at the inactivity of the Day. Says we have here now 10,300 and odd rank & file of Regulars exclusive of officers who may be near 2,000 more." As the month of August dribbled away with Clinton still doing nothing, Arnold's disgust mounted. On the twenty-fifth he was at Smith's house again, telling the loyalist that "none of his propositions of Service are listened to & he dispairs of any Thing great or small from Sr. H. Clinton, who he suspects aims at prolonging the war for his own Interest."

Smith himself had an interview with Clinton, in which he asked him why he was immobile while Washington was marching all around him. This produced a small explosion from Sir Henry. "He held," Smith says, "that the French were 5,000 and Washington 7,000. He said a late letter . . . said the Rebels dealt out 10,000 rations—He allowed for 3,000 less—the Rebels had no Women."

As an intelligence expert, Smith knew better. "I recollect Parsons [the letter writer] made both armies about 8,000 as Henry Van Schack had it from Col. Ja: DeLancey who saw and del'd the letters," he wrote in his diary. "Sir Henry also asserted to render his Supposition the more probable that Washington had left the Highland forts to 400 Invalids—Of his own force he had before August 11 when the Troops arrived from the Weser (the German reinforcements) but 9,200 rank and file, that Cornwallis had near 8,000 and Lord Rawdon above 7,000, which last I much wondered at but he took up his pen and figured out the number rather above 7,000. He said the idea in England is that I keep a great army here & yet it is nearly equally divided between N.Y., Virginia & South Carolina."

This incomparable picture of the commander in chief wallowing in self pity is one explanation of why the British did nothing while Washington marched around them with an army which, contrary to Clinton's assertions, did not exceed 7,000 men, including officers. Washington did everything in his power to add confusion to Clinton's exaggerations of allied strength.

In a conversation the American Commander in Chief had with an "old inhabitant of New York," who was a known British spy, Washington blandly asked this gentleman what he knew about the water supply and the quality of the landing beaches on Long Island, and terrain conditions around Sandy Hook. There was no special reason why he was asking, Washington explained. He was just "fond of knowing the Situation of different parts of the Country, as in the Course of the war he might unexpectedly be called into that part of the Country." Then, as if suddenly remembering he was a general, he gave the old Tory an alarmed look, and urged him "by no means to lisp a Word of what had passed between them."

Around the same time, Washington sent orders into New Jersey to erect a large camp near Chatham. The messenger passed so close to British lines that he was inevitably captured. Meanwhile, around Chatham, French cooks began constructing four huge ovens, certainly proof that Washington had every intention of converting the site into a permanent camp. Finally, the allies carried with them across the Hudson and on their line of march into New Jersey some thirty large flatboats on wheels. Putting it all together, the British were convinced that Washington intended to attack New York via Staten Island.

Another reason why Sir Henry did not strike a hammer blow at the flank of the allied army as it wound along the roads of New Jersey was his passion for working on several plans at once. The one that obsessed him during August was a seaborne attack on the French camp at Newport, which was protected only by a French rear guard of 400, plus 1,000 local militia. This would have been a masterful move, if Sir Henry had brought it off. All the French siege guns, as well as vital supplies would have been lost to the allies. Sir Henry bombarded the newly arrived British admiral, Thomas Graves, with suggestions for the operation, always with the proviso that the admiral approved them. But Graves, after first warmly endorsing the idea, became evasive and vague. He found a thousand reasons for delaying the final decision. The planning degenerated into an exchange of letters as fruitless, if not as acrimonious, as Sir Henry's correspondence with Cornwallis.

Meanwhile, some of Clinton's more intelligent officers began to doubt Washington's intentions, even when he sent a detachment tramping through the broiling August heat in the direction of Sandy Hook. On August 18, Lieutenant Colonel Ludwig Johan Adolph von Wurmb informed Clinton that his spies reported depots of food and forage for the allied army all the way across New Jersey. He also learned that a French officer had sent his American mistress to Trenton. Von Wurmb was thus convinced that the allies were marching south, but Clinton brushed off his warnings. On August 22, a New Jersey agent known as "Squib" wrote nervously to Clinton: "It is said they will go against New York, but some Circumstances, induce me to believe they will go to the Chesapeake. Yet for God's sake be prepared at all Points."

Again Clinton paid no attention, though plenty of other people in New York were worrying out loud. On August 31, Smith wrote in his diary, "The town much agitated this morning because no troops are in motion to stay the Progress of the Rebels Southwardly." The next day Smith was even more certain: "Reports from Jersey last night that the whole

Rebel army are still moving South. . . . Some say the Southern delegates carry the Sway in Congress & that Washington
moves South against his own Opinion." On September 3
Smith was close to despair: "There is no Spirit of Enterprise.
The general Dulness kills the Spark that happens to rise in
the Mind of any Man. Washington's present movement from
the Hudson is the severest Censure upon the British Commanders in this Quarter."

If the loyalists had their worries, so did Washington and
Rochambeau. Even before the march began, they realized by
counting noses and estimating supplies that one of the big-
gest problems they faced was feeding the allied army after it
arrived in Yorktown. At Newport was 1,500 tons of salt beef,
reserve provisions for the French army. This was the answer
to their food shortage, and they requested the French admiral, the Comte de Barras, to transport it to Virginia by sea.
Equally vital were the French siege guns, also left behind at
Newport. Would the admiral kindly put these too on his
ships and rendezvous at Yorktown?

The admiral decided he would most kindly do no such
thing. He was feeling petulant because Admiral de Grasse
was arriving from the West Indies with twenty-nine ships to
Barras' eight. Yet Admiral Barras was the senior of the two
by several years; in fact, De Grasse had served under him as
a cadet. Honor could not permit Admiral Barras to put himself in a position where he had to accept commands from
his erstwhile subordinate. He planned instead to cruise off
Newfoundland and attack British fishing boats.

Frantic pleas from Washington and Rochambeau changed
his mind. Reluctantly, he loaded salt beef and siege guns,
and sailed for Virginia on August 23. Four days later, with
the allies halfway across New Jersey, a messenger arrived at
the door of Washington's tent with news that made Washington and Rochambeau wonder if they had given Barras
the right orders. General David Forman, who manned a

lookout near Sandy Hook, had in the morning of the same day written:

> Sir: I am this minute informed that eighteen large ships of war appeared standing in from the southward to Sandy Hook this morning at seven o'clock—by nine their colours was discovered British . . . if it should prove to be Adml. Rodney which at present appears most probable . . . I shall not send any other information—if any other fleet your Excellency will hear from me again as soon as possible.

Rodney! That meant the ships were from the British West Indies squadron. For the first time Washington and Rochambeau realized that the French Admiralty was not the only one capable of sending a formidable fleet to the American coast. If Rodney brought eighteen ships and Graves in New York had eleven, that meant there were twenty-nine British ships of the line ready to cruise off the Chesapeake—more than enough to annihilate Barras with his salt provisions and siege cannon—and then turn and give De Grasse a mauling which would make him abandon all thoughts of trapping Cornwallis. Aside from his numbers, the very name Rodney was enough to send shivers down any Frenchman's spine; he was one of the heroes of the Seven Years' War, in which one French fleet after another had gone down before British guns.

In the next few days, more reports came in from Forman on Sandy Hook. The British numbers were revised. Graves had only seven seaworthy ships of the line in New York, and the West Indies Fleet had brought thirteen. The numbers were a little more comforting—but the rest of the message was distinctly ominous. The entire British fleet had sailed from New York on the 31st of August. Barras was undoubtedly still at sea. The British chances of intercepting him were painfully good.

Meanwhile, Washington had ended his feinting in New

Jersey and turned the heads of his columns toward the Delaware. On September 2, the first day that Sir Henry Clinton received definite word from his secret agents that the Americans were heading south, the American column marched in blazing heat through Philadelphia, raising "a dust like a smothering snow." Although half the city turned out to cheer them, Rochambeau and Washington found little to make them smile. Robert Morris had almost nothing to offer in the way of water transportation. Any hope of sending the troops south by ship had to be abandoned. Artillery and heavy stores were committed to the few vessels Morris had been able to commandeer. As for money, Morris could only proffer the totally worthless continental paper.

A tense moment arose when the American troops made a direct request to Congress for at least a small advance on their back pay. Washington supported the request. Hurried conferences between Robert Morris and the congressmen resulted in a decision to borrow enough hard cash from the intendant of the French army to give the men a few dollars. The next day Washington had the satisfaction of announcing that one month's pay in specie was to be distributed to all ranks except those who "lost to all sense of honor, the pride of their profession and the love of their country, had deserted the Standard of Freedom at this critical moment."

Washington visited the Congress and could hardly have been cheered by what he saw there. The great names who had formulated the Declaration of Independence were almost all gone. Most had been lured away by the politics of their individual states, which seemed far more important than the Congress. The weak Articles of Confederation had left Congress without the power to tax or to command the separate states in almost any other sphere. It could only recommend, and it had long since grown used to being ignored. So pointless had it become as a political body by the summer of 1781 that as many as five states did not even bother to send representatives. The morale of the members who did come was low.

The French troops arrived in Philadelphia on the third and fourth of September. If the American arrival caused excitement, the French were a sensation. They wanted it that way. Chastellux noted with evident satisfaction: "The arrival of the French troops . . . was in the nature of a triumph. The troops made a halt about a mile from the city, and in an instant were dressed as elegantly as ever were the soldiers of a garrison on a day of royal review. They then marched through the town with military music playing, which is always particularly pleasing to the Americans. The streets were crowded with people, and the ladies appeared at the windows in their most splendid attire. All Philadelphia was astonished to see people who had endured the fatigues of a long journey so ruddy and so handsome." Cromot du Bourg declared that the Soissonnais Regiments, with their parade uniforms of white and rose and their grenadier caps with white and rose-colored feathers, "struck with astonishment the beauties of the city."

The Philadelphians, so used to sober Quaker attire, could hardly believe some of the French costumes were real. The French chaplain, Abbé Robin, was vastly amused "at the mistakes of the people who thought that one of these men whom our Lords have in their service, to go ahead of them or to carry their messages, was a general. His embroidered jerkin, his tunic with silver fringe, his emblazoned headdress, his cane with its golden knob, were the sources of this mistake. Each time that he approached his master to get orders they thought that he was giving them." The abbé also thought poorly of the "long black coat" the President of Congress, Thomas McKean, wore to an exhibition exercise of the manual of arms which the Soissonnais Regiment performed the day after they arrived. But he balanced his criticism with a neat compliment: "The worthy Pennsylvanians are as far below the French in etiquette as the French are below them in the Science of Legislation."

By the fifth of September, the entire allied army was on the march once more, the Americans in the first division and the slower moving French behind them. Without shipping, the march now became a race against time. They had to get to the Chesapeake, where Washington felt certain there would be shipping to carry them on the last leg of their journey. He had written to a number of his friends on the eastern shore to collect every possible ship. Racing ahead of the army were other messengers urging the Governors of Maryland and Delaware to accumulate supplies for the army en route and reminding them to rouse their militia.

Still another messenger carried a letter to Lafayette, which gives a clear picture of Washington's deepening anxiety about the expedition. In Philadelphia he had hoped that there might be some word waiting for him from Admiral de Grasse. Instead there was only silence.

"I am distressed beyond expression to know what is become of the Count de Grasse, and for fear the English fleet, by occupying the Chesapeake (towards which my last accounts say they were steering) should frustrate all our flattering propsects in that quarter. I am also not a little solicitous for the Count de Barras." He then urged Lafayette to continue to block Cornwallis' retreat by land, and ended with a frank summary of the American position: "You see how critically important the present moment is: for my own part I am determined still to persist with unremitting ardor in my present plan, unless some inevitable and insuperable obstacles are thrown in our way. Adieu, my dear Marquis! If you get anything new from any quarter, send it, I pray you, on the Spur of Speed, for I am almost all impatience and anxiety. . . ."

From Philadelphia, Washington rode toward Chester. Rochambeau went by water, because he wanted to see the forts of the Delaware, over which the British and Americans had fought more than one sanguinary battle during the campaign of 1777. When the little ship on which he made his journey pulled up to the dock, Rochambeau and his staff were treated to a unique sight: George Washington had totally abandoned his habitual reserve, and was acting like a man possessed. He had his hat in one hand and his handkerchief in the other and was waving them both in wide, whooping circles. When the French general came down the gangplank, Washington threw his arms around him and announced the glorious news: a messenger had just arrived from De Grasse's fleet. He was in the Chesapeake, with twenty-eight ships and 3,000 troops. The soldiers were already ashore. Cornwallis was trapped!

"I never saw a man more thoroughly and openly delighted than was General Washington at this moment," said the Duc de Lauzun. Colonel William de Deux-Ponts added: "He seemed to put aside his character as arbiter of North America and contented himself for the moment with that of a citizen, happy at the good fortune of his country."

Washington immediately issued a bulletin to his marching army, announcing De Grasse's arrival. Gone was the pessimism which had dogged his preparations for the venture south. "The General anticipates the glorious events which may be expected from the combined operations now in contemplation. As no circumstance could possibly happen more opportunely in point of time, no prospect would ever have promised more opportunely of success. Nothing but want of exertion can blast the pleasing prospect before us . . ."

This was not entirely true. De Grasse had neard nothing from his fellow admiral, Barras, conveying the indispensable provisions and siege guns. Moreover, the shipping available at Chester was as disappointing as it had been at Philadelphia. On September 6 Washington pushed on to Head of Elk, where the Elk River met the Chesapeake. Here was where the ships of his Maryland friends were supposed to be collected. All he found were apologies. British cruisers had destroyed or captured almost every vessel of decent size in the Chesapeake. Washington and Rochambeau held a hurried conference, and decided to embark 2,000 troops, about 1,200 French and 800 Americans, on the available ships, and send the rest of the army to Baltimore.

General Mordecai Gist of Maryland brought Washington some good news at Head of Elk. The state had raised 1,800 men and they would be ready to serve in the allied lines at Yorktown. Many of them were sons and brothers of men who had died so heroically at the battle of Long Island in 1776. "They are young, terribly young," said Gist, "but they are lions whelps and now they are under way. Some are riding, some are sailing, some are walking; they will be there, General, before you are."

Washington now decided that everything he could do to hurry the arrival of the army at Yorktown was done. By riding ahead, he saw a chance to visit his beloved Mount Vernon and repay Rochambeau and his fellow French officers some of the overwhelming hospitality they had showered on the Americans in the camp at White Plains. He also wanted to reach Lafayette and give that impulsive young general his personal attention as soon as possible. On the eighth of September, he started for Baltimore in the dawn, riding as he always did several hours before breakfast.

His pace was too much for the French. They let him go on ahead, and he was in Baltimore by evening. September 9 was a Sunday, but Washington did not rest. Instead he took his ever-present mulatto servant, Billy, and one member of his staff, Colonel David Humphreys, with him and produced one of those feats of horsemanship which left so many of his contemporaries openmouthed. From dawn until six-twenty that evening, he pounded onward, the full sixty miles from Baltimore to Mount Vernon. Finally, in the deepening twilight, he cantered up the path to the stately white house on the hill. For the first time in six years and four months, he was home.

It was a moment of vast excitement for Mount Vernon. The slaves flocked up from their cabins to see "The Master" and all the household servants crowded around. Old Bishop, who had marched to war with Washington against the French in 1756, hobbled up to exchange a warm greeting. Everyone probably discussed how much he had aged in the past six years. But the weight of those frustrating years undoubtedly seemed light to Washington, as he looked from his veranda down the broad lawn of Mount Vernon to the Potomac. Here was the kind of peace which he genuinely treasured. Only a few months before he had written to a friend: "A person of my years . . . pants for retirement and for those domestic and rural enjoyments which in my estimation far surpass the highest pageantry of this world."

Now he was home, not to retire, but to catch his breath on the way to battle. Still, it was a precious chance to see his family. Martha was there to greet him; but she had spent the winter with him at New Windsor, so Washington's special attention was undoubtedly given to his four grandchildren, whom he had never seen, and next to their parents, his stepson, twenty-six-year-old Jacky Custis, and his pretty wife, Eleanor. Washington had been strongly opposed to the marriage, on which Jacky had insisted when he was only twenty. But as usual, Martha had ruled in her son's favor. She had invariably managed to spoil Jacky and frustrate every attempt by Washington to give his ward's life some discipline and direction. Though Jacky, at twenty, had the advantage of an estate worth $500,000, a stupendous sum in the eighteenth century, he had none of the personal qualities Washington wanted in a son. He was a catastrophe as a scholar, showed no interest in pursuing a career, and if he had any inclinations to join his stepfather in the war, Martha suppressed them. But he had plenty of charm and he was re-markably handsome; in spite of his shortcomings, Washington was genuinely fond of him. And of course the children, three girls and a boy, must have given him special pleasure, especially the six-month-old lad named George Washington Custis.

After an evening with his family, Washington spent the next day preparing the house and plantation for the arrival of his distinguished guests. Washington's staff arrived just at mealtime, Rochambeau and his aides a few hours later. The following morning General Chastellux arrived. The French thought the house was "simple" and Martha Washington "somewhat fat, but fresh and with a pleasant face." The view from the dining room down the lawn to the glistening Potomac they found superb.

On September 11, host and guests enjoyed the pleasures of Mount Vernon, which impressed Connecticut-born Jonathan Trumbull, Jr., Washington's aide, with its "great appearance of opulence and real exhibitions of hospitality and princely entertainment." They were disturbed only by news that already the commissary was having trouble feeding the troops in the lines around Cornwallis. The militia were living on "roastening ears" of corn, four a day per man. Washington appealed to the Governor of Maryland to ship food down Chesapeake Bay.

Sometime on the eleventh Washington received a rather startling request from Jacky Custis. Dazzled and delighted by the dashing young Frenchmen on Rochambeau's staff, Jacky had decided he wanted to go to war. Could he serve on his stepfather's staff as an amateur aide? Washington was dubious, knowing how much his wife might worry. But when he consulted Martha, she gave her permission. No doubt Jacky had charmed her into saying yes in advance.

The next day, September 12, everyone was up at dawn for the journey from Mount Vernon to Williamsburg. They were on the road little more than an hour when a horseman came riding up to them with dispatches for Congress from Lafayette's headquarters. He told them dismaying news: De Grasse had abandoned the blockade at the mouth of the Chesapeake. A British fleet had appeared on the horizon, and the French had gone to sea to battle them. Sounds of gunfire had been heard from shore, but both fleets had vanished into the vast Atlantic, so no one knew whether France or Britannia ruled the waves.

Washington and Rochambeau could only look at each other mutely. No words were necessary. Both knew that everything they had planned and hoped for the past month was being decided out there on the stormy September ocean. There was only one thing to do. Ride on, and pray for good news.

The man who held all of Washington's hopes—and America's future—in his hands was Comte François Joseph Paul de Grasse, Marquis de Grasse-Tilly. Born in Provence of a noble family which could trace its lineage back to 993 A.D., he had entered the navy at the age of twelve, but he was not promoted to the rank of *lieutenant général* (rear admiral) until March 22, 1781. He was thus exercising his first independent command at the age of fifty-nine. Physically he was an imposing man. He was six feet two, and his sailors liked to say he was "six feet six on battle days." He had the impulsive temper of the Provençal. In his early days as a cadet, he once gave an order to a sailor who chose to disregard it; De Grasse picked him up and threw him bodily across the ship.

At a glance, this would seem to be the sort of man who won battles. But there were many other things involved in winning sea fights in the eighteenth century—and Washington, with his thorough knowledge of naval strategy, was undoubtedly aware of them. Almost all the intangibles favored the sailors of England—and thus what happened on the Atlantic during the next five days, as De Grasse collided with his traditional enemy, is doubly astonishing.

Though personally brave, De Grasse suffered from limitations which few French naval officers in the eighteenth century were able to overcome. The French were land animals. The sea was foreign to them, and their concept of naval warfare, their seamanship, their gunnery, were consistently inferior to that of the British. As sailors they were especially deficient. When De Grasse was a captain, the French Admiral d'Orvilliers took a squadron out to sea to practice evolutions. After ten weeks of maneuvers, the admiral declared De Grasse "was the best skilled captain in the squadron. Although his vessel was very inferior in quality, he nevertheless gave to the evolutions all the precision and brilliance possible. His frequent collisions with other ships during the cruise seems to demand something more perfect in his estimate of a situation at a glance, but they show his confidence in approaching vessels. . . ."

A British captain with a record of frequent collisions would have been run out of the service. To the French it was part of naval routine. The captain of another line-of-battle ship in De Grasse's squadron, the *Zélé*, had fourteen collisions in a thirteen-month cruise. But this ineptitude did not mean that the French squadron blockading Cornwallis was a contemptible force. On the contrary, it was visible evidence of what every Frenchman felt was the rebirth of a genuine fighting navy, which would restore the empire France had lost to Britain in the Seven Years' War. At the end of that sanguinary conflict France had lost ninety-three ships. The French minister Choiseul had embarked on a vigorous campaign of shipbuilding and an equally thorough naval training program. By the time the American revolt gave France its opportunity to strike at her old enemy, she had 67,000 trained seamen, eighty ships of war and well stocked arsenals at Brest, Toulon and Marseilles. In the very first battle of the war, a single ship slugging match between the frigates *Belle Poule* and *Arethusa,* the Frenchman forced the English captain to strike his colors—an almost unprecedented event.

De Grasse's squadron was the strong right arm of France's efforts to recapture control of the West Indies. Ironically, the French regarded these islands as infinitely more important than any possessions in North America. Thirty per cent of France's imports and thirty-five per cent of her exports were directly involved in West Indian trade. The British found it equally lucrative: "rich as a West Indiaman" was a proverbial expression in eighteenth-century London. When the Franco-American treaty of alliance was signed, one of Congress' first proposals was a joint expedition against Canada—a project which they thought the French would accept with alacrity. But the French Ambassador's secret instructions ordered him to quash the idea; France had already decided to let the British keep Canada. The reasoning: with a powerful British possession on their northern border, the independent United States would be much more likely to remain allied to France.

From the day they entered the war, the French had prosecuted the West Indian campaign far more vigorously than they had fought in America. An army of 8,000 men and a fleet of twenty-five ships of the line attacked vastly outnumbered British forces in the first year, and captured Dominica, St. Vincent and Grenada. Americans looked on these exertions with more than a little pique. They began to suspect that there was some truth in the British contention that

France was merely supporting the Americans to tie down British ships and men, while she made her real conquests elsewhere.

The terms under which De Grasse came to America were shrewdly within the limits of this grand design. His fleet was intended for West Indies service, and his orders for America were added almost as an afterthought. Under no circumstances was he to remain on the American coast later than October 15. Since August through October was the hurricane season in the West Indies, when no fleet dared venture out of its harbor, this was hardly a sacrifice.

De Grasse's sailing gives us a glimpse of the parlous state of French finances. Before he could get under way from Brest on March 22, 1781, the French Minister of Marine, De Castries, had to hurry down from Paris to satisfy the sailors' demands for back pay. He found the money only by "knocking at a hundred doors, the treasury being empty." The minister watched the fleet stand out to sea and was said to be most impressed by the seamanship displayed; there were only two collisions.

The British had a well-paid, highly expert intelligence service in France, and they knew De Grasse's destination and plans almost as soon as he did. But the King's ministers, with almost incredible ineptitude, sent their warning to the fleet in the West Indies by a slow-sailing cutter which reached the islands a month after De Grasse and his convoy. It was, remarked one British writer, a case of the tortoise beating the hare.

On station in the islands was Sir George Rodney, the most gifted admiral then in England's service, and a fleet of twenty-one ships of the line. Unfortunately for Great Britain, Rodney had attacked and captured the Dutch island of St. Eustatius in February, 1781, shortly after England declared war on Holland for her passive cooperation with France. The island had been a key center for the exchange of goods between European merchants and the colonies. Over 150 richly loaded ships and several square miles of warehouses were taken without firing a shot. The goods were valued at three million pounds sterling, and the King graciously gave the spoils to the army and the navy.

Rodney was a wild gambler and speculator; until 1778 he had been forced to live in Paris to avoid his creditors, and he had come home to fight only when a patriotic nobleman gave him a thousand guineas to quiet his would-be jailors. The vision of unlimited wealth in St. Eustatius almost undid his judgment. Instead of taking to his ships and guarding the sea lanes, he spent three months haggling and conniving with the British general, John Vaughan, leaving his subordinate, Sir Samuel Hood, to cruise on station with an inadequate squadron of seventeen ships.

On April 28, De Grasse arrived off Martinique with twenty ships and a convoy of 150 merchantmen. Waiting in Fort Royal were four more ships of the line. Hood could only spar ineffectually and then retire to warn Rodney of this unexpected development. If Rodney had been there with his entire fleet, he could have almost certainly whipped De Grasse, encumbered as he was by a convoy. Instead, the French fleet sailed into Fort Royal untouched.

De Grasse now outnumbered the British in the West Indies, and he spent the rest of the spring on the offensive, landing troops who captured Tobago and came close to seizing St. Lucia, the only good harbor the British held in the northern Caribbean. Sir Henry Clinton meanwhile had sent copies of Washington's intercepted letter to Rodney and begged him to bring the West Indies fleet to New York to protect the port from the French squadron which was certainly coming to Washington's support.

Rodney's opinion of Clinton was low. He had written to the Ministers after a visit to New York in the previous year that Clinton preferred the comforts of the city to a campaign in the field, and this explained why he was cooped up by Washington's inferior army. Nevertheless Rodney believed that the threat of De Grasse's movement to the American coast was very real. He had already received orders from Lord George Germain in London to watch De Grasse closely, and he had assured the Secretary that he would watch the Frenchman "like a lynx." He was as good as his word, up to a point. On the fifth of July a British frigate patrolling off Fort Royal counted twenty-three French ships of the line, the fifty-gun *Experiment,* and 200 home-bound merchantmen standing out to sea. Off Grenada they were joined by another ship of the line, the *Hector.* No convoy needed twenty-five battle ships; De Grasse was obviously sailing for America. Rodney instantly dispatched sloops to New York to warn the British admiral there, and to Jamaica, where a small British squadron was ordered to detach two battleships for America immediately. But Rodney himself did not follow De Grasse north. The months of negotiation and intrigue over the fortune on St. Eustatius had broken his health. Rodney was prone to terrific attacks of gout, among other things, and he now found himself incapable of continuing in his command.

It took Rodney almost three weeks to decide to haul down his flag. His second in command, Sir Samuel Hood, was in a fury at him, and wrote home: "It is quite impossible from the unsteadiness of the Commander in Chief to know what he means three days together; one hour he says his complaints are of such a nature that he cannot possibly remain in the country and is determined to leave the command to me; the next he says he has not thought of going home." Not until July 24 did Rodney turn over the fleet to Hood, and order him to sail north with fifteen ships of the line. Rodney did not sail for home until August 1, and even then he was so loath to surrender his authority that he ordered the frigate *Pegasus* to accompany his flagship *Gibraltar* as far as Bermuda in the hope that the sea air in the more northern latitudes would improve his health enough to make for New York and take charge of the combined fleet.

Putting himself in De Grasse's place, Rodney reasoned that the French admiral would not dare to detach more than twelve or fourteen battleships from his precious West Indian convoy. Two days before he sailed, Rodney detached three battleships and a frigate from Hood's fleet, and ordered them to shepherd a convoy to Jamaica, and then "without one moment's loss of time" two of the battleships were to head for the American coast. Even though Hood's squadron was now reduced to ten ships, he could add four under Rear Admiral Drake at St. Lucia, and this would be more than enough, with the ships already at New York, to give the enemy a "proper reception on their arrival."

Rodney did everything a sick man could do before he sailed for home. But Jean François Paul de Grasse was under no compulsion to conform to Sir George's expectations. He had taken his fleet and the West Indian convoy to Cap Français (modern Cap-Haïtien), on the island of Saint-Domingue (modern Haiti) where he picked up four ships of the line and received his dispatches from Rochambeau, which described the desperate state of the American cause and the need for troops and money. The admiral instantly made an historic decision. Although his orders from home instructed him to take twelve ships, leaving the rest to protect the convoy, he decided to take every ship and every man he could find to North America with him. He canceled the convoy's sailing date and commandeered his entire fleet for the trip to the Chesapeake.

This required considerable courage. Admirals and generals in the eighteenth century disregarded orders only at the risk of their reputations—and even their lives. How important the West Indies convoy was can be gleaned from the anxiety which England felt for hers. In 1779, when Rodney was delayed in escorting the outward bound convoy, the

First Lord of the Admiralty was almost hysterical. "For God's sake go to sea without delay," he wrote. "You cannot conceive of what importance it is to your self, to me and to the public that you should not lose this fair wind; if you do I shall not only hear of it in Parliament, but in places to which I pay more attention."

De Grasse found troops easily enough. He persuaded the Royal Governor of Saint-Domingue to give him 3,000 infantry, 100 artillerymen, 100 dragoons, ten field cannon and some siege guns and mortars, on the promise that they would be returned in time for a winter campaign their Spanish allies were hatching against British Jamaica. But money was another matter. The local French treasury was bare, and even when De Grasse and one of his captains offered as security the extensive plantations they owned on the island, not a banker or a citizen was willing to put up a sou. The admiral finally buttonholed the Spanish director general of customs, who happened to be in Cap Français, and begged him to raise the money in Havana. To everyone's amazement, the gentleman from Spain proved most agreeable, and De Grasse was soon told he could dispatch a frigate to pick up 1.2 million livres (or their equivalent in gold piastres). Some of the money came from the public treasury, the rest from private citizens; many local Havana ladies were said to have offered their diamonds to help defeat the hated English, who had stormed and captured the city in 1762.

De Grasse's voyage did not begin auspiciously, from a sailor's point of view. In the week before he sailed, two of his ships, one of the line and the other a frigate, caught fire while drawing brandy by lantern-light, and blew up with a loss of over 200 men. On August 5 he put to sea and again showed his courage by attempting something few French admirals had the seamanship to dare. Instead of following the usual mid-Atlantic route north, he chose the route between Cuba and the Bahamas, partly to rendezvous with his frigate from Havana and secure the vitally-needed cash, and partly to avoid British ships which might warn of his approach.

Soon, with the aid of Spanish pilots, De Grasse's ships were threading their way through the channel off Baracoa on the northern coast of Cuba. For three days they were trapped in the narrowest part of the passage by contrary winds and came within a whisker of losing one of their battleships, the *Northumberland,* which got into the breakers near the reefs when a helmsman gave the wheel a wrong turn. By the seventeenth of August the fleet was in the Bahama channel, a ten-mile belt of water which flows northward from the islands and carries ships along at a daily rate of twenty to thirty miles, even with contrary winds.

Meanwhile, all of Rodney's precautions began to unravel. Sir Peter Parker, admiral in command in Jamaica, totally disregarded the order to dispatch two ships of the line immediately for New York. The sloop *Swallow* which Rodney had dispatched to warn New York of De Grasse's sailing arrived there on the twenty-seventh of July and found Admiral Graves and his squadron had gone cruising off Newport to intercept a French convoy carrying supplies and reinforcements for Rochambeau. The senior naval officer in New York opened Rodney's letter, made a copy and sent the sloop off to find Admiral Graves at sea. The *Swallow*'s captain was scarcely out of New York harbor when he saw a Yankee privateer, and with visions of prize money dancing in his head, attacked and captured her. Hours after he had won his battle, he was in turn attacked by three other privateers and driven ashore on Long Island, where his ship and the precious warning letter went up in smoke.

Equally doleful was the fate of a brig which Sir Samuel Hood had dispatched to New York on August 1 warning Graves of his impending arrival and urging him to rendezvous with him at sea so they could be instantly ready to take on the enemy. It too was captured by privateers and taken to

Philadelphia. There the captain, who knew the importance of his message (something the imperious Rodney did not bother to tell the *Swallow*'s captain), bribed a loyalist sympathizer to get the message to New York overland. But it arrived much too late.

Not until August 16 did Graves return to New York. There he found the copy of Rodney's letter, but nothing which gave him definite news of Hood's probable arrival date. Moreover, he soon had his hands full with Sir Henry Clinton, who wanted him to transport men and supplies for his attack on the undefended French base at Newport. Graves finally deflated this idea by maintaining that one of his ships had to be refitted, another remasted.

To do him justice, Sir Henry Clinton had admirals who would have driven a better balanced man to raving. Before Graves, the British sea commander had been Vice Admiral Marriot Arbuthnot, an aging, vacillating, irritable has-been, whom Clinton finally unseated by threatening (once more) to resign. Graves was a little younger, but otherwise no improvement. He had never held an independent command before, and his record as a captain was totally undistinguished. The reason such men were given vital commands was entirely political. The savage animosities aroused by the American Revolution were by no means confined to Parliamentary exchanges. A number of distinguished admirals who had refused to serve against the Americans had come into the war reluctantly when France entered. Sandwich, First Lord of the Admiralty, did nothing to improve relations with these officers when he tried one of their most outspoken leaders, Admiral Keppel, in a court martial after an indecisive battle with the French fleet off Ushant in 1778. Keppel's acquittal was the signal for anti-government riots in London, which were suppressed only by armed troops. Thereafter, no admiral felt he was safe against the political meddling of Sandwich, and even with the French threatening invasion, many refused to serve until the First Lord resigned. "Out Twitcher must" was the cry, which doubly insulted Sandwich by identifying him with stool pigeon Jemmy Twitcher in *The Beggar's Opera*.

Sir Samuel Hood, the one man capable of redeeming England's collapsing fortunes in American waters, sailed from the West Indies with fourteen ships on August 10, five days after De Grasse. But because his ships had copper bottoms, and De Grasse had chosen the longer route up the Bahama Channel, Hood beat him to the Chesapeake by five days, hauling his wind off the mouth of the great bay on August 25. If Graves had received his messages, he would have undoubtedly been there to meet him, and when De Grasse arrived, he would have found a British fleet blockading the mouth of the Chesapeake. But the loyalist messenger from Philadelphia was still trudging across New Jersey, and Graves and Clinton were in New York arguing about the expedition to Newport. Hood found the Chesapeake empty and peaceful, and pushed on to New York, reaching Sandy Hook on August 28.

The day he arrived, the complacent Graves wrote him a dispatch: "No intelligence as yet of De Grasse. Accounts say that he has gone to Havana to join the Spaniards. A little time will shew us. All the American accounts are big with expectation and the Army has lately crossed to the Southward of the Hudson and appears in motion in the Jerseys as if to threaten Staten Island. For my own part I believe the mountain in labour."

Hood sent a boat into New York and asked Graves and Clinton to join him for an immediate conference. Instead Graves urged him to bring his ships over the bar and join him in the harbor, because they were "exposed to the enemy as well as to the violence of the sea" where they were. Hood, in language only slightly less than scalding, urged him in turn to order his own ships out of the harbor, so that they would be ready for sea. Graves took his suggestion, but from the very first meeting it was evident that the two men had small regard for each other.

Most of the contempt was from Hood's side of the table. Sir Samuel was on his way to becoming one of England's greatest admirals. A lean, acerbic man with a hawk nose and gimlet eyes (William Smith called him "the image of a Yankee Colonel both in person and stiff behavior"), he was also one of the greatest letter writers of his day, and in these so-called personal and private missives, he spared no one from his vitriol. Unfortunately for England, Graves was the senior admiral by several years. Hood had been edged aside in the fierce infighting which promotion in the navy entailed and in 1778 was mouldering as Commissioner of the Portsmouth Dockyard. The scarcity of admirals willing to serve had forced Sandwich to give him a non-political appointment as second in command to Rodney. Ironically, he was chosen as "likely to second you properly and with proper subordination"—which only suggests that Sandwich was a poor judge of personality as well as ability. In later years, Nelson called Hood "the best officer take him all together, that England had to boast of."

While Hood urged Graves to go to sea immediately, and the latter dallied, a frigate came tearing in from the Newport patrol with the news that Admiral Barras had sailed from Newport. This left Graves with no choice, and on the 31st of August he put to sea, heading for the Chesapeake, Barras' logical destination. He was confident that he was on his way to annihilate the French eight-ship squadron with his own fleet of nineteen ships of the line. Disregarding all the warnings from Rodney, he wrote to the Admiralty on the thirtieth: "The *Richmond* came in on the 29th from the Chesapeake in four days where everything is quiet and I have had two frigates before the Delaware for some time past. Whether the French intend a junction or whether they have left the coast is only to be guessed at."

Admiral Graves had a surprise waiting for him in the Chesapeake. On August 30 Admiral de Grasse's fleet stood into the mouth of the bay, after a most successful voyage up the American coast. Off Charleston they had the satisfaction of capturing three small British ships, one of them carrying Lord Rawdon, Cornwallis' lieutenant in South Carolina, who was going home to rest. Another ship was carrying four other English officers and "several young women." One of the French nobles in De Grasse's fleet, who published a journal of the voyage under the pseudonym Chevalier de Goussencourt, declared the ladies "were greatly rejoiced at their adversity and said that the French even on the sea were better than their countrymen. There is one style in which they surely would not prove it—being very knowing. I would willingly rely on their judgment, so far as their experience goes."

Only a few hours after the French dropped anchor in the Chesapeake, a number of small boats came out from shore. One of them carried a man identified only as "one of the Principal citizens of Virginia." They pulled alongside, and the astonished French heard a voice ask in eager tones which was Lord Rodney's flagship. One of the sailors on deck spoke English quite well, and invited the whole party on board. They were marched to the main cabin, where the ship's captain politely informed them that they were prisoners. In the boat were "excellent melons and many other refreshments which the delighted officers promptly ate, with frequent toasts to Lord Rodney."

Admiral de Grasse was not wasting his time with such drolleries. By September 2, he had ships moving up the James River, covering the landing of the 3,300 troops he had brought from the islands under the command of the Marquis de Saint-Simon, to assist Lafayette in his blockade of Cornwallis. Over 1,800 men and 90 officers from his fleet were put ashore to collect fresh vegetables and water. The frigate *Concorde* was sent up the bay to Baltimore with the dispatches which were to give Washington such joy. Everyone seemed to be meshing with almost unbelievable efficiency except Admiral Barras. Not a word had been heard from him, and unless he arrived safely with the artillery and provisions chaos might still be the final result.

On September 5 about ten o'clock, a French scouting frigate came scurrying inside the capes of the Chesapeake and reported sails on the horizon. At first there was rejoicing; the French thought it was Barras, because ten ships had been the frigate's count. But by eleven o'clock, the count had risen to twenty-seven, and De Grasse knew it was the English fleet on the attack. They could not have arrived at a worse moment; he still had those 1,800 men and 90 officers on shore. Almost all his smaller craft were busy landing troops, and three of his capital ships were blockading the York and James Rivers. But he had to go out and fight. He could not leave Barras' little squadron to certain annihilation. At eleven-thirty he gave the order to slip cables and stand out to sea, but it was noon before the tide allowed him to get under way.

If De Grasse was surprised, Admiral Graves was thunderstruck to find not Barras' piddling squadron, but an immense battle-fleet confronting him. In his dispatch after the battle, he still echoes his shock, even speaking in the third person. "The British Admiral . . . had discovered a number of great ships at anchor which seemed to be extended across the extreme of the Chesapeake from Cape Henry to the Middle Ground . . ."

The sudden realization that he was facing a superior enemy seemed to have numbed Graves's brain. He completely forgot his advantages—all his ships were coppered, and thus half again as fast as the French (who had about half their twenty-four big ships coppered), besides the fact that the English could count on superior seamanship, firepower and fleet condition. Moreover, his ships were already in battle formation, while De Grasse was frantically trying to get free of the Chesapeake and form a line. He was only outnumbered by five ships—hardly a significant difference. The English channel fleet had recently stood off a combined Spanish-French fleet of fifty ships with twenty-five of their coppered bottoms. Above all, Graves had the wind—an absolutely vital advantage in the age of sail.

For a full hour the French fleet straggled out of the bay. De Grasse in his flagship, the great three deck *Ville de Paris,* with its 110 guns, was the eleventh ship to clear the capes. Their position was made doubly difficult by the peculiar nature of the Chesapeake's mouth. The main channel is between Cape Henry and a shoal called the Middle Ground. Thus ships that were stationed on the northern side of the bay had to sail almost ten miles, tacking several times, to get into the open sea. Not until 1:45 did the *Ville de Paris* clear Cape Henry.

"The Fifth of September was a moment of ambition to me," Graves admitted later. No doubt, as he saw the size of the French fleet, he had a vivid image of a victory dispatch which might make Quiberon Bay a mere splashing match. But at that climactic naval battle of the Seven Years' War, the British admirals had driven into a stormlashed bay like a pack of ravenous hounds and torn the French to pieces. Off the Chesapeake, while the ten ships of the French van were milling around waiting for orders, what was Graves doing?

Nothing. Ignoring an opportunity which one writer has called "beyond the wildest dreams of a sea commander," he fell back on the rigid rules which governed the tactics of the British navy in the eighteenth century. The "Fighting Instructions" specified that in a fleet-to-fleet battle, ships were to form in a precise line, so as to give each other supporting fire and reduce the danger of any ship being cut off and overwhelmed. In 1744 off Toulon, Admiral Thomas Matthews had made the mistake of abandoning the line and attacking with only half his fleet, when his rear squadron did not obey his signals. Though the battle was a draw, Matthews was court-martialed and drummed out of the service. Since that day, hardly a single English admiral dared to vary the tactics of the line, as long as his enemy maintained a line formation opposite him. Gifted admirals, such as Rodney, knew the limitations of line tactics; it always tended to produce drawn battles, because each ship engaged its opposite in the enemy line, gave some damage, took some, and then hauled away. Two years before, Rodney had written: "To fight ships for ships was contrary to common sense, and the duty of an Admiral is to keep all his fleet in order to attack the half or a smaller portion of the enemy."

But such thinking was rare, especially among unimaginative men such as Graves. Moreover, the admiral had had one close brush with ruin for failing to follow the regulations in his youth; when captain of a frigate, he had refused to pursue and capture a merchant ship, which he had mistaken for a ship of the line. He was court-martialed and censured for an "error of judgment." On the same day, in 1757, Admiral John Byng had been court-martialed and shot to death on his own quarter-deck by a firing squad of marines for "negligence." Ironically, Byng, by adhering too literally to the strategy of the line, had allowed a French amphibious army to capture Minorca. More than a few observers were to note that the kind of battle Byng had fought and the kind Graves now was to fight were almost identical: a French squadron in disarray, an English army besieged, an admiral who refused his chance to attack and destroy his enemy on the sea because his fleet was not properly in line.

Graves was also hamstrung by the primitive state of British signaling. The fighting admirals of earlier wars had looked down on signals. They said too many flags only hampered the initiative of the individual captains, and for proof pointed to the French, who had a far more elaborate signal system which kept each captain so busy straining to see what the admiral was telling him to do that he could not command his ship. As a result, Graves had only two signals to choose from as he approached De Grasse. One was "line ahead," the other "general chase." But a general chase was only supposed to be used when a fleet was defeated or fleeing, and De Grasse was coming out to fight. Another admiral, Sir Charles Knowles, had come close to meeting Admiral Byng's fate for ordering a chase of an unbeaten Spanish fleet off Havana in 1748.

So Graves clung to the safe but sure line formation, and let De Grasse's fleet pile out of the Chesapeake and straggle into a semblance of a line. Then, finding his own forward ships approaching too close to the shoals of the Middle Ground, he shifted his course so that by 2:15 both fleets were heading out to sea on a roughly parallel course, with the British still in possession of the wind.

Even then, Graves still had a chance for what Hood later called "a rich and most delightful harvest of glory." The five leading ships—the "van" of the French fleet—were by Graves's own admission "very particularly extended." With his superior speed, Graves could easily have cut them off from the rest of the fleet and annihilated them. A French eyewitness admitted the French were courting disaster. "The fleet formed in very bad order, for to tell the truth, there were only four vessels in line, the *Pluton,* 74 guns, the *Bourgogne,* 80, the *Marseillois,* 64, and the *Diadème,* 74. The *Réfléchi,* 64 guns, and the *Caton* came next, half a league to the lee of the first; the rest of the fleet more to the lee of the latter; the *Ville de Paris,* 110, in the center. The British were in the best possible order, bowsprit to stern, bearing down on us."

Once more Graves's devotion to the rule book caused him to miss his chance to save America for the Empire. Still flying the signal, "line ahead at half a cable length," he actually

brought his flagship *London* to a stop. In the ship's log is the
almost unbelievable entry: "brought to in order to let ye
Center of the Enemys Ships come a Brest of us." Signals were
sent flying aloft to five of his ships to "gett in line or gett to
her station." All told, Graves gave De Grasse a "full hour and
a half" to bring up his center and rear, according to the enraged Hood, who was bringing up the British rear. It all
seemed very sensible to Graves, who did not see how he could
fight in line unless the French were neatly in line opposite
him.

At 2:30 Graves went from missing chances to making blunders. With the two fleets about three miles apart on their
parallel lines, he made a signal for "ye leading Ships to lead
more to starboard"—toward the French. Since the French
stayed on their course, and Graves still kept the line ahead
signal flying, this meant his whole fleet followed the lead ship
and came in at the French at a thirty degree angle.

Ships of the line in 1781 were huge, unwieldy creatures,
really little more than floating gun platforms. Moreover,
their guns were fixed and could only fire straight ahead.
Thus a ship that came in at an angle could bring practically
none of its guns to bear, while it was exposed to the full
broadside of the enemy. This is precisely what happened
to Graves's leading ships. At 4:03, six hours after he had
sighted the enemy, Graves finally opened fire. "Seeing the
enemy ships advancing very slow and the evening approaching," he says, "the English Admiral made ye signal for ye
ships to bear down and Engage."

Now was the moment when every sailor said his prayers.
No fighting on land could equal the carnage that ensued
when these massive old square-riggers hauled alongside one
another, and at point blank range poured in broadsides of
80 to 100 shots. British gun crews were capable of firing two
shots every three minutes, and they had the additional advantage of carronades, large calibre cannon of very short

range, that could be loaded and fired even faster. They had been introduced into the fleet in 1779 and had already proved themselves ferociously effective weapons.

Every man in both battle fleets was at general quarters. On the lower gun decks, hatches were bolted to make sure no one deserted his station. The French, helpless to maneuver while the British had the wind, could only watch as the British leader, the *Shrewsbury,* captained by a grizzled sea dog named Mark Robinson, cut through the water at them. Now they could see everything—the grim-faced gunners with their black silk kerchiefs on their heads, shirtsleeves tucked up, most but not all wearing the familiar blue jacket and white trousers (there was as yet no official uniform for seamen), the powder boys sitting coolly on their full boxes of high explosives, the captains of guns with their boxes of equally explosive priming powder buckled around their waists, the officers in blue and gold with their swords drawn, standing by their respective divisions, the captain on his quarterdeck, more exposed than most of his men.

A Spanish officer, who once watched the English go to quarters on a line-of-battle ship, remarked in awed tones that they reminded him of a squadron of devils. There was undoubtedly something spectral about the relish they seemed to show for battle. But on September 5, 1781, the French were equally determined, and they were seamen enough to take advantage of Graves's blunders. Before the *Shrewsbury* could fire a shot (because of her oblique approach), the captain of the *Pluton* caught her with a broadside from the port half of his seventy-four guns. A cannon ball tore off Captain Robinson's leg, killed his lieutenant standing beside him and fourteen of the crew, and horribly wounded fifty-two others. Bearing up behind the *Shrewsbury* was the *Intrepid,* whose captain, A. J. P. Molloy, tried to come to her assistance, but was himself staggered by a broadside from the *Marseillois,* the second ship in the French line.

One after the other, the first six ships of Graves's van came grimly into battle on the precise line ahead of the fighting instructions, knowing they were going to be mauled before they could defend themselves.

In his own defense, Graves maintained that he never intended to keep the precise line formation right up to the moment of engagement. At 4:11, he avowed, he pulled the signal down and sent up "ye signal to engage close." Whereupon his flagship *London* started for the enemy, though Hood considered the ship's opening broadside was "from a most improper distance." Then, at 4:22, Graves rehoisted the signal for line ahead, "ye ships not being sufficiently extended." Consternation instantly seized the entire English fleet, especially the nine ships behind Graves, who was tenth in line. The two signals were contradictory, as far as they were concerned. On the extended angle at which they were approaching the French, if they stayed in line formation, they could not engage at all, much less engage close.

Graves later swore that he only put up the signal for the line to stop his ships from bunching; he was emphasizing the last half of the signal's message: "line ahead *at half a cable.*" He also said that he took it down again at 4:27. But Sir Samuel Hood and his captains swore it flew continuously until 5:30. This left them with the unhappy choice of disobeying the sacred line orders or sitting at the end of Graves's weirdly angled battle line, watching their comrades up ahead fighting for their lives without firing a shot in their support. Which is, alas for England, exactly what they did.

The anguish and indignation of Hood's captains can be glimpsed in these words from Thomas White, testifying that Graves kept the signal for the line flying while close action was also up. "If the *London*'s log, or the log of any other individual ship in the fleet confirm this statement [that the signal for the line was hauled down], I shall be induced to fancy that what I that day saw and heard was a mere chimera of the brain and that what I believed to be the signal for the line was not a Union Jack, but an *ignis fatuus* conjured up to mock me."

While Hood strode his quarterdeck sputtering with the same rage and contempt for his commander in chief that Cornwallis on the shore felt for Sir Henry Clinton, the ships of the British van were giving a more-than-adequate account of themselves. In spite of the raking they had taken on their approach, they went to work on the French van with their traditional ferocity. The *Princessa,* flagship of Rear Admiral Francis Drake, flung a broadside into the *Réfléchi,* fourth in the French line, which killed its captain and wreaked dreadful havoc on the crew. The English always fired low in sea battles, going instinctively for the most crucial target area. The French always fired high, because it was part of their naval theory to disable an enemy fleet rather than to sink it. To the French, a sea battle was never an end in itself, but always a part of some "ulterior object"—usually an operation on the land. Because of this contradiction in theory, French casualties were always higher when they faced an English fleet. The wooden walls offered little or no protection for the forty and fifty pound shot that came hurtling through the French lower gun decks.

Minutes after Drake's flagship opened fire, the *Réfléchi* fell out of line, reeling in defeat. The *Caton,* seventh in the French formation, soon followed it in bloody retreat. Once more the British had a superb opportunity to chop De Grasse's fleet into separate sections. Here is how it looked to a French eyewitness:

> The four ships in the French van found themselves . . . entirely cut off from the rest of the fleet, and constantly engaged with seven or eight vessels at close quarters. The *Diadème* was near Rear Admiral Drake, who set fire to her at

every shot, the wadding entering her side. This vessel was
constantly engaged with two and sometimes three ships. . . .
The *Diadème* was utterly unable to keep up the battle, having only four 36 pounders and nine 18 pounders fit for use
and all on board killed, wounded or burnt.

With three French ships out of the line, Graves once more
had a magnificent opportunity to break through the French
fleet and devour it piecemeal. But his rigid line formation
prevented most of the ships in his center squadron from getting close enough to give the French a real fight. Hood
summed up Graves's tactical ignorance in a letter he wrote
home the following day:

> Had the centre gone to the support of the van and the signal
> for the line being hauled down, or the commander in chief
> had set the example for close action, even with the signal for
> the line flying, the van of the enemy must have been cut to
> pieces and the rear division of the British fleet would have
> been opposed to those ships the centre division fired at, and
> at the proper distance for engaging, or the Rear Admiral who
> commanded it would have a great deal to answer for. Instead
> of that, our centre division did the enemy but little damage,
> and the rear ships, being barely within random shot, three
> only fired a few shots. . . .

In the melee at the van, the French in several instances
more than held their own. The years of training in gunnery
and discipline were paying off at last. The Chevalier de
Goussencourt tells how the captain of the *St. Esprit,* though
himself wounded, came to the assistance of the staggering
Diadème and "opened a terrible fire that the gentlemen
from Albion could not stand and had to haul their wind."
Admiral Bougainville, in command of the van, came within
a whisker of boarding the *Princessa,* Admiral Drake's flagship, and then turned his fire on the *Terrible* which he "rid-
dled."

The Swedish officer, Karl Gustaf Tornquist, who was fighting with the French, tells how Admiral Bougainville had his foretop bowline blown off and how sailors who twice tried to climb aloft to repair it were shot down. Bougainville, noticing that no one was inclined to make a third attempt, and needing every sail he could get, offered his purse to the man who would put the bowline in shape. An ordinary seaman immediately went out on the yard and repaired the damage. Then called back: "My Admiral, we do not go there for money."

At 5:30, Graves finally hauled down the signal for the line, and Hood immediately brought his rear squadron down upon the enemy. But the French had had enough fighting for the day, and De Grasse signaled his fleet to "bear up" and thus avoid the oncoming Hood. This gave the French a chance to reform their line, and at six P.M. De Grasse made the signal to "wear"—come about and take the wind on the opposite side—signifying his readiness for another attack on those parts of his hulls which were undamaged. But at 6:30 Graves ran up his old reliable "line ahead" signal once more and held his fleet on a parallel course. He knew his outnumbered squadron had been roughly handled, and he was not going to attack again until he found out how many ships were still in fighting condition. Frigates were sent racing up and down the line to gather reports from the Captains.

The news was bad. The *Intrepid* had sixty-five shot holes in the starboard side, the *Shrewsbury* had lost her main topmast and her foremast was almost severed in three places, the mizzenmast in two. At 8:05 she made the signal of distress and abandoned her leadership of the column. The *Alcide* reported many shot holes under water, making the ship leaky, and three shot through the mainmast; the *Ajax* had "two guns wounded and one dismounted;" the *Europe* had four shot in the mainmast, twelve shot between wind and water, and a great number in the upper works. The *Montague*'s hull was "much shattered by shot, rigging and sails very much cut, four guns dismounted." The ancient *Terrible,* which had been fighting a bad leak and a sprung mainmast before the battle began, had taken two cannon balls through the mainmast and many others in the hull, and was in sinking condition. All told there were 90 sailors dead and 220 wounded.

On the morning of the sixth Graves peered through the early light at the French fleet and decided they "had not the appearance of near so much damage as we had sustained." He then tried to pass the buck to Samuel Hood. He sent a captain over to the *Barfleur,* Hood says, "desiring his opinion whether the action should be renewed." Sir Samuel's answer was: "I dare say Mr. Graves will do what is right. I can *send* no opinion, but whenever he, Mr. Graves, wishes to see me, I will wait upon him with great pleasure." Face to face in a council of war, Hood was perfectly willing to share his views. But he was not about to do so through third parties who could later testify against him if things went wrong. Such sparring shows the state of mind of the best officers in the navy, as a result of the political interference of the government in purely naval matters.

The day was calm, and the two fleets lay in sight of each other while the carpenters and shipwrights and gunners worked furiously on rigging and hulls to repair the damages. The British admirals spent their time wrangling. Graves sent a memorandum to the rest of the fleet, explaining his ideas about the use of the line ahead signal. His explanation was as foggy as his tactics:

When the signal for the line of battle ahead is out at the same time with the signal for battle, it is not to be understood that the latter signal shall be rendered ineffectual by a too strict adherence to the former. The signal for the line of battle ahead is to be considered as the line of extension for the fleet, and the respective admirals and captains of the fleet are desired to be attentive not to advance or fall back, so as to intercept the fire of their seconds ahead and astern, but to keep as near the enemy as possible while the signal for close action continues out; and to take notice that the line must be preserved parallel to that of the enemy during battle, without regard to a particular point of bearing. . . .

Hood seized this bit of doubletalk, and wrote on the back of it:

It is the first time I ever heard it suggested that too strict an adherence could be paid to the line of battle; and if I understand the meaning of the British fleet being formed parallel to that of the enemy, it is that if the enemy's fleet is disorderly and irregularly formed, the British fleet is, in compliment to it, to form irregularly and disorderly also. Now the direct contrary is my opinion; and I think, in case of disorder or irregularity in the enemy's line, that the British fleet should be as compact as possible, in order to take the critical moment of an advantage opening and offering itself, to make a powerful impression on the most vulnerable part of the enemy.

It was the voice of the next century, speaking to a man thinking and working with tactics already a century old, and there was simply no communication. The manner of Hood's message certainly did nothing to improve relations between him and Graves. Later in the day, the commander in chief sent for his two junior admirals and discussed the situation. Hood's advice to Graves was simple: you have copper bottoms and can sail the canvas off De Grasse. Make for the Chesapeake at this very moment, throw a line of battleships across the entrance, and let the Frenchman figure out how to break through it. Graves thought the maneuver too risky. Already outnumbered, he was afraid of being trapped. As a sop, he decided to send two frigates into the bay and cut the cables of the French anchor buoys.

On the seventh of September, the wind shifted, and De Grasse found himself in possession of it. But he did not try to attack. It would have been a foolish move on his part. If he could keep between the English and the Chesapeake, Barras and his eight ships had a good chance of slipping in unchallenged. For forty-eight hours, the entire seventh and eighth of September, the two fleets cruised about three miles apart, with the French usually, but not continually in possession of the wind, while Graves worried over the state of his fleet. He betrays his thinking in his dispatch: "We had not speed enough in so mutilated a state to attack them had it been prudent and they showed no inclination to renew the action for they generally maintained the wind of us and had it often in their power." Like Sir Henry Clinton, Graves's first principle of military success was to do nothing wrong. He was thinking and acting like an admiral on maneuvers, rather than as the savior of 7,500 trapped British soldiers on the shore.

The condition of Graves's damaged ships added nothing to his collapsing confidence. On the eighth, the *Intrepid*'s main topmast went over the side and her foreyard was expected to go at any moment. Toward evening the *Terrible* made the signal of distress, and it soon became apparent that the ship would not last out the night. Crew and stores were transferred to nearby ships, and around midnight the *Terrible* was set on fire and soon blew up.

On the ninth of September, De Grasse's ships suddenly shook out every sail they had, and disappeared over the horizon toward the Chesapeake. Graves made no attempt to follow them; instead he let a northeast wind carry him farther south, until he was off Cape Hatteras. Hood was almost incoherent with anguish. On the tenth he sent a letter to Graves:

I flatter myself you will forgive the liberty I take in asking whether you have any knowledge where the French fleet is, as we can see nothing of it from the *Barfleur* [Hood's flagship]. By the press of sail De Grasse carried yesterday, I am inclined to think his aim is the Chesapeake, in order to be strengthened by the ships there, either by adding them to his present force, or by exchanging his disabled ships for them. Admitting that to be his plan, will he not cut off the frigates you have sent to reconnoitre, as well as the ships you expect from New York? And if he should enter the Bay, which is by no means improbable, will he not succeed in giving most effectual succour to the rebels?

This letter forced Graves to summon Hood and Drake to another council of war. When Hood came on board Graves's flagship he found "to my great astonishment Mr. Graves as ignorant as myself where the French fleet was, and that no frigates were particularly ordered . . . to watch and bring an account of the enemy's motions." Graves now asked Sir Samuel what they should do, and he answered "we should get into the Chesapeake to the Succour of Lord Cornwallis and his brave troops if possible." Hood pointed out that they had only sixteen damaged guns in the whole fleet, and in Hood's squadron not a man or a ship had been touched. But Graves preferred to dally. Not until the eleventh of September did he decide to sail for the Chesapeake and send the frigate *Medea* ahead to reconnoitre. On the twelfth, the *Medea*'s captain brought to off the great bay and counted thirty-six French battleships riding confidently at anchor. Barras had made it safely into harbor and now gave De Grasse an overwhelming superiority. Back dashed the *Medea* to Graves with the doleful news.

It was so demoralizing, Graves actually humbled himself before the disgusted Hood. He sent him another note: "Admiral Graves presents his compliments to Sir Samuel Hood and begs leave to acquaint him that the *Medea* has just made the signal to inform him that the French fleet are at anchor above the Horse Shoe in the Chesapeake and desires his opinion what to do with the fleet."

He got the following answer: "Rear Admiral Sir Samuel Hood presents his compliments to Rear Admiral Graves. Is extremely concerned to find by his note just received that the French fleet is at anchor in the Chesapeake above the Horse Shoe, though it is no more than what he expected, as the press of sail the fleet carried on the ninth and in the night of the eighth made it very clear to him what De Grasse's intentions were. Sir Samuel would be very glad to send an opinion, but he really knows not what to say in the truly lamentable state we have brought ourselves."

Driven by their anxiety for news of De Grasse, Washington
and Rochambeau rode with hardly a stop all day on the
twelfth of September. Messengers had already been sent to
the troopships coming down the Chesapeake to put ashore
until further orders arrived. It would be the end of everything if the allied army sailed into the guns of an English
fleet. The two generals spent the night in a tavern in Fred-
ricksburg, Maryland, and pushed ahead the next morning at
dawn. More than a few of their party fell behind, unable to
keep the pace Washington set. But another day ended without
Williamsburg in sight, and it was not until the afternoon of
the fourteenth that the dust-covered cavalcade rode through
the streets of Williamsburg, past the handsome red brick "palace" where the Royal Governor had lived.

Only when they reached the camp of the French West Indian division did they call a halt. Washington's keen sense of military etiquette came to the fore, and he realized that the French officers would be mortified if they did not have time to prepare the troops to receive such distinguished visitors. After a few minutes, down the avenue of tents rode Lafayette and Governor Thomas Nelson of Virginia, and the French general, the Marquis de Saint-Simon.

The irrepressible Lafayette leaped off his horse, and while bystanders watched goggle-eyed, he rushed toward Washington with his arms outstretched. St. George Tucker, a young Bermudian who had moved to Virginia to join the Revolution, was standing only a few feet away, and wrote his wife a vivid description of the scene. Lafayette "caught the General round his body, hugged him as close as it was possible, and absolutely kissed him from ear to ear once or twice . . . with as much ardor as ever an absent lover kissed his mistress on his return." Meanwhile the French regiments poured out of their tents and fell in on either side of the road, as eager to see *le grand Washington* as he was to see them.

After a brief review, Washington rode on to his Americans, who had had more time to prepare a reception. Drums rolled and cannon boomed a twenty-one gun salute as he entered the camp, and the ragged Light Infantry of Lafayette and the tattered Pennsylvania Line stood in trim formation, presenting their well-kept arms. They did not look as flashy as the white and gold regiments of France, but Washington undoubtedly looked upon them with considerable pride. Outnumbered four to one, these men had defended the general's beloved Virginia with stubborn courage.

But the burning question was: what news of De Grasse? Had Admiral Barras arrived? At dinner in General Saint-Simon's tent, there were only glum shakes of the head, and worried, regretful *no's*. Nevertheless, the French were determined to be gay. Saint-Simon's food was good, his wine was superb, and Lafayette filled Washington in on all that had been happening while the latter was on the road south. General Wayne had been wounded in the leg by a sentry when he failed to give the proper countersign while coming to visit Lafayette. The Marquis himself had spent two weeks in bed with malaria, and in fact had staggered from his cot to his horse only to meet Washington. Baron von Steuben was in camp, miraculously freed from his gout, which had prevented him from serving with Lafayette. (The Baron had written to his friend Nathanael Greene, that the moment he heard of the French arrival, "my gout was cured at once.")

Not until ten o'clock did the toasts and serenades of the French army band end and let Washington retreat to his tent, and Lafayette to his sickbed to shake and shiver for another feverish night. Around twelve o'clock, before anyone could have been well asleep, considering the anxiety De Grasse was causing them, an excited messenger came charging into camp with the wonderful news that the French fleet was back in the Chesapeake with a victory, and the English had retreated to New York. The next day Claude Blanchard, the French commissary, also arrived in camp with more news. He had had dinner aboard the *Ville de Paris* two days before, and had heard the admiral speak with much modesty of the sea battle, saying that it was "only an encounter between two advanced guards." In his diary, Washington seemed inclined to agree, calling the clash between the fleets "a partial engagement."

To everyone in the allied camp, it seemed probable, even inevitable, that the British would return for another attempt to save Cornwallis. This, plus the deadline De Grasse had mentioned for his stay on the coast, made speed essential. But speed was the one thing Washington and Rochambeau could not command. Their armies were still far up the Chesapeake. Washington fired off a letter to Major General Benjamin Lincoln, who was shepherding the troops, urging all pos-

sible speed. "Every day we lose now is comparatively an age,"
he wrote. But he must have known Lincoln could not command the wind and tide. All anyone could do for the time
being was worry and wait.

Their first communication from De Grasse did not decrease
their worries. The moment he learned the good news of his
victory. Washington had written to the admiral suggesting
the "honor of an interview" with him. From what he had
heard from Lafayette, Washington had undoubtedly already
realized the admiral might be the weak link in their siege.
The moment De Grasse had arrived in the Chesapeake, and
put ashore Saint-Simon with his 3,300 troops, the admiral
had wanted Lafayette and the West Indian army to launch
an assault on Cornwallis' entrenchments. They had wisely
declined the opportunity, pointing out their combined army
was barely as strong as the English, who were dug in up to
their chins. The suggestion had reminded everyone ominously of an earlier French admiral, the Comte d'Estaing,
and an earlier siege, that of Savannah in 1779. There the
French had insisted on a premature frontal assault against
the well-entrenched English, and over a thousand French
and American troops had been mowed down in a dreadful
slaughter.

De Grasse's answer to Washington's request for an interview, while it showed a soldierly regard for the problem of
getting more troops down the bay (the admiral had already
dispatched transports to Baltimore) and cordially welcomed
the idea of a conference ended with the same note of nervous
impatience. "I am annoyed by the delay . . . time is passing, the enemy is profiting by it, and the season is approaching when against my will, I shall be obliged to forsake the allies for whom I have done my very best and more than could
be expected."

But De Grasse was by no means the only worry. Supplies,
that perpetual problem, were alarmingly low. Four days be-

fore, Lafayette, in the midst of his malaria attack, had written frantically to Virginia's Governor Thomas Nelson: "I could wish to sleep tonight but I fear it will be impossible with the prospect that is before us tomorrow. There is not one grain of flour in camp whether for the American or French army."

The nine thousand men already in the allied camp were living from day to day on a trickle of food from the surrounding countryside. Yet the harvest in both Virginia and Maryland had been exceptionally rich; it was a question of organizing the transportation and spending freely the money De Grasse had brought from Havana. The two generals handed over to Monsieur Blanchard 800,000 gold piastres and told him to get busy.

The commissary, who was the very model of the government worker—fussy, precise, proud of order and in love with organization—was appalled. Everything—his staff, his supplies, his secretary—were still on the Chesapeake with the rest of the army. "I set to work," he says, "though without a piece of paper or an employee or a bag of flour at my disposal; I was completely overwhelmed." Lafayette, used to dealing with the Virginians, volunteered to help, and won M. Blanchard's heart completely. Though he found fault with almost everyone else, including Rochambeau (whose manners he pronounced far from courteous), on the young Marquis he showered compliments. "It is difficult to employ more order, patience and integrity in the discussion of business manners; he reminded me of Scipio Africanus in Spain; as young and as modest as he, he already had the reputation of a skillful warrior. . . ." The commissary ordered ovens to be built, "but I was in want of tools and had to run about much and negotiate to obtain even a hammer." The climax to his woes was a nocturnal catastrophe; the house in which he had stored the 800,000 gold piastres was old and weak; in the middle of the night M. Blanchard was frightened from his bed on the second floor by a tremendous crash. He rushed downstairs to find his servant in the cellar, up to his neck in gold coins. The whole first floor had given way under the weight of the hard cash.

Meanwhile, Washington had given warm approval to Baron von Steuben's suggestion that he improve the polish of the American army with a little drilling. Both the Baron and Lafayette were determined to show their European compatriots that their American "sansculottes" (Von Steuben had coined the word at Valley Forge) could be as professional as the gaudiest French grenadier. Soon Lieutenant Ebenezer Denny of the Pennsylvania Line was noting in his diary:

> Discipline the order of the day. In all directions troops seen exercising and maneuvering. Baron Steuben our great military oracle. The guards attend the grand parade at an early hour, where the Baron is always found, waiting with one or two aides on horseback. These men are exercised and put through various evolutions and military experiments for two hours. Many officers and spectators present. A good school, this.

Almost certainly, the Baron was in the same rare form which had endeared him to Americans since Valley Forge. When he arrived in the New World, he could not speak any English, and it took him months to learn more than his favorite word, "Goddam!" When the drilling men misunderstood a command, and started marching in the wrong direction, he would curse them in French and German and then order his aide, linguist Captain Benjamin Walker of New York, to take over and curse them in English. *"Viens Walker, mon ami, mon bon ami, sacre,"* he would roar. "Goddam de Gaucheries of dese badauts. *Je ne puis plus.* I can curse dem no more."

In spite of all his thundering, there were few generals in the army to whom the men were more devoted. The Baron was always bankrupt, because he could not stop handing out his money to soldiers in distress. He spent as much again on feeding his junior officers at his famous suppers. "Poor fellows," he would say, "they have field officers' stomachs without their pay or rations."

While the Baron drilled, Washington showed his gift for personal leadership. The day after he arrived he held a reception before his tent for all the officers in the American camp. Young Denny noted in his diary: "Officers all pay their respects to the Commander in Chief. Go in a body. Those who are not personally known, their names given by General Hand and General Wayne. He stands in the door, takes every man by the hand. The officers all pass in, receiving his salute and shake. This is the first time I had seen the General. . . ."

On the seventeenth of September, Washington and Rochambeau journeyed to their face-to-face confrontation with Admiral de Grasse. The admiral sent up the James River the captured British ship, *Queen Charlotte*. In wiltingly hot weather, she stood out into the bay, and after an all night sail, reached the French men-of-war at anchor just within the capes of the Chesapeake. In a moment Washington and his commander of the artillery, General Henry Knox, two young aides, Tench Tilghman and Jonathan Trumbull, Jr. and French generals Duportail and Rochambeau were mounting the ladder of the great triple-decked *Ville De Paris*. De Grasse, in his admiral's uniform of blue and scarlet, lavishly decorated with gold lace, and bearing diagonally across his breast the broad flame-coloured ribbon of the Order of St. Louis, was on deck with his officers to receive them, while the fleet's guns boomed in salute.

According to one story, Admiral de Grasse strode forward, and hugging Washington with Gallic enthusiasm, kissed him on both cheeks, exclaiming, *"Mon petit Général!"* Washington's sturdy six feet towered over most of his fellow Americans, and hearing him called *petit* by the slightly larger De

Grasse forced several of the visitors to control their smiles. The story even has Henry Knox, the jolly fat man of Washington's staff, exploding in helpless laughter—but this is hard to believe—amid the punctilious protocol of meeting all the officers of De Grasse's staff.

Formalities over, the admiral and the generals then retired to the main cabin for the business of the visit. The methodical Washington had his questions written out in advance. His aide Tench Tilghman, educated in Europe, took down De Grasse's answers in French beside each one.

After complimenting and thanking De Grasse for the generous assistance he had brought them, Washington wasted no words:

"The measures which we are now pursuing are big with great events—the peace and Independence of this country and the general Tranquility of Europe will, it is more than probable, result from our complete success—Disgrace to ourselves, Triumph to the Enemy and probable Ruin to the American Cause, will follow our Disappointment. The first is certain if the powerful Fleet, now in Chesapeake Bay or such part of it as will be competent to the purpose, can remain to the close of a regular operation, which from various unforseen causes, may be protracted beyond our present Expectations. The Second is much to be apprehended, if from the fear of loosing the aid of the Fleet, the operations by land are precipitated faster than a necessary Prudence and regard to the lives of men will warrant. The first may be slow but sure, the second must be bloody and precarious.

"Under this state of Matters, General Washington begs that the Count De Grasse will have the Goodness to give him a Resolution of the following questions:

"Is your Excellency restricted to any certain time for the continuance of the fleet upon these coasts? If any time is fixed, beyond which your Orders will not warrant your Stay in this Bay or if the Pursuit of any other Object should more attract your Attention, be pleased to name the day to which your Departure is determined?"

The admiral replied:

"The instructions of Count de Grasse fix his departure to the 15th of October and some engagements which he has made for other operations oblige him to be punctual. But having already taken much upon himself, he will also engage to stay to the end of October."

"If your Excellency should find yourself under a Necessity to return the troops under the Command of the Marquis De St. Simon to the West Indies, however to be lamented such Circumstance must be, may I not be assured that a Detachment of the fleet may be employed as a Convoy to those troops and that the Main Fleet may remain in the Bay to form a sufficient Cover to our operations against the Enemy—to prevent their receiving Supplies by Water and to protect us from any attempt from the British to give Relief to Ld Cornwallis, and raise our siege and this fleet to remain until the close of operations?"

The admiral answered:

"The troops under the orders of Marquis de St. Simon have a particular destination, and I am not altogether at liberty to dispose of them; but as my vessels will not depart before the 1st of November, you may count upon these Troops to that period, for the Reduction of York."

"Will it in your Excellency's opinion, be practical to force with your ships the passage of the York River, so as to get above the Enemy? This measure if effected will be attended with almost infinite advantages, not only as it will secure our Communication on both sides of the River, which otherwise must be very lengthy and tedious, but will give us the Navigation of the River, and enable us to draw the Supplies of the Country throughout its whole Extent and will also form the compleat Investiture of the Enemy's Posts."

The admiral hedged on this request:

"The Thing is not impossible with a good Wind and favorable Tide: but I do not find that operation very useful. Our communication can be established, and our provisions drawn from the East side of York River without requiring the men and the Vessels in their passage between the Batteries; But I suspend my definitive answer until I can reconnoitre the local situation and force of the Enemy; I shall certainly do everything in my power."

"So long as the Enemy possesses both sides of the River, it will be necessary to keep up our Force on both sides. To aid our Efforts in this operation, will it be in your Excellency's power to spare us any Number of Men from on Board the Fleet, to continue so long as this Measure is necessary? If any, what number?"

The admiral's answer to this was precise:

"I have offered, and I again offer 1,800 or 2,000 men from my ships; but I wish that these troops may not be employed but in a surprise attack."

"If in the Prosecution of our Operations, our Prospects of Success should wear a Favorable Aspect, I shall be glad to be decided whether your Excellency will be able to detach some suitable Vessels from your Fleet, sufficient to block in the British Troops at Wilmington and to Possess the Harbour of Charleston."

This exceeded the bargain De Grasse had made.

"The form of my vessels do not admit of the enterprise."

"If our Operations should be of such a Nature as to require it, will your Excellency be able to lend us some heavy Cannon and other Artillery—Powder also—and in what number & quantity of each?"

The admiral disliked this request.

"I can give some Cannon and powder—the two combats which I have had admit of my sparing but a small quantity of the latter."

Washington had played the part of the bargainer well. He

had deliberately asked for more than he could expect to get —he did not really hope De Grasse would assist him in operations against Wilmington and Charleston, but he obviously saw no harm in asking for his help. The one point on which he noted his unhappiness in his diary was De Grasse's refusal to send ships above Cornwallis' position on the York River. This meant Cornwallis in effect controlled the ninety miles above him, and could use it for a night escape.

But Washington was too good a diplomat to argue with De Grasse about it. Instead he relaxed and enjoyed a formal dinner with the admiral and his officers, and then went on a tour of the magnificent French flagship. Aide Jonathan Trumbull, Jr. was particularly amazed at the beautiful flowers and tropical plants the French sailors were growing between the guns. At sunset the allied generals set sail again in the *Queen Charlotte*, and once more the fleet's guns boomed a military salute. As an added honor, every ship in the fleet manned the yards and tops.

The trip back to Williamsburg should have taken no more than twenty-four hours. But the weather changed unexpectedly, and the *Queen Charlotte* found herself totally becalmed on the following morning. On the evening of the nineteenth a breeze came up at last, but it was the wrong one, and in a few minutes the little ship was keel deep in a sandbar. The generals spent a fretful night, and the next morning ordered a boat which took them to the frigate *Andromaque*. The frigate's captain was more than happy to transport his distinguished visitors to Williamsburg, and they raced off under a favorable wind, only to find the *Queen Charlotte* spanking along, afloat once more. Not wanting to tie up a fighting ship, they returned to their original transport, which promptly went into another decline. A headwind came up that was so strong the captain lost all hope of getting up the James River, and so the two commanders spent another night, pitching and tossing in the shelter of land, and in the morning the gray clouds and rattling wind promised nothing better.

Their only consolation, on September 19 and 20, was sighting the collection of miscellaneous transports which was bringing the men and cannon down the Chesapeake from upper Maryland. If they—and the troops—could ever get ashore, operations could begin. But the twenty-first of September came and went, with the *Queen Charlotte* struggling in vain against the wind, while the transports pitched and tossed at anchor. The next morning at dawn, the generals had had all they wanted of the *Queen Charlotte;* the allied party disgustedly boarded rowboats, and the sailors hauled them slowly up the river and then up College Creek to Williamsburg, which they reached at noon. Their face-to-face confrontation with Admiral de Grasse had cost them four-and-a-half days they could not afford to lose.

Later that day and the following day, the transports began working their way up the James River. Some of the less fortunate soldiers in the scratch fleet Maryland's gentlemen had pulled together spent fourteen days in open boats. Every mile they sailed, they kept a nervous lookout for British cruisers, which had been ravaging the bay for months. Even the ones who had been lucky enough to sail from Philadelphia did not make much better time. Joseph Plumb Martin, our sergeant in the sappers and miners, thought his trip down the Delaware and up Christiana Creek would never end. "In the morning we got under weigh, the winds serving, and proceeded up the creek fourteen miles, the creek passing the most of its course through a marsh as crooked as a snake in motion. There was one place in particular near the village of Newport [Delaware] where you sail four miles to gain about forty rods."

Martin had survived the starving winters at Valley Forge and Morristown, and some harrowing days and nights in the forts on the Delaware. He had the enlisted man's approach to soldiering. Let the generals worry about timetables and deadlines; his chief worry was where his next drink and his next meal were coming from. He and a small number of his fellow sappers and miners boarded the schooner *Birming-ham* for the trip down the Chesapeake. There were only "six or eight officers and a commissary, who had a small quantity of stores on board, among which was a hogshead containing twenty or thirty gallons of rum."

"To prevent the men from getting more than their share of the liquor," Martin says, with wry disillusion, "the offi-cers, who loved a little of the 'good creature' as well as the men, had the bulkhead between the hold and the cabin taken down and placed the hogshead in the cabin, carefully nailing up the partition against it, when they thought that they had the exclusive disposal of the precious treasure. But the sol-diers were as wily as they, for the very first night after the officers had snugly secured it, as they thought, the head of the cask being crowded against the bulkhead, the soldiers con-trived to loosen one of the boards at the lower end, so as to swing it aside, and broached the hogshead on the other head, so that while the officers in the cabin thought they were the sole possessors of its contents, the soldiers in the hold had possession of at least as good a share as themselves."

Their "mosquito fleet," as Martin called it, poked warily down the bay, with a French cutter preceding them to make sure all was well ahead. At the mouth of the James River, the storm was as frustrating to them as it was to Washington and Rochambeau. In the distance they could see the masts of the French fleet, resembling "a swamp of dry pine trees." Better still they could also see dry land—but it remained tantalizingly beyond their reach for days.

The officers on Martin's boat were not the only ones who liked a drop of the "creature." While the wind was still blowing a gale and all the ships were still anchored, the offi-cers in a nearby vessel sent a soldier off in a small punt to another ship where some friends had an ample supply of the hard stuff. One of the officers had apparently offered him his hat as a reward for the errand, which was no small task in the stormy Chesapeake. The rum-bearer completed the first half of his journey, but on the way back his punt swamped, and the poor fellow had to start swimming for his life. "He exhibited a rather ludicrous figure," Martin says acidly, "with an officer's large cocked hat upon his head, paddling away with one hand and holding his canteen in the other." The captain of Martin's company tried to rouse the swimmer's ship, but the storm was blowing so hard they were all below decks. He finally seized a musket and discharged it several times. French seamen on a nearby ship lowered a boat and rescued the nearly drowned soldier. "Our officers pretended to blame the others greatly for sending the poor fellow upon such an errand in a storm," Martin says. "But it is to be remembered that they had a plenty of liquor on board their vessel and therefore had no occasion to send anyone on such business."

The next night, Martin's ship was anchored in the James River just below Williamsburg, and his officers sent him across the river with two men in a borrowed boat to fill a cask with water. "It was quite dark before I got ready to return," he says, "and I had to cross almost the whole river (which is pretty wide here) and through the whole fleet before I reached our vessel. I could not find her in the dark among so many and when I hailed her the soldiers in almost every vessel in the river would answer me.

"What could I do? Why just what I did do. Keep rowing one way and another till nine or ten o'clock at night, weary and wishing every man in the fleet, except ourselves, had a toad in his throat. At length by mere good luck I found our vessel, which soon put an end to my trouble and fatigue, together with their mischievous fun."

Martin's troubles did not end with his landing at Williamsburg. His regiment had nothing to eat—by now a thoroughly familiar predicament for a Continental soldier—and Martin and another sergeant "concluded to go after the provisions, to stretch our legs after so long confinement on board the vessel." They took their cook with them, "for he as usual had nothing to do at home."

When they arrived at the camp commissary, they found dozens of other units ahead of them; it would obviously be hours before they were served. They therefore spent some of the precious hard money they had received at Philadelphia ("the first that could be called money," Martin said, "which we had received as wages since the year '76 or that we ever did receive till the close of the war, or indeed ever after") to buy a side of beef from the butchers. They sent their cook back to camp with it on his back, so he could have it ready for them when they returned. It was a fatal mistake.

"The cook," Martin says, "who had been a bank fisherman and of course loved to wet his whistle once in a while, set off for home and we contented ourselves till after dark before we could get away. . . . When we came home we went directly to our tent to get our suppers, when, lo, we found Mr. Cook fast asleep in the tent and not the least sign of cookery going on. With much ado we waked him and inquired where our victuals were. He had got none, he mumbled out as well as he could.

" 'Where is the pluck you brought home?'

" 'I sold it,' said he.

" 'Sold it! What did you sell it for?'

" 'I don't know,' was the reply.

" 'If you have sold it, what did you get for it?'

" 'I will tell you,' said he. 'First I got a little rum, and next I got a little pepper and—and—then I got a little more rum.'

" 'Well, and where is the rum and pepper you got?'

" 'I drank the rum,' said he, 'there is the pepper.'

" 'Pox on you,' said the sergeant. 'I'll pepper you.' " He started to thrash Mr. Cook but Sergeant Martin intervened in his favor. "But truly," he admitted later, "I was hungry and impatient enough to have eaten the fellow had he been well cooked and peppered."

Within a day or two of his return from his visit with De Grasse, Washington could have begun an advance against Cornwallis in his Yorktown defenses. But Washington was determined to make sure every possible guarantee was on his side before he marched. He decided to wait until the last of the ships came in, and meanwhile build up his supplies of food and ammunition.

Patrols reported the British working day and night on their fortifications and their progress worried Henry Knox; he began to think he might need reserve supplies of ammunition. In a September 23 letter to the Board of War, Washington explained why: "Should we be under the necessity of slackening our fire on account of the consumption of our stock, the loss to us would be perhaps irretrievable." That same day he wrote to the President of the Congress, telling him he was "embarrassed for Want of sufficient Stores of Provisions and means of Transportation. By Superior Exertions, however, I hope to surmount these Difficulties, and in a few days find myself before the Enemy's Works at York and Gloucester."

The letter was in answer to a report the President had received from New York. It was little more than a rumor that another British admiral, Robert Digby, had arrived in New York with reinforcements, thought to be anywhere between three and ten ships. Because it was a naval matter, Washington asked Rochambeau's aide, Baron von Closen, to take the message out to Admiral de Grasse immediately. Even if Digby had actually brought ten ships, it would still leave the British inferior to De Grasse, and Washington passed the rumor on more in the spirit of courtesy than urgency.

Two days later, Von Closen was back in camp with news which left Washington and Rochambeau momentarily speechless. De Grasse had heard the rumor of Digby's arrival before Washington, and he felt it called for a complete revision of his plans. As Von Closen noted in his diary: "These . . . turbulent men of the sea . . . think of nothing but cruising, with no desire to cooperate with the land forces." De Grasse was going to sea, abandoning the Chesapeake!

> The enemy [De Grasse wrote in the dispatch Von Closen brought from him] are beginning to be almost equal to us, and it would be imprudent of me to put myself in a position where I could not engage them in battle should they attempt to come up with relief. Accordingly I have the honor to propose to Your Excellency that you leave at the mouth of the river York two vessels, which following my instructions ought to remain there, and that all others approach nearer to me, with the exception of the sloops and frigates which have been blockading the River James since my arrival. . . . I shall recall here all the rest, in order to hoist sail and hold out in the offing, so that if the fleet come to force the entrance I can engage them in a less disadvantageous position; but it can happen that the course of the battle may drive us to leeward and put it beyond our power to return. In this case, what would you do and what would be the resources of Your Excellency? I cannot sacrifice the army I command, and the position I occupy is neither favorable for a battle nor safe in case of a gale. . . . If my troops and those of M. de St. Simon remain with you, the two ships and the sloops in the James will suffice you. I would set out for New York with my forces where perhaps, I could do more for the common cause than by remaining here, an idle spectator. . . . I shall set sail as soon as the wind permits me.

It was an incredible about face. De Grasse seemed incapable of realizing how important his part in the capture of Cornwallis was. He saw the situation in wholly nautical terms;

the only way he wanted to help was by fighting the British fleet. But if he left the Chesapeake open only for a day, this might be all the faster British ships needed to carry Cornwallis to safety.

Frantically, Washington rushed to a conference with Rochambeau, who agreed to do everything in his power to stop the admiral's departure. Washington summoned John Laurens just arrived from Paris, and dictated the following letter, to be translated into French:

> I cannot conceal from your Excellency the painful anxiety under which I have labored since the receipt of the letter with which you honored me on the 23rd inst. . . . Give me leave in the first place to repeat to your Excellency that the enterprise against York under the protection of your Ships is as certain as any military operation can be rendered by a decisive superiority of strength and means that it is in fact reducible to calculation—& that the surrender of the British Garrison will be so important itself and in its consequences; and that it must necessarily go a great way towards terminating the war, and securing the invaluable objects of it to the Allies.
>
> Your Excellency's departure from the Chesapeake by affording an opening for the Succor of York, which the Enemy would instantly avail himself of would frustrate these brilliant prospects, and the consequence would be not only the disgrace and loss of renouncing an enterprise upon which the fairest expectations of the allies have been founded after the most extensive preparations and uncommon exertions and fatigues, but the disbanding perhaps of the whole Army for want of provisions. The present theater of the war is totally deficient in means of land transportation, being intersected by large rivers and its whole dependence for interior communication being upon small vessels. The Country has been so much exhausted besides by the ravages of the enemy, and the subsistence of our own army that our supplies can only be drawn from a distance, and under cover of a fleet

Mistress of the Chesapeake. I most earnestly entreat your Excellency rather to consider that if the present opportunity should be missed, that if you withdraw your maritime force from the position agreed upon, that no future day can restore to us a similar occasion for striking a decisive blow—that the British will be indefatigable in strengthening their most important maritime points; and that the epoch of an honorable peace will be more remote than ever. . . .

Washington recapitulated these arguments in the rest of the letter, even lecturing the admiral briefly on naval tactics: "However the British Admiral may manoeuvre . . . I can hardly admit a belief that it can be his serious intention to engage in a general action with a fleet whose force will be superior." It was an earnest, pointed letter. It was also a daring letter. De Grasse might suddenly remember he was not under Washington's orders and decide to drop the whole operation. Then there was the suspicion that if the admiral felt like sailing away, his captains were even more inclined to do so. In the disgraceful Franco-American operation against Newport in 1778, Admiral d'Estaing had begged his captains to help him support the American army under General John Sullivan. They had refused to a man, and forced him to sail off to Boston, leaving the horrified Sullivan to extricate himself and his men from the British as best he could.

The one man who might persuade both the admiral and the captains was Lafayette. Fortunately, his malaria had left him, and he was full of his old energy. Washington gave him the letter, and with Baron von Closen, the Marquis left instantly for the Chesapeake. They boarded the frigate *Richmond* at College Landing on the James River and by morning they were in the bay. The frigate *Iris* carried them out to Lynnhaven Bay, De Grasse's supposed anchorage off Cape Henry, only to find not a trace of the French fleet. But the frigate captain assured them they had not gone to sea; he would certainly have been notified; obviously they had only changed their anchorage. It took another twelve hours of sailing before they finally found De Grasse and his ships, anchored at the mouth of the York River.

On board the *Ville de Paris,* Lafayette and Von Closen found their trip had been totally unnecessary. The admiral and his captains had had a conference, and to the soldiers' agreeable surprise, the captains had totally vetoed De Grasse's plan. While the admiral's ideas were "the most brilliant and glorious, they did not appear to fulfill the aims we had in view." Obviously, the captains had a better grasp on the over-all strategy of the campaign than the admiral. It was they who urged him to anchor the major part of the fleet at the mouth of the York River and to patrol the James with four or five ships. They also wanted the army to erect a battery of mortars on Point Comfort, to protect them against intruders from the sea.

Lafayette showered De Grasse with compliments for his decision to stay in the Chesapeake. But the Marquis was less than happy with the admiral's decision to use his entire fleet to blockade the mouth of the York River. This left a vast stretch of coast along the inner bay, as well as the James River, wide open to the landing of a British army to relieve Cornwallis. He urged the admiral to return to the mouth of the bay, where he would be in a position to deal with the enemy the moment they appeared. After a few hours of meditation, De Grasse agreed. He had already discovered it was difficult to provision the fleet at the mouth of the York, since the nearby shore was mostly dismal swamp, and the allied army was using every scrap of local food and water. He gave this as his sailor's reason for returning to Lynnhaven Bay at the Chesapeake's mouth.

Back in Williamsburg, Washington hurled himself once more into preparing the army for the march on Yorktown. There was an appalling shortage of horses, oxen and wagons. Without them, they would never be able to haul the heavy artillery from the ships in the James River. Governor Thomas Nelson was beseeched to find the equipment somewhere, anywhere. He went to work, ignoring Mr. Jefferson's laws by commandeering wagons, drivers, horses and slaves from farms for dozens of miles around Yorktown. He did the same thing for food to feed the constantly swelling army at Williamsburg, often giving notes drawn on his own personal credit if the farmers protested.

Another major decision was the distribution of army commands. Here Washington proved he stood by his soldiers, even when they were criticized by his fellow Virginians. He appointed Lafayette and Steuben to command a division each. For the Baron who had been publicly condemned in the Virginia legislature, it was a special vindication. To his other major general, solid, devoted Benjamin Lincoln, Washington gave a third division, as well as the command of the American wing of the allied army. Each division contained two brigades, each under the command of a brigadier general. It was all crisply professional; the Americans had come a long way from the inchoate mass of amateur farmers who had marched out to battle the neatly brigaded, well-officered British army at Bunker Hill.

The brigades were also an interesting revelation of how far the Americans had come from those early days in Massachusetts, when much of the continent looked upon the disagreement with England as the "Yankee's War." The first two brigades were light infantry, the best and toughest soldiers in the army selected from every state purely on the basis of merit. The Chevalier d'Acteville, who came to Virginia with the French West Indies division, described them as "all soldierly looking and, for the most part, big men. . . . They meet privations and delays without murmuring and are capable of sustaining great fatigue and long marches, and these, of course, are admirable and most desirable qualities for an organization of real light infantry." The Third brigade in Washington's General Orders for September 24 were "Colonel Gaskins Virginia Regiment and the two Battalions of Pennsylvania . . . to be commanded by Brigadier General Wayne." The Fourth Brigade was "the Third and Fourth Maryland Regiments, to be commanded by Brigadier General Mordecai Gist." The Fifth Brigade was "the two Jersey regiments and the Rhode Island Regiment, to be commanded by Colonel Elisha Dayton." The Sixth and last was "the First and Second New York Regiments to be commanded by Brigadier General James Clinton."

On the twenty-seventh of September, Washington and Rochambeau received a letter from De Grasse announcing his intention to stay in the Chesapeake. The generals' relief can be glimpsed in the letters they wrote him. Washington declared the "resolution that your Excellency has taken in our Circumstances proves that a great Mind knows how to make personal Sacrifices to secure an important general Good." Rochambeau wrote in more comradely fashion: "You are the most amiable admiral I know. You meet all our wishes, and I believe we are going to turn this into a good business."

That the admiral was far from amiable was amply demonstrated by a letter he wrote to Washington on the twenty-seventh. Worried about their forces in Gloucester, which consisted only of militia and Lauzun's legion of 600 men, the generals had decided to ask the admiral for seven or eight hundred marines to reinforce the lines. The admiral exploded once more.

> Your Excellency should see from the answers given by me to the questions you put to me on board the *Ville De Paris* that I only promised these troops for a surprise attack, and not to remain on land during the entire attack. . . . When I promised them, the enemy were not strong enough by sea to make me fear an attack. . . . It is not so today, and the number of sick which daily increases for lack of fresh sup-

plies, makes it impossible for me to lend troops from my ships. . . . Nevertheless I do not want to refuse the eight hundred men you require, but I earnestly beseech your Excellency to dispense in future with the necessity of demanding men from my vessels.

The admiral then proceeded to advise Washington on how he should deploy the troops on the Gloucester side, should Cornwallis attempt a breakthrough there. "I ask your Excellency's pardon for making you participate in my reveries, but it is permitted to an idle sailor to idly dream. . . ."

This was sarcasm, but now came a more ominous tone. De Grasse had received new dispatches from the French Minister of Marine in Paris. The admiral warned Washington that they "direct me to repair toward the end of October to the place appointed, where I should be joined by an expeditionary force. You can observe what my position is at the moment, either I leave you and lose the entire profit of the campaign, or by failing to be at the rendezvous at the prescribed time, I cause the project of the Court to fall through. . . ."

There was only one answer to such a letter: March! On September 28th, at five A.M., even before he had received this latest warning from the admiral, Washington had started his Franco-American army down the road from Williamsburg to Yorktown. The American light infantry were the advance guard, moving with field artillery interspersed among their companies, so that they would be ready to give battle the instant they encountered opposition. In his General Orders, Washington told the soldiers what to do if they were attacked: "The General particularly enjoins the troops to place their principle reliance on the Bayonet, that they may prove the Vanity of the boast which the British make of their particular prowess in deciding Battles with that Weapon." He went on to hope that a "generous Emulation will actuate the Allied Armies. . . . The Justice of the cause in which we are engaged and the Honor of the Two Nations must inspire every breast with sentiments that are the presage of Victory."

Sergeant Joseph Plumb Martin did not see the march in quite as lofty terms, but his thoughts on it were effective enough, in their own way. "We prepared to move down and pay our old acquaintance, the British, at Yorktown, a visit. I doubt not but their wish was not to have so many of us come at once as their accommodations were rather scanty. They thought, 'the fewer the better cheer.' We thought, 'the more the merrier.' We had come a long way to see them and were unwilling to be put off with excuses."

What were Cornwallis and his men doing, while the storm gathered around their heads? Cornwallis himself continued his war of letters with Sir Henry Clinton. As late as August 20, while Washington and Rochambeau were crossing the Hudson, Cornwallis was still explaining to Sir Henry why he had crossed the James River and retreated to Portsmouth in July—in order to embark the men Sir Henry had ordered to New York. His tone was now that of the corrected subordinate. "Being unacquainted with the instructions of Administration, ignorant of the force at your command from other services, and without the power of making the necessary arrangements for execution, I can only offer my opinions for consideration, certainly not as plans. . . ." In equally frigid tones, he suggested that if Sir Henry had any ideas about future operations in the Chesapeake, he ought to undertake to direct them in person. If the commander in chief wanted Lord Cornwallis to conduct such operations, "I shall, if employed, hope to be honoured with explicit instructions from your Excellency on all points that will admit of them."

At the same time, the noble Earl persisted in refusing to send a single man to Sir Henry's aid in New York. In other letters he told him, no doubt with carefully concealed relish, that evacuating Portsmouth, their already established base which Sir Henry had suddenly found unsatisfactory, had involved numerous engineers, artificers and laborers. He pointed out that constructing fortifications in Virginia summer sunshine was slow and difficult business, and he was short of Negro labor. For some never-explained reason, Cornwallis spent the first weeks of August working largely on the fortifications of the Gloucester side of the York River. Not until August 22 did he begin serious work on the Yorktown defenses. In a letter written that day, he told Sir Henry that he had just approved the engineer's plans, and he did not see how the labor of his whole force could complete the job in less than "five or six weeks." He then proceeded to tantalize Clinton by asking him soberly whether he wanted 1,000 or 1,200 men sent to him. Cornwallis could spare them from every other purpose "but that of labor." Or did Sir Henry wish to send explicit orders that "the whole of the troops here should be employed in expediting the works?"

In the same letter, Cornwallis casually mentions that "There being only four 18's and one 24 pounder here, more heavy guns will be wanted for the sea-batteries at this place; and we are likewise in want of many other artillery and engineers stores, the returns for which I take the liberty to enclose."

On August 27, in a letter to General Alexander Leslie, now commanding in South Carolina, Cornwallis in the same casual tone wrote: "We are busily employed in fortifying this post, which will be a work of great time and labour, and after all, I fear, not be very strong. Our troops are remarkably healthy for this season."

The fighting general who had annihilated whole armies, who had burned his supply wagons and marched into the North Carolina wilderness in pursuit of Nathanael Greene, had disappeared. The man who wrote these letters might have been the disgruntled commander of a minor garrison post—which is more or less what Cornwallis considered himself to be. He did not have the smallest notion that inside a month he would find himself fighting for the fate of North America. Up in New York, Sir Henry Clinton did nothing whatsoever to wake him up. In a letter written on August 27, he tells his chief lieutenant that Washington had crossed the Hudson and was encamped in New Jersey. "I cannot well ascertain Mr. Washington's real intentions by this move of his army," he says. "But it is possible he means for the present to suspend his offensive operations against this post, and to take a defensive station at the old post of Morris-town, from whence he may detach to the southward."

Because of this possibility, and because Sir Henry had recently received substantial reinforcements of German troops at New York, he tells Cornwallis "to keep with you all the troops you have there." Then, in a move obviously designed to conciliate his unhappy subordinate, he informs Cornwallis that he is sending him "such recruits, convalescents, etc." as can leave immediately for Yorktown. "Towards the latter end of next month . . . if this post should not be threatened, I propose to reinforce the Chesapeake army with all the troops that can possibly be spared consistent with the security of this important post."

After two months of petty squabbling which had reduced Cornwallis to a state of indifferent disgust, Clinton was now buying the Earl's plan to launch a full scale invasion of Virginia, where a "single battle may give us America." On September 2 Clinton's intelligence reports made it unmistakably clear that Washington and Rochambeau were marching to attack Cornwallis. He promptly notified Cornwallis of the move, and added: "Your Lordship . . . may be assured that if this should be the case, I shall either endeavour to reinforce the army under your command by all the means within the compass of my power, or make every possible diversion in your favor." In the same letter he told Cornwallis that Captain Stanhope of the frigate *Pegasus* had sighted eight French ships of the line off the coast. "However, as Rear Admiral Graves, after being joined by Sir Samuel Hood with fourteen coppered ships of the line, sailed from hence on the 31st ult., with a fleet of nineteen sail, besides some fifty gun ships, I flatter myself you have little to apprehend from that of the French."

It took two weeks for Cornwallis to get this letter. Long before it arrived he was writing (on September 4) to Sir Henry: "Comte de Grasse's fleet is within the Capes of the Chesapeake. Forty boats with troops went up James River on the 1st instant. . . ." He got this letter out by a small boat, and it reached New York in two days. Clinton's reply was full of energy and optimism. "I think the best way to relieve you is to join you as soon as possible, with all the Force that can be spared from hence. Which is about 4,000 men. They are already embarked, and will proceed the Instant I receive Information from the Admiral that we may venture . . ."

Between the second of September, when he had told Cornwallis he would either reinforce him or create a diversion, and the sixth, when Sir Henry felt he had better come personally to Yorktown, he had already launched his favorite mode of making war, the "desultory expedition." While Washington had been maneuvering in New Jersey, Clinton had decided to unleash Benedict Arnold in a raid on New London, Connecticut. According to some reports, he was persuaded to do this, in part at least, to get Arnold and his ceaseless demands for action out of town. Arnold was notified of his command on August 28; by September 3, Clinton knew Washington was heading south, but he let Arnold go anyway, probably in the hope that it would force Washington either to turn back or at least detach part of his army northward again. No less than 1,700 men, including the fortieth, fifty-fourth and thirty-eighth British Regiments, were committed to this operation. Three battalions of loyalist volunteers, and several Hessian detachments were also put aboard the transports, which with their man of war escorts became a fleet of more than forty ships.

Arnold arrived off New London on the morning of September 6, and with his customary energy, attacked at once. Most of the forts protecting the town fell instantly, but Fort Griswold, containing about 140 state militia under Lieutenant Colonel William Ledyard, put up a ferocious resistance. It was completely unexpected; Arnold had left the reduction to his second in command, Lieutenant Colonel Edmund Eyre. Twice Eyre led his men in a frontal assault, only to be driven back with heavy losses. Eyre was carried out of the battle mortally wounded, but his men returned to the attack, and carried the walls on the third try.

The American commander promptly offered to surrender. According to eighteenth century rules of war, once the walls were breached, resistance was pointless. Ledyard offered his sword to loyalist Lieutenant Colonel Van Buskirk of the New Jersey Volunteers. Buskirk took it and plunged it to the hilt in Ledyard's body.

This was a signal for total slaughter. The attackers went after the surrendered and defenseless Americans like madmen, pursuing them under gun platforms and into the barracks where they bayoneted and shot them without mercy. By the time the massacre was over, eighty-five of the fort's defenders were dead and sixty wounded, many of them mortally. Meanwhile, Arnold's detachment was in the town of

New London, setting fire to warehouses and ships containing merchandise and war material. One of the warehouses, unknown to the British, contained gunpowder, and this soon exploded, spreading the fire to the rest of the town, destroying 140 buildings before it burned itself out.

Even if Washington had maintained his whole army on the Hudson, he would have been unable to defend the New England coastline from such brutal raids, so Arnold's venture could not possibly detain the allied plunge southward after bigger game. Clinton professed himself shocked at the British casualties, which were, considering the nature of the nature of the operation, high: 48 killed, 145 wounded. But by the time he got this news from Arnold, he was involved in much more serious worries in Yorktown.

Cornwallis, unaware of this idiocy in New York, was meanwhile doing his best to make Yorktown defensible. He decided, he told Clinton in a letter of September 8 (the day before Washington reached Mount Vernon), that "his works were not in a state of defence," so he took "a strong position out of town."

Above the town on the British right, Yorktown creek had worn a deep ravine which extended from the river nearly halfway across the peninsula. On the other side Wormley Creek created an impassable swamp. These two natural obstructions were nature's gift to Yorktown's outer defenses, leaving only the center relatively unsecured. Virginians called this center the "gorge" or throat of land over which ran the road to Hampton and the main road to Williamsburg. Cornwallis had his engineers build three redoubts in this half-mile stretch, which was slightly elevated above the land running down to the town. Two of these little forts covered the Williamsburg Road, in what was known as Pigeon Quarter. The third, farther to the left, commanded the Hampton Road. Near the head of Wormley Creek, at a place known as Moore's Mill, other entrenchments were constructed, while on the extreme right flank, by the bank of the York River, a star-shaped redoubt was built and garrisoned by the Twenty-third Regiment, the famed Royal Welsh Fusileers who had fought in America from 1776.

All this heavy building was not begun until the first week in September. The rest of Cornwallis' army was toiling just as hard on the inner defenses around the town of York itself. Here Cornwallis' engineers had laid out a line of earthworks, two covering the right and the river road to Williamsburg, three in back of the town, three on the left looking down the river. Two redoubts, known as numbers nine and ten, stood slightly in advance of the others to add strength to the left flank, which the British felt to be their weakest point. In the center of the semi-circle stood a projecting redoubt, known to the British soldiers as "the hornwork" because of its shape. In these ten redoubts Cornwallis was able to mount sixty-five guns in fourteen batteries—but few were larger than 18 pounders, and most of these were obtained by stripping the frigate *Charon,* tied up in the river. These inner lines were about 1,200 yards long and 500 yards wide. As September lengthened, and Cornwallis learned from Clinton's letters and loyalist spies that Washington was arriving and the British relieving fleet had been defeated, the Earl drove his weary men to greater efforts. Hundreds of trees were chopped down in front of the entrenchments. Whole houses were ripped down to create a barren field about a half mile wide before the inner defenses.

During this month, Cornwallis continued personally to cling to several illusions. One was the certainty that Clinton was coming to help him. The second was the certainty that the British fleet would clear the way for this reinforcement by decisively defeating De Grasse. Another conjecture which he told his officers and men was that the allies were weak in artillery, which would make their siege a relatively feckless affair. He did not see how they could have possibly transported anything heavier than field artillery, whose shot would bounce off his redoubts like tennis balls. The arrival of Admiral Barras with the French siege guns from Newport apparently never even occurred to Cornwallis. After all, wasn't the British fleet patrolling the sea lanes off New York?

Most of his men remained equally sanguine about their chances. Samuel Graham, twenty-five-year-old captain of the Seventy-sixth Regiment, composed of unruly Scotch Highlanders, had no great opinion of Americans after his view of the Pennsylvania Line at Green Spring Farm in July. It was the Seventy-sixth and their fellow Scots from the Eightieth who won that little battle. "At the Highlander's charge," he wrote, "the enemy disappeared in an instant, almost by magic." Graham and his soldiers, many of whom could speak only Gaelic, had come down to Virginia in May, and the young captain worshiped Cornwallis. He told of the emotion with which they greeted Cornwallis' army after their grueling campaign in the Carolinas. "Words can ill describe the admiration in which this band of heroes was held by the two Scot regiments. . . . The gallant Earl and his brave officers, who had shared with him in his long and arduous marches, as well as in his laurels, were almost idolized."

With our homogenized civilization, it is hard for us to believe how thoroughly Scottish the men of the Seventy-sixth were. Graham tells of an amphibious operation in European waters, when, the night before the landing, the soldiers got possession of a whetstone and spent the night sharpening their basket-hilted broadswords, their favorite weapons. The officers had been told to land in boots and uniform. Graham awoke to find in the dawn a fellow officer, a member of one of the most ancient families of the Macdonalds, dressed out in the full Highland costume. Graham reminded him of the commander's wishes respecting their dress. " 'It was not an order,' " the Macdonald replied, " 'and as this is the dress in which I determined to die, I have put it on.' "

A similar spirit animated "an old Highland gentleman, a lieutenant," whom Graham saw one evening standing on one of the outer redoubts, fondling his drawn sword, and saying: " 'Come on, Maister Washington, I'm unco glad to see you; I've been offered money for my commission, but I could na think of gangin hame without a sight of you. Come on.' "

Not quite as sanguine as Captain Graham was twenty-nine-year-old Lieutenant Bartholomew James of the Royal Navy. He was aboard the *Charon,* but was appointed temporary commander of a captured American sloop, which the British naval commander, Captain Thomas Symonds, wished to use as a tender. From the day the French fleet arrived Lieutenant James lived a dangerous existence. On September 1 he "guarded" an express boat with dispatches for New York, escorting it at midnight past the French ships blockading the York River's mouth, and past the rest of the enemy fleet at the entrance to the Chesapeake. Then with a lucky breeze he made it back to York before dawn revealed his cockleshell tender with its crew of thirty to the 19,000 sailors of De Grasse's armada.

On the ninth of September, he was sent down the river in the tender to "reconnoiter the enemy's fleet" which had, of course, disappeared to fight Admiral Graves. He was to signal the York garrison what he found out from this close observation. For two days and two nights, he prowled about the bay reporting that he counted "thirty-six sail of the line, besides frigates, fireships, bombs and transports." Casually in his journal he notes: "I made signal of the enemy's remaining at anchor in Lynnhaven Bay, and stood off and on in sight of them all night." On the tenth he noted De Grasse's fleet had moved from Lynnhaven Bay and anchored at the part of the bay known to sailors as the "Shoe." Then, the morning of the eleventh, Lieutenant James had the unpleasant experience of seeing the entire French fleet weigh anchor and start straight for him while he lay totally becalmed. De Grasse was just shifting position again. He had no interest in attacking the gnat that poor James was commanding, but the leading frigates came racing for him, more than willing to snap him up. James was about three miles from them when this chase began. "By bringing with them a sea breeze they came very near me before I could get any wind; at six o'clock one of the headmost ships fired a shot at me, at which time, having received the wind, I cut away my boat and hopped off, with all I could drag on her, and fortunately escaped *'Monsieur.'*"

When the French seemed to be loitering, James waited, to see which way they were going. Then they came after him again. "At noon I made the signal for a further advancement of the enemy, and at four o'clock ran up the harbour like a scalded cock, the French fleet having anchored in the mouth of the harbour at Too's Marsh." This put James and his tender out of business, and he hauled her up on shore and rejoined the *Charon*.

For James this kind of duty took special courage. He had been captured three years before in the Caribbean doing exactly the same thing, a few weeks after war with France had been declared. The admiral had sent him out to warn English ships that the French fleet was at sea; James had been taken by a frigate, and spent a year of dreadful imprisonment in the native village of Ou-Trou on Saint-Domingue before being exchanged. He recalled the experience with horror; his best friend had died of fever and semi-starvation at his side, and he had no desire to be taken prisoner by *'Monsieur'* again.

Lieutenant James's adventures were by no means over. His report on the enemy fleet revealed an interesting fact to his superior officers. De Grasse had an embarrassing shortage of small ships capable of navigating the rivers and creeks with which this part of Virginia abounded. (This was one of the reasons why he had refused Washington's request to send ships up the York River to blockade the British from that direction.) This shortage immediately suggested an idea to

Cornwallis and his naval advisers: fire ships. The mouth of the York was being guarded by two frigates and a ship of the line. If these frigates could be destroyed by fire ships, the admiral might withdraw all his ships from the river's mouth, giving Cornwallis at least a fighting chance of sneaking away some dark night and landing on the southern side of the bay, where he could leg it for the Carolinas.

There was one established fire ship, appropriately named the *Vulcan,* among the ships tied up at York. The British seamen and officers lost no time in converting four schooners into more of the same. Any amateur can construct a fire ship. All it requires is a plentiful supply of tarred faggots and sailors with good nerves. Lieutenant James promptly volunteered for command of one fire ship. Lieutenants Conway and Symonds, also of the Royal Navy, asked for and received two others. The fourth was assigned to the captain of a loyalist privateer, on whom the regular navy men looked with considerable suspicion. On September 22 (the day Washington returned from his conference aboard the *Ville de Paris*), the wind was between the north and west, and this meant it was just right for a fire ship assault.

"We cut our cables at midnight, and ran down the river," Lieutenant James relates. "At two o'clock we came within sight of the enemy, and were advancing with every probability of success when from some cause, unaccountable as strange, Mr. Campbell of the privateer set fire to his vessel. This proved as unfortunate as dangerous, for the enemy, who was before keeping no lookout, cut their cables, beat to quarters, and having fired twenty or thirty shot at us, retreated in a precipitate and confused manner."

A few moments later, Lieutenants Conway and Symonds set fire to their vessels. This meant the whole river was now aglow, and James could see French launches rowing toward him. There was no quarter asked or given to sailors aboard fire ships, and so James "set fire to my vessel, with no other view than to prevent her falling into the hands of the enemy," and took to his boat. Only Captain Palmer of the regular fire ship *Vulcan* clung to what invisibility the night still offered. Sailing apart from the four makeshift vessels, he waited until the last possible moment to ignite his vessel. James, from his rowboat, watched her blaze up "within her own length" of a seventy-four gun ship of the line's bow. But the French ship, (the *Vaillant*) avoided her, and when she bore down on another ship, the *Triton,* she gave her a broadside and the *Vulcan* veered off to consume herself in the dark waters of the bay.

The disgruntled James never knew that the French, far from "keeping no lookout," were waiting for the five British fire ships all the time. Swedish Lieutenant Tornquist, who was aboard the *Vaillant,* told in his journal how the barque from their regular fire watch had run down a schooner from York earlier that evening and the loyalist captain had talked freely, telling the French that the fire ships were scheduled for midnight.

Even so, Tornquist admitted that the *Vaillant* had a close call. When the *Vulcan* exploded into flames and headed toward their accommodation ladder "with standard sails, pennant and flag ablaze," Tornquist reported they had no time to do more than cut their anchor rope and fall off downstream with the wind and current. Only the current, which fortunately for them was running with the wind, saved them. Aboard the *Triton,* the pandemonium was so great that the pilot ran the ship aground, and the broadside beat off the *Vulcan* so narrowly that not a man could stand the fantastic heat on the afterdeck as the blazing ship slid past.

If Lieutenant James had his worries about French captivity, they were mild compared to the anxiety of other men in Cornwallis' army. By far the most concerned was Lt. Colonel John Connolly, who had spent five years in American jails for his royal sympathies. Connolly's story was a picture, in miniature, of the sufferings and anguish of the American loyalists. He had once been one of the most prominent men on the Virginia frontier, with a notable reputation as a woodsman and Indian fighter. In February, 1775, Washington himself wrote to him about conditions on the frontier, and remarked, "If the journal of your proceedings in the Indian war is to be published, I shall have an opportunity of seeing what I have long coveted."

When, six months later, Washington was appointed commander in chief of an American army of rebellion, Connolly's conscience could not make the transition. Like many other Englishmen on the frontier, he had been too long engaged in negotiating with Indian nations in the name of his King to switch loyalties, no matter how many of his fellow citizens seemed so inclined. Moreover he had a deep personal bond to Lord Dunmore, the Royal Governor of Virginia, who had distinguished himself in the same frontier fighting which had made Connolly locally famous.

Connolly was a powerful man in the vicinity of Pittsburgh. When the patriots tried to seize him for openly avowing loyalty to the Crown, a small army of his followers gathered, and quickly persuaded the rebels to let him go. But he made the mistake of leaving his home grounds and traveling to New York to obtain official approval of a plan to assault Virginia from the west with a loyalist Indian army, which Connolly was eminently qualified to gather and lead. The British generals gave him their enthusiastic approval, and with his papers and his commission he was on his way back to Pittsburgh when a vigilant Committee of Safety member spotted him in Hagerstown, Maryland, and promptly had him arrested.

Connolly was, as he described himself, "the first person of influence who had attempted to support the Royal cause by raising troops in America." The Americans recognized him as a leader extremely dangerous to their cause. He was transported to Philadelphia and lodged in the town jail, and thereafter, for five years, wherever Congress went, Connolly went. When they retreated hastily to York, Pennsylvania, during the British occupation of Philadelphia, "Dr. Connolly," as they insisted on calling him (he had studied medicine briefly in his youth), was carted along with the records and a few other equally valuable political prisoners.

The British attempted to exchange captive Americans of equal rank for him, but Congress always managed to find some excuse to keep poor Connolly behind bars. In the course of his confinement his health broke down completely, he almost died of cholera, and he became subject to spells of terrific depression. There were times when he was confined in jails with as many as 150 captured British soldiers jammed into a room designed to hold seven men. He was, by his own description, "subject to all the indignities and low insults of an illiberal gaoler and turnkey, and placed upon the same footing with horse-thieves, deserters, Negroes and the lowest and most despicable of the human race." Yet when Congress granted an amnesty to all loyalists who would swear their allegiance to the United States within a stipulated time, and also guaranteed to return all lands confiscated on charges of disloyalty, Connolly absolutely refused to take this chance to regain his freedom and his property. He thereby forfeited no less than 4,000 acres of land in the vicinity of Pittsburgh and a very considerable sum of money due him from the Assembly of Virginia for his public services as a soldier and Indian diplomat.

Finally, on the twenty-fifth of October, 1780, Congress agreed to exchange Connolly. After five years they no doubt assumed that he had lost all influence on the frontier, which the Continental Army had recently pacified by severely punishing the Indian tribes. Connolly went to New York, and in spite of his weakened health, promptly proposed to Clinton a plan for "attacking outposts on the frontiers of the Middle Colonies, to possess myself of Pittsburgh, fortify the passes of the Allegheny Mountains and with Provincial troops and Indian auxiliaries, act as emergencies might require." Clinton approved this adventure. Why not? He had nothing to lose if Connolly failed.

The only way Connolly could get to Pittsburgh, however, was via the St. Lawrence River and the Great Lakes. There wasn't time for him to make this journey and fight in the coming campaign. So Clinton asked him, in June, 1781, if he would like to join Cornwallis in Virginia. Connolly had been trying in vain to raise a loyalist regiment in New York, to give him something to do with his lieutenant colonel's commission. He now "flattered myself I might be enabled to compleat my corps to the southward," and accepted Sir Henry's offer.

He must have been depressed by what he found when he arrived in Virginia. Cornwallis had with him a forlorn band of thirty-three loyalists who had followed him from North Carolina, about the same number of King George's true believers from Virginia, and a detachment of "York Volunteers" —a paltry 114 in all. Late in August, Cornwallis ordered Connolly to take command of this bobtail outfit, and march south to Back River, where the loyalist inhabitants had complained that they were being plundered by rebel raiders sailing from the eastern shore of Virginia. Connolly had gone exactly five miles with his first independent command when he was informed that the French fleet had arrived, and two ships of the line were blocking the mouth of the York River. Naturally, he returned hastily to Cornwallis.

That was the end of John Connolly's military operations in the Revolutionary War. For the month of September he sat inside the British lines at Yorktown, slipping steadily into another physical and mental decline. His description of the sanitary conditions inside the camp are revealing: "the men underwent excessive fatigue in an inclement climate; had been obliged to drink noxious water; the horses in the legionary camp were lying dead in numbers; the Negroes that followed the army could hardly be buried fast enough." It was too much for the "small remains of vigour" in Connolly's constitution. He came down with dysentery, and decided his only hope was "a change of air"—almost any place other than the swamps of Yorktown. Some loyalist gentlemen on the peninsula had already invited Connolly to their homes, and now, with Cornwallis' permission and best wishes, he accepted the invitation.

He was too weak to ride on horseback, so on September twenty-first he set out in a small sulky, attended by two servants. He had not gone more than ten miles when three American sentries with drawn bayonets leaped out of a thicket and took him prisoner. Washington had ordered all prisoners to be brought to headquarters, and though they had captured Connolly two dozen miles away from Williamsburg, the Americans insisted on obeying the order literally. They put Connolly on board Admiral Barras' flagship for the night and the admiral treated him "with all tenderness and humanity, which the feelings and politeness of gentlemen could dictate." The next day he was sent ashore to Washington's second in command, General Benjamin Lincoln, who was good enough to loan Connolly his own horse to carry him to Williamsburg and his confrontation with his old friend, Washington.

"I was now to see a man with whom I had formerly been upon a footing of intimacy, I may say of friendship," Connolly wrote. Like so many loyalists, Connolly seemed to think that the war had left no scars on hearts and souls of the other side. "Politics might induce us to meet like enemies in the field," he thought, as he rode to his meeting with Washington, "but should not have made us personally so."

He was wrong. Washington met him on horseback, while on the way to review the allied camp. The meeting was cold and utterly formal. Connolly's words are a crushed whisper even at this distance; "I can only say the friendly sentiments he once publicly professed for me, no longer existed."

Washington treated him humanely, nonetheless. He ordered Connolly taken to Lafayette's quarters, where the Marquis gave him "every civility and attention" for three days. Then, at Connolly's own request, he was paroled on his word not to bear arms against America and sent to a small town sixty miles back in the country, where he disappears from the revolution's drama, a plaintive, almost pathetic figure, who made the wrong choice at one of history's great turning points.

If "prisoner of war" had a horrible sound in Connolly's ears, it rang like the knell of doom in the ears of other men in Cornwallis' army. These were Americans who had deserted from Washington's ranks and were now wearing British uniforms, thus enjoying—at least until De Grasse arrived—the pleasures of steady pay, pittance though it might seem to us, and the regular rations of His Majesty's army. We know the names of only a few of these men—but other evidence indicates that there were three hundred or more of them in Cornwallis' army. They were mute testimony to the confusion which had seized more than one person's mind as the long years of war rolled past. It is hard for us to remember, at this distance, how blurred were many of the motives in the conflict between King and colonists. If in one place, such as New London, enemy brutality might seem to inspire every able-bodied man to the revolutionary cause, in another place the British could be so considerate it was hard to believe they were fighting a war.

Lieutenant James tells some delightful stories of his adventures in Virginia before the siege began. At one point he and a party of armed men were prowling through the streets of Hampton in the middle of the night. They burst into one house, which they thought contained rebel militia, only to find a Virginia merchant named Jones and his terrified wife and daughters. "The ladies were almost in fits," James reported, "which gave me an opportunity, from a very particular attention on this night, to become a favourite of the family." (James rarely missed an opportunity to become friendly with a man who had daughters.) "Having relieved them from all the fears and apprehensions our visit had thrown them into by directing the soldiers and seamen to remove to the bottom of the street, I sat with them myself in a friendly manner upwards of an hour."

Another time, in a raid up the Nansemond River, he entered another house in the middle of the night to find a "lovely young lady alone, sitting by the fire, weeping immoderately." This gave the dashing lieutenant another chance to exert his charms. "Having by every possible means and persuasive argument removed her apprehensions and dried up the tears of her distress," he says, "I flattered myself she would discover to me though a stranger, wherein she was unhappy, that I might have the felicity of sympathising with so amiable a fair."

" 'Indeed,' " she replied, sounding in James's report like a heroine from Jane Austen, " 'my own fears being removed, and my apprehensions of your using me ill totally vanished, gratitude obliges me to feel for the safety of so generous an enemy in return.' "

"The generous fair," as James now called her, proceeded to tell the lieutenant that her father was a colonel of the militia, and that he was at that very hour raising 400 men in the countryside to block James's retreat to the sea. She even told him of the mill where her father planned to guard the river and added that he did not intend to attack until daylight, to make the shooting more accurate. James and his fellow officers immediately decided a "precipitate retreat" was necessary, and sure enough, at the mill lower down the river, they sailed in the pre-dawn darkness through a shattering volley of musketry from the colonel's men—which only wounded one sailor.

With the so-called enemies on such strangely friendly terms, it is easy enough to see how a man could be persuaded to desert from one side to the other. British desertion was equally heavy. When Lord Rawdon marched the Volunteers of Ireland, a regiment he had raised from Irish immigrants in New York, through the Irish settlements in the back country of the Carolinas, half his men evaporated, and he was so exasperated he offered ten guineas for the head of a deserter.

Also important was the habit on both sides of the conflict of trying to persuade prisoners to enlist. More than a few of the Americans in British uniforms had undoubtedly enlisted as an alternative to dying in the rotten hulks in New York harbor which the British used as prison ships. Although Washington condemned the practice, the Americans regularly tried to enlist British and German prisoners and deserters. Of the 5,891 men in Burgoyne's army captured at Saratoga in 1778, no less than 815 had deserted within the year. The foreign officers fighting for America often saw the prisoner of war as a perfect recruit. Count Pulaski, for instance, enlisted many in spite of Washington's warning.

If there were men in the British ranks at Yorktown with confused allegiances, there were even more with no allegiance whatsoever to the flag they were supposedly supporting. These were the 1,765 German troops, part of the 29,875 whom George III had literally purchased to do his fighting for him in America. We have been used to calling these men Hessians; but actually only half came from the territories of the Landgrave of Hesse-Cassel, and few of these were at Yorktown. There were five other German princes who were more than happy to exchange subjects for British gold, at the going rate of 7 pounds, 4 shillings, and 4½ pence per soldier. It was the bargain of the century for a ruling prince. The British also agreed to pay fabulous subsidies—11,517 pounds to the

Duke of Brunswick, 1,108,281 to the Landgrave of Hesse-Cassel—while the troops were serving in America, plus blood money of 30 crowns (about $35) for every soldier killed and a lesser sum, $11.66, for every one maimed. The British did not even have to approach the smaller princes. Once they heard of the bargain struck by Brunswick and Hesse-Cassel, they rushed to offer their men at the same price. The minister of one prince wrote a pamphlet defending the practice. He pointed out that in all ages men had slaughtered each other, that the Swiss had long been in the habit of fighting as mercenaries all over Europe, that ten thousand Greeks under Xenophon did the same, and that this was the tenth time in the century that Hesse-Cassel had bartered its men for cash.

Not everyone felt the same way; Freiherr von Gemmingen, minister to the Margrave of Anspach, wrote to his agent in London: "It is very hard for me to deal in troops, but the Margrave is determined to set his affairs in order at any price, and to pay all his own debts and those of his predecessors. So the good that may come out of such a treaty will far outweigh the hatefulness of the business."

In the English House of Lords, the idea was castigated as contrary to the ideals of the nation. The Duke of Cumberland lamented that these German troops, some of whom had fought beside English soldiers against France in the name of liberty, should now be sent "to subjugate constitutional liberties in another part of this vast empire." But the British ministry had to find men somewhere, and the unpopularity of the war against America made recruiters despair of raising a respectable army in England. The "mercenary bargains" were passed by crushing majorities in both houses of Parliament.

At Yorktown the principal German detachment was two regiments from Anspach-Bayreuth, whose minister had admitted the "hatefulness" of the business of selling them but had not boggled at going through with the job. In their ranks was a lively young corporal named Stephan Popp who kept a diary of his journey to America. Popp describes what happened the first night the Anspachers sailed from the town of Ochsenfurth, on the Main about a hundred miles above Hanau. The men went aboard the crowded smelly troopships at evening and by daybreak they were in a mutinous mood. Some daring fellows laid a plank to shore and walked over it. They then dragged the other boats to shore, and soon there were 1,200 angry farm boys shouting and yelling insults to their officers, refusing to move until they were given better food and quarters.

The officers wisely listened to their grievances, but they also stationed Jagers—professional riflemen—on the hills to make sure everyone stayed for the trip. When a few men tried to escape, the Jagers fired, whereupon the enraged men fired back, wounding several of the sharpshooters. For a while it looked as if civil war were imminent. The burghers of Ochsenfurth shut the town gates and pulled up the drawbridges. But the Roman Catholic Bishop of Würzburg, who controlled the surrounding territory, sent some of his hussars and dragoons down to stop the show.

The Margrave of Anspach, meanwhile, had heard the bad news and reacted with alarm. As one commentator on the scene put it, "here were twelve hundred men, eighteen thousand good English pounds and next winter's little journey to Paris, all in danger of making off at once." Without even stopping to pack his bag, the Margrave leaped on his horse and rode all night to Ochsenfurth. There he interviewed each man personally, as he walked down the line of the paraded regiments. He listened to their grievances and assured everyone of his forgiveness, if they would go freely to America. "He asked whether they would go freely or not," Stephan Popp says. "There were none who wanted to say no." He would be happy to release any man who did not want to go freely, the Margrave said, but of course this meant that he thereby forfeited his home, his property and the "princely favor." In other words, he became a penniless exile.

The Anspach Regiments arrived in New York in 1777, but in four years they had seen little fighting. Most of their time was spent in garrison duty in New York and in Rhode Island, where they suffered more from cold and rotten provisions than from the enemy. "Oatmeal which had been discarded for two or three years was what we received. Of this we baked bread. The disgust with which we ate was great—but the hunger which we had was much greater. Codfish which is stinkier than anything else, so that everyone else considered it valueless, was still good enough for us." One Christmas Eve in Newport, nine men froze to death.

But Corporal Popp, who was twenty-six years old, never became bitter at such treatment, nor was he especially nonplussed to find himself risking his life for a foreign flag. He admitted some sadness at leaving the "fatherland" but elsewhere Popp seemed delighted at this opportunity to see the world. Popp and his fellow Anspachers had arrived in Virginia in June, 1781, under General Phillips' command. During September, the corporal was working too hard to do much more than scratch a few lines in his journal, testifying to the energy with which Cornwallis now pushed his fortifying. But he also hints that until the French fleet arrived, things were allowed to progress much more slowly. "Everything that could be done in a hurry was done," he says. Popp also reported many men in his regiment sick as early as September 2. "There were said to be 1,300 men in the hospital," he noted on that day.

Another German soldier, Johann Conrad Doehla of the Bayreuth Regiment, gives an even more detailed account of the early stages of the siege. He tells of toiling on "unloading duty" bringing ashore munitions and provisions from the ships in the harbor. "The lower tiers of guns from the warships and frigates were brought into the earthworks and all the ships completely emptied." In the beginning of September, he was hard at work felling trees and creating tangled barricades on all the roads leading into Yorktown.

Doehla also reports growing sickness, and complains bitterly of the food. "We get terrible provisions now," he wrote on September 12, "putrid ship's meat and wormy biscuits that have spoiled on the ships. Many of the men have taken sick here with dysentery or the bloody flux and with diarrhea. Also the foul fever is spreading, partly on account of the many hardships from which we had had little rest day or night, and partly on account of the awful food; but mostly, the nitrebearing water is to blame for it."

If there were men in Cornwallis' army who might justifiably be dubious soldiers in a crisis, there were others on whom he could rely to stand by their colors as long as they could fire a gun or heft a bayonet. One of these was Sergeant Roger Lamb of the Twenty-third Welsh Fusileers. A tough professional who had marched into capture with Burgoyne and then escaped to New York, Lamb had also made the harrowing 1,500 mile tour of the Carolina backlands with Cornwallis. Nothing was likely to surprise or dismay him or his battle-hardened fellow Fusileers. There were little more than 150 of them left now, out of a normal regimental strength of 360, but they had some superb officers, notably Captain Thomas Saumerez. In 1779, when he was only nineteen, Saumerez had so distinguished himself in fighting around New York that he was allowed to purchase a captaincy in the Royal Welsh. He and his men were put in charge of the star-shaped redoubt which Cornwallis had constructed far in advance of his right wing fortifications. Putting the Royal Welsh in this post of danger was the Earl's way of stating his confidence in them, and they returned the compliment by defending the position with savage skill throughout the siege.

But Cornwallis was not so fortunate in his senior officers.

A general in Cornwallis' situation needed advice, and he was only able to get it from other generals who were capable of speaking frankly to him. The only other officer above the rank of colonel in the Yorktown camp was General Charles O'Hara. He and Cornwallis were old friends. They had been aides to the Marquis of Granby during the Seven Years' War, and had been side by side in the bloody battle of Minden. O'Hara was personally brave; in spite of two agonizing wounds, he had rallied the retreating Guards, and done much to retrieve the Battle of Guilford Court House from impending disaster.

But O'Hara was best known for the fabulous uniforms he wore, which were in the style of twenty years past, and for his tendency to play himself in a real-life romance. Extremely handsome, he was the illegitimate son of James O'Hara, second Lord Tyrawley. While traveling on the continent, he fell passionately in love with a beautiful British expatriate and after a fifteen year courtship was finally rejected. He never married thereafter, though he fathered numerous children, whom he always was careful to provide for, as his father had done for him. A contemporary called him "the most perfect specimen of a soldier and a courtier of the past age." It was a lovely compliment—but a courtier of the past age was not likely to give Cornwallis brilliant tactical advice on how to rescue the present from imminent disaster.

There was one officer in Yorktown who might have been able to infuse the British general with his old fire. But the fortunes of war had dimmed the reputation of Banastre Tarleton, the young cavalry colonel who had cut a path of blood and fire across the South at the head of his legion.

Already Tarleton's exploits had made him a legend in Europe. In America his name was synonymous with raw terror, and the American militia often fled at the sound of his hoofbeats. He was infamous for what the Americans called "Tarleton's quarter." At Waxhaws, in 1780, Tarleton had made a daring night march and surprised a little army of 400 partisans under General Abraham Buford. Charging into their camp in the darkness, he routed them totally, and they ceased to exist as a military organization. Everywhere men tried to surrender, only to go down, hacked to death beneath the flailing of the razor-edged cavalry sabres. Some say half, some say two-thirds of the men were slaughtered after they had given up all hope of defending themselves.

For a while, Tarleton and his legion, which was largely composed of American loyalists, seemed invincible. But at the Cowpens on the Broad River in South Carolina he came up against Daniel Morgan and a mixed army of Continentals and militia, and before the morning was over Tarleton's 600-man detachment of infantry and most of the legion were prisoners, and the young colonel himself was lucky to get away on a fast horse. The blow had done much to cripple Cornwallis' army in its march through the Carolinas. The light infantry, his best troops, had been lost to a man at Cowpens. But the Earl generously forgave Tarleton for the blunder, which had been created almost entirely by his impetuosity. He exonerated him from blame, although he confided to Lord Rawdon: "The . . . affair almost broke my heart." Between Cornwallis and Tarleton there had been a father-son feeling, similar to the friendship between Washington and Lafayette.

Although Cowpens in many ways marked the collapse of Cornwallis' hopes to pacify the South for England, he still wrote to Tarleton, two weeks after the disaster: "You have forfeited no part of my esteem as an officer by the unfortunate event of the action of the 17th: the means you used to bring the enemy to action were able and masterly, and must ever do you honour. Your disposition was unexceptionable; the total misbehaviour of the troops could alone have deprived you of the Glory which was so justly your due." Generous words, and shrewd ones, too. After a month of hand wringing and despair, Tarleton took to his horse, refilled his ranks, and was the terror of the South once more. But there was never again that close personal communion between the cavalry hero and his general.

After O'Hara and Tarleton, the two officers with the best reputations were Lieutenant Colonels Robert Abercromby and Thomas Dundas. Abercromby was a good example of the fierce political conflicts which the American Revolution had evoked. His older brother, Ralph, was a hero of the British victory at Minden in the Seven Years' War and one of the outstanding soldiers in the British army. Ralph flatly refused to serve against the Americans, and sat out the war sniping at the government from a seat in Parliament. Robert and another brother, James, were in the war from 1776, and James died at the Battle of Long Island. Dundas was a sturdy Scot with a reputation for tough common sense. But neither of these men were in a position to advise Cornwallis directly, as a fellow general could.

This lack of seasoned senior officers explains (along with his disgust for Clinton), the strange inactivity which characterized Cornwallis' behavior throughout the month of September. He made no attempt to prevent the landing of De Grasse's West Indian troops and their junction with Lafayette's forces, although one French officer noted that a single cannon, judiciously placed, could have wreaked havoc on their operation. Once these troops joined, Cornwallis still had an opportunity to march out and thrash them while Washington was marching south. One of the cherished tactics of the day was to defeat an enemy force *en détail*. Even with the addition of the West Indian reinforcements, Lafayette's army was barely equal to Cornwallis' in numbers, and the young Marquis had given ample evidence that he was hardly the Earl's equal in generalship.

Moreover, the West Indian troops were by no means the equals of the crack regiments Rochambeau was marching south. Like most European soldiers who spent any time in the tropics, their ranks had been thinned by disease (Tarleton estimated their real strength at little more than 2,000), and even those who were still fit for duty had little stamina. Their discipline was also alarmingly lax, with drunkenness a special problem. One boozing captain of the Gâtinais, "Cask" Mirabeau, was famous for his habit of drinking rum from his boots. Tarleton was convinced the British could have routed them with one charge.

There was, it would seem, a moment when Cornwallis did contemplate attacking. Urged by Tarleton, the Earl made plans to march the army at night, and assault Williamsburg on September 17. Even then, an all-out attack could have been a master stroke. Washington and Rochambeau had just arrived in the American camp, but their troops were still moving south by land and water. Lafayette's Americans and the under-strength French West Indian regiments were still the only opposition. But in the midst of preparations for the attack, Sir Henry Clinton's letter of September 2 arrived in camp, and Cornwallis' aide, Major Alexander Ross, convinced his chief that its contents forbade him to make such a risky gamble. Since Clinton was sending reinforcements, it was contrary to all the rules of military behavior for an attacker to move before he had achieved his maximum strength. So the plan was put aside.

Ross apparently had a great deal to do with the spirit of sullen obedience which possessed Cornwallis at this time. The handsome aide had taken the victory dispatch home to England after the battle of Camden, and had done some assiduous politicking on his general's behalf while there. When he returned to the army, he had filled Cornwallis' ears with stories of his fame in England, and the certainty that he was to succeed Clinton as commander in chief. Many people felt that Ross was responsible for inflaming the Earl's latent insubordination against Clinton and for keeping this resentment smoldering at Yorktown.

An older, more mature advisor such as William Phillips might have helped Cornwallis to a more balanced view. With a minimum of sound advice, he might have disregarded Clinton's nagging and taken what seemed to his bulldog instincts a magnificent opportunity to thrash Lafayette. Instead, the Earl had only the snide flattery of Major Ross and the benign friendship of O'Hara, both of whom were inclined to feed rather than correct his mood.

Throughout the month of September Tarleton was industrious at gathering information, and reconnoitering the American positions. One night, he relates in his memoirs, he, three other officers and six men rode all the way to Williamsburg and explored the whole layout of the American camp. On the Hampton Road, he regularly "drove in the pickets of the militia," so that he could confer with a spy. By the twenty-sixth of September, thanks to his vigorous cavalry commander, Cornwallis had a very clear picture of the formidable army that was gathering around him.

Still, he made no attempt to retreat, nor did he try to plan ambushes or delaying actions which might interrupt Washington's schedule. The Earl seemed to have no idea that the American general was working against a harrowing deadline. Cornwallis stayed with his fortifying. As he saw it he would have been foolish to do anything else. His commander in chief had promised he was coming to his aid with large reinforcements. On the sixteenth of September, he wrote to Clinton: "If I had no hopes of Relief, I would rather risk an Action than defend my half-finished Works. But as you say Admiral Digby is hourly expected, and promise every Exertion to assist me, I do not think myself justifiable in putting the fate of the War on so desperate an Attempt." To risk a battle with a small army, and lose it, would be an open invitation to military disgrace. Far better to hold out expertly, with as little loss of men as possible, until the time when Clinton arrived. Then, yes then, might come that "single battle that will give us America."

But the grim facts of his situation also dogged Cornwallis. On September 17, Lieutenant Conway of the navy was exchanged for a French naval officer captured by a British patrol while he was foraging. He told Cornwallis that the French fleet numbered thirty-six sail of the line. Cornwallis added this news as a postscript to his letter of the sixteenth, and then added: "This place is in no state of defence. If you cannot relieve me very soon, you must be prepared to hear the Worst."

Then came that sunny September morning, the twenty-eighth, when the British patrols heard the sounds of the advancing Franco-American army. Minutes later, the scouts were upon them and the rifle balls hissed between the trees. The British pickets returned the fire, but fell back quickly on their fortifications. On the British right, Tarleton's dragoons galloped across the line of advance, but also fell back when the French opened on them with cannon. The next day they watched the Americans crossing Beaverdam Creek where it ran more or less parallel to the Yorktown-Williamsburg Road, and moving to their right, toward the York River. At the same time, the French wing moved to their left, and made an exploratory attack on the Fusileers' redoubt. It was beaten back with furious cannon fire and musketry. Stephan Popp, far in the rear, reported to his diary that the French had lost over 400 men in fifteen minutes. The official count of the French army gave one dead, two wounded. Johann Doehla's regiment was in the hottest part of this skirmishing. On the twenty-ninth of September, he tells how Private Zeilmann was mortally wounded on his picket post, how he helped bury him, and how at noon he helped hold down another sentry while a surgeon extracted a musket ball from between his shoulder blades. "Today over thirty men were shot and wounded on the detached outposts," he records somberly.

Throughout the entire British army there was a tremendous sense of imminent battle. American and French officers were seen repeatedly on the twenty-ninth studying the British lines, trying to find the weakest link in the chain of natural and man-made fortifications. If they had any hope of reducing Cornwallis to surrender the British reasoned they would have to storm the outer fortifications, and in that storm, they would lose so many men it would make them think twice about doing the same thing against the inner lines. But the day passed without anything more ambitious than the little French probe, and at midnight the men in the lines received what was to them an incredible order: retreat.

At one A.M., the British regiments quietly abandoned their advanced positions and silently stole back across the open meadow to the inner fortifications circling Yorktown. It was a disheartening experience, and Stephan Popp's diary leaves little doubt of the impression it made on the men. "The regiments in the line moved back to the city because the enemy always came nearer and stronger. . . . In the night three of the men of our company deserted."

What happened? What was going on in Cornwallis' mind? Once more, the explanation was not to be found in the British command at Yorktown, but in headquarters at New York. During the day, Cornwallis had received the following letter from Sir Henry Clinton:

> My Lord: At a meeting of the General and Flag officers held this day, it is determined that above five thousand men, rank and file, shall be embarked on board the King's ships, and the joint exertions of the navy and army made in a few days to relieve you, and afterwards co-operate with you.
>
> The fleet consists of twenty-three sail of the line, three of which are three deckers. There is every reason to hope we start from hence the 5th October.

P.S. Admiral Digby is this moment arrived at the Hook with three sail of the line.

This was Cornwallis' reason for retiring to his inner lines. If he waited for the allies to advance, some at least of these forward redoubts might have been cut off by a successful flank attack. Hence the army left to defend the inner line would have been so much smaller. This way, he would have the best chance of retaining a compact striking force when Sir Henry arrived with his reinforcements. Undoubtedly he knew that a retreat would dampen the morale of his men. But there are times when tactics are more important than morale. That night Cornwallis sat down at his desk in the Nelson mansion, and wrote to his commander in chief:

> Sir: I have ventured these last two days to look General Washington's whole force in the face in the position on the outside of my works, and I have the pleasure to assure your Excellency that there was but one wish throughout the whole army, which was, that the enemy would advance.
>
> I have this evening received your letter of the 24th, which has given me the greatest satisfaction. I shall retire this night within my works, and have no doubt, if relief arrives in any reasonable time, York and Gloucester will be both in possession of his Majesty's troops.

Colonel Alexander Scammell, officer of the day for the American wing of the allied army, was among the first to discover the astonishing fact that the British had abandoned their advanced redoubts and forts. The sentries must have noticed the remarkable silence of the British works at dawn on the thirtieth of September, and hastened to inform the colonel, who hastened even faster to inform General Washington. The French and Americans could not believe their good fortune. Not until noon did they send detachments of men into the works. Washington, meanwhile, immediately began to worry about what Cornwallis might have had in mind. The move made no sense, unless he had an ulterior motive for wanting to draw his army into a compact body. What could be more logical than a dash for the exits? The allied generals could not think of any other reason why the British general, so famed for his fighting instincts, would have surrendered positions that would have cost the allies considerable time and blood to possess.

Pressured by De Grasse, Washington had marched without his heavy artillery, which on the morning of the thirtieth was only just being unloaded from the ships at Trebell's Landing in the James River, six miles away. The necessary oxen, wagons, and other transportation equipment were still excruciatingly scarce. The allies would have had to wait for this vital siege artillery to come up before attempting any move against the outer positions.

Would Cornwallis have abandoned his outer lines if he knew that Washington and his chief of artillery, Henry Knox, were holding the trump card in readiness, back there on Trebell's Landing? Probably not. Among the multiple ironies of Yorktown, the concentration not merely of men, but of superior military equipment, has been seldom noticed. After six years of inferiority in firepower and expertise, Washington had assembled in this unlikely place an immense superiority in guns, trained artillerymen, and engineers.

No matter how harshly time pressed on him, Washington had decided before they marched that an impulsive attempt to storm was to be avoided at all costs. The memory of Savannah was constantly before him. The approach was to be conducted with the prescribed ritual of a formal siege, as laid down by the French general, Vauban, in a manual written almost one hundred years before. This called for "regular approaches," digging trenches parallel to the enemy lines, and the extensive use of artillery to destroy enemy defenses before anything so rash as an assault was attempted. Cornwallis had saved them the trouble of going through all this labor, against the first line of defense.

Washington himself knew little about the ritual of siege

warfare. The only officer in his army who had ever actually taken part in a siege was Baron von Steuben, and it was to him and a few others such as Timothy Pickering, his quartermaster general, that Washington turned for advice. These military pedants loved a siege. It gave them a marvelous opportunity to demonstrate their knowledge of textbook punctilio. Pickering, who had a low opinion of Washington's generalship, tells of a conversation he had with him and Henry Knox, shortly after the British had abandoned the outer works. Knox began it by asking: " 'Colonel Pickering, the General thinks we ought to move and encamp nearer to the enemy's works: What is your opinion?' "

"I answered instantly," Pickering says, "expressing precisely all the following ideas, and I am sure, nearly in these words:

" 'The duties of troops at a siege are severe. Those off duty ought to be so situated as to take their rest in security. We must look for repeated sallies from the enemy, and if any of them are made in great force, they will beat the guards of the trenches and compel them to retreat. If the camp be near, the soldiers will not have time to rouse from sleep and to recollect themselves, before the enemy will be upon them. Shot from the enemy's outworks reaches where we are now. For these reasons I think we are near enough.' "

" 'Well, but we must invest the place,' " said Washington.

"This remark," Pickering says, "I confess surprised me: while in a moment I replied:

" 'The object of an investment is to prevent the besieged from receiving succour, or making their escape. The American army now extends so as to command the ground from York River, below the town, round to the morass on our left. Above the town, the French army commands the ground from the morass to the river. Duke Lauzun's legion and General Weedon's brigade of Virginia militia are at Gloucester Point, opposite to Yorktown, and Count De Grasse, with his fleet, commands the mouth of the river. No passage is open except that up the river; and Lord Cornwallis will not attempt to escape by marching into the heart of the country. So I think, Sir, the place is completely invested already.' "

"The General made no further observation," Pickering says, "and the troops continued on the ground they then occupied."

The most amazing thing in this little drama is not, as Pickering felt, that Washington did not know the meaning of the word investment; Washington never claimed to be a walking encyclopedia of military information. But that he allowed one of his colonels to lecture him so disdainfully is certainly a tribute to his forbearance.

Colonel Pickering, smug in his military lore, which he had garnered almost entirely from books read in his study, may have scoffed at the idea of Cornwallis sailing away up the York River. But Washington, who had been trapped twice with a river at his back and an enemy army facing him (at Brooklyn and Trenton), did not think it was by any means an improbable move. The abandonment of the outer works promptly intensified his suspicion that Cornwallis had it imminently in mind. In his diary on the twenty-ninth of September Washington had noted with some vexation that "a plan of attack and approach" had to be worked out "without the assistance of the Shipping above the Town, as the Admiral (notwithstanding my earnest solicitation) declined hazarding any vessels on that Station."

Making an attack without De Grasse's assistance was one thing; it was more or less legitimate for the admiral to let the army worry about problems on terra firma. But letting Cornwallis escape by water was another matter, which seemed to Washington to fall within the admiral's responsibility. So, with due caution, he decided to risk De Grasse's explosive Provençal temper once more, and re-demand ships to be stationed in the York River above the British positions.

On October 1 he wrote the admiral, explaining his reasons, which were cogent enough: the British had close to 100 large and small craft in Yorktown harbor and they controlled the river with their armed vessels for more than twenty-five miles above York. They had already intercepted supplies of the greatest value on the way to the allied camp. Because of the mobility water transport gave the British, the allies were forced to leave seven or eight hundred men in Williamsburg to guard the magazines and stores. The British could steal around the left flank of the allied army in their boats, and "by a very short march effect the most destructive purposes." Also, it took a trip of ninety miles to communicate with the allied troops in Gloucester. But by far the most important point was that "Ld Cornwallis has by the York River an outlet for his retreat, and that he may by embracing a leading wind and tide, and stealing a march proceed unmolested to West Point—where upon debarking his troops he will have the Pamunky on one flank and the Mattapeny on the other, and that finally he may by mounting the greatest part of his men and successive forced marches—push his way with a compact, disciplined army thro' a Country whose population is too scattered to be collected for sudden opposition, and make it impossible for us to overtake him."

A glance at a map of the region shows that Washington's thinking on this matter was by no means naïve. By a short sail up the York, Cornwallis could have landed at West Point between the above-mentioned two rivers, where he would have had natural barriers between him and Washington which would immensely retard a pursuit. It took days for an eighteenth century army to ford a river with its artillery and baggage. There were no pontoon bridges to be flung across water in a matter of hours. It was the move Washington would have made, if he and Cornwallis were in opposite positions. But Admiral de Grasse could not see it—at least not vividly enough to risk his ships. His reason was not the cannonade the ships would receive from York and Gloucester, but the danger of fire rafts. Above York the river was too narrow to give a sailing vessel much room to maneuver. There would be no way to escape the blazing attackers, as the French had done at the mouth of the river, simply by cutting loose and sailing with the tide into the open bay. De Grasse recommended batteries on the banks of the York River instead. He also assured Washington that the army's mortars, once they began operating, would set fire to many of the British ships in Yorktown's harbor.

Washington undoubtedly knew that his mortars could do these things. But he was worried about what Cornwallis was liable to do before the mortars and their ammunition were dragged from the James River and wrestled into position. As for batteries on the bank of the river, they would guarantee nothing. Cornwallis was not likely to sail up the York while the sun was shining. He would go in the blackest part of the darkest night.

It was maddening to have De Grasse refuse to blockade Cornwallis' best escape hatch. But fortunately there was more than enough to keep Washington from worrying about it too much. Men were marched into the abandoned British positions, and they began converting them into American fortifications without an hour's delay. They also began throwing up companion fortifications linked to the standing British works, so that Cornwallis and his men would have to fight their way past a formidable barrier if they attempted a breakout down the center of the peninsula. Since this was improbable, the real purpose of the works was partly psychological, partly a precautionary defense which would protect the army encamped beyond them on the peninsula. It was also part of the ritual of a siege. Any work captured from the enemy was, Baron von Steuben insisted, to be converted instantly into a fort which made their investment more total and secure.

How grateful Washington was for Cornwallis' retreat is evident in a letter he wrote October 1 to the President of Congress:

> In the morning we discovered that the Enemy had evacuated all their Exterior line of Works and withdrawn themselves to those near the Body of the Town. By this Means we are in possession of very advantageous Grounds, which command, in a very near Advance, almost the whole Remaining Line of their Defence.

The French were equally delighted. Colonel William de Deux-Ponts wrote in his journal:

> I followed the Count de Rochambeau in his rounds reconnoitering these redoubts. The places evacuated allowed us to see and to judge of all the land which surrounds the town and the works which are to defend it; and it seems to me for this reason that the enemy ought to have kept these redoubts until they were forced to abandon them, although in themselves, these works were of no great importance. It would have compelled us to feel our way, and held us in doubt; it would have retarded our works, perhaps, instead of leaving us masters of all the approaches to the place, to the distance of six or eight hundred yards.

In the afternoon of the same day, Washington had news that reminded him acutely that the British were by no means ready for a passive defense. As officer of the day Colonel Alexander Scammell decided to reconnoiter the enemy inner lines, and rode out with a few other officers on horseback to do so. He could not have been more than a few hundred yards away from men working on the new fortifications, but before anyone could seize a musket or shout a warning, out of a clump of woods whirled a squadron of Tarleton's dread dragoons, sabers drawn, and cut them off from the American lines. There was no choice but surrender. Scammell and his men did not even try to defend themselves.

One of the officers leading the dragoons came charging up, pistol in hand, while other dragoons were already seizing the reins of Scammell's horse, and without a shadow of provocation shot him in the back. They wheeled around and carried him into Yorktown, where Cornwallis had British surgeons dress his wound, and under a flag of truce had an officer conduct him to the American lines as a paroled prisoner. The American doctors who examined Scammell's wound shook their heads mournfully. It was undoubtedly fatal.

Washington had seen dozens, even hundreds of officers he liked and admired die, but Scammell's death must have been especially wrenching for him because the colonel had been his adjutant general—thus a member of his official family— for over two years. Scammell's personality was extremely attractive; he had a talent for telling funny stories and was one of the few men who could invariably make Washington laugh. In the numerous diaries of the siege his barbarous wounding drew forth an amazing number of anguished regrets and vows of revenge. Scammell had been a young Harvard graduate reading for law in the office of John Sullivan when the war broke out. Sullivan's exertions on behalf of the American cause won him a generalship, and his example inspired Scammell to follow him into battle.

To replace his old friend as commander of the First Light Infantry Regiment of the Second Brigade, Washington named his Parisian emissary, John Laurens. Nothing could have delighted Laurens more than this appointment. Although he was uniquely fitted by his education to serve the commander in chief as an aide, Laurens' romantic temperament chafed under headquarters routine. He wanted to be on the firing line. "The Bayard of the Revolution" is what some writers have called him, and Laurens was in many ways a figure almost too romantic to be real. His fearlessness in battle was legendary. During the siege of Charleston, when he was attached to Light Horse Harry Lee's cavalry, several officers resigned rather than ride under him, because the chances he took were often foolhardy. Laurens had challenged and shot Major General Charles Lee when that strange character maligned Washington after the battle of Monmouth. The erratic ex-English cavalry officer was so impressed with Laurens he afterwards said: "How handsomely the young fellow behaved. I could have hugged him."

Laurens' idealism also inspired him to attempt one of the most daring of all schemes to widen the American Revolution's high-flown statements about liberty. He obtained his father's permission to raise a "black battalion" from among the Laurens' slaves, the forerunner of what he hoped would be a 3,000-man division of Negroes, who would be promised freedom and land in return for their services on the revolutionary battlefields. The elder Laurens was frankly sceptical that his fellow South Carolinians would ever tolerate such a daring breach in the already rigid "peculiar institution" of slavery, and he was right. Young John managed, with his father's help, to get the Continental Congress to pass a resolution recommending the enlistment of the black battalion, but the South Carolina legislature contemptuously voted the idea into oblivion.

Young Laurens was crushed by the rejection. Even before the war began, he had written to a friend: "I think that we Americans, at least in the Southern colonies cannot contend with a good grace for liberty until we shall have enfranchised our slaves. How can we whose jealousy has been alarmed more at the name of oppression than at the reality reconcile to our spirited assertions of the rights of mankind the galling abject slavery of Negroes?" He had hoped his black battalion would be an opening wedge which would eventually bring the whole edifice of slavery crashing down.

Few Americans had more personal reasons for fighting at

Yorktown than John Laurens. Victory here would mean the liberation of his father from the Tower of London and his own reunion with his wife and daughter. But even as he took command of his regiment, one of these hopes had tragically vanished. Exhausted by her clandestine trip to France, "Patty" Laurens had become seriously ill after her husband left and sometime during October died at Lille.

With the slow pace of the sea mail in 1781, Laurens was not to learn this bad news for months. So with his zeal undiminished, he stepped back into active command, and was undoubtedly delighted to find himself fighting beside an old friend, another young lieutenant colonel named Alexander Hamilton. It was in many ways a strange friendship; for Hamilton has come down to us as the supremely cynical realist of the Revolution and after. Laurens was perhaps the supreme romantic. When Hamilton demonstrated his bravery in battle, it was for a clear-cut personal purpose: his reputation and his ambition inspired him as much as his adopted country's cause. Nor had this impoverished son of a West Indies planter neglected his war-won opportunities. Thanks to his valor and flamboyant personality, he had won the hand of Betsy Schuyler, daughter of General Philip Schuyler of Albany, richest of the great New York landowners. For Laurens, born to wealth, the Revolution was a crusade, into which no breath of personal ambition ever intruded. He even declined the honor of being sent to Paris as Special Ambassador, and suggested Hamilton as a better choice. Hamilton could not afford such generous gestures.

Moreover, where Laurens had worship, Hamilton had only a limited regard for Washington. On February 16, 1781, the general and the twenty-six-year-old-aide abruptly parted company, as the result of a quarrel which Washington did everything he could to repair. Here is how Hamilton described the incident in a letter to his father-in-law, General Philip Schuyler:

Two days ago, the General and I passed each other on the stairs. He told me he wanted to speak to me. I answered that I would wait upon him immediately. I went below, and delivered to Mr. Tilghman a letter to be sent to the commissary, containing an order of a pressing and interesting nature.

Returning to the General I was stopped on the way by the Marquis de La Fayette and we conversed together about a minute on a matter of business. He can testify how impatient I was to get back, and that I left him in a manner which, but for our intimacy, would have been more than abrupt. Instead of finding the General, as is usual, in his room, I met him at the head of the stairs, where, accosting me in an angry tone:

"Colonel Hamilton," he said, "you have kept me waiting at the head of the stairs these ten minutes. I must tell you, sir, you treat me with disrespect." I replied, with petulancy, but with decision: "I am not conscious of it, sir; but since you have thought it necessary to tell me so, we part." "Very well, sir," said he, "if it be your choice."

Less than an hour later, Washington sent aide Tench Tilghman to Hamilton with an outright apology and a testament of the General's admiration for Hamilton's talents. Anyone but Hamilton would have been more than satisfied. Instead, he coolly humiliated Washington by insisting on a transfer to active service. In a letter to ex-aide James McHenry, he reveals his attitude toward Washington:

The Great man and I have come to an open rupture. Proposals of accommodation have been made on his part, but rejected. I pledge my honor to you that he will find me inflexible. He shall for once at least repent his ill-humour. . . . Except to a very few friends our difference will be a secret, therefore be silent. I shall continue to support a popularity that has been essential—is still useful. Adieu my friend. May the time come when characters may be Known in their true light.

Hamilton had the gall to insist that Washington himself remain silent on the subject while he wrote his version of the story to everyone he chose. When Lafayette finally mentioned it in a letter, Washington could only confess he was bewildered by Hamilton's conduct. Yet, in April, when Hamilton pressed him for an assignment to a regiment of the line, Washington went calmly about the business of finding him a combat job. This was not easy. Regimental officers frequently resented a lieutenant colonel who had risen in rank while a general's aide. Earlier appointments of such rank had produced wholesale resignations.

In July, Hamilton grew impatient, and wrote a cold letter, resigning his commission. Once more Washington sent the faithful Tilghman to beg him to retain his commission and promise him that a command would be coming his way soon. Hamilton wrote his bride, Betsy, "Though I know you would be happy to hear had I rejected this proposal, it is a pleasure my reputation would not permit me to afford you. I consented to retain my commission, and accept the command."

Lafayette, who as a major general was commander of the light infantry "division" of 1,500 men, must have joined in the reunion of Hamilton and Laurens. They had all been aides and the closest of friends during the campaign of 1777 and the grim winter at Valley Forge. But Lafayette was by now already looking beyond America, to France. On October 1 he wrote Washington one of those candid requests which only he could make without evoking condemnation and cavil. Major General Benjamin Lincoln was acting as second in command, not because he was especially talented, but because he had been the only senior major general available and willing to make the trip to Yorktown. Why not, Lafayette suggested, send Lincoln over to Gloucester to command there, and let Lafayette take charge of the whole American wing? "As command of the right wing in this siege is of the highest importance to me—as it cannot have any similar effect upon General Lincoln's reputation and military prospects in Europe and the future course of his life, I am sure you will be so very kind to me as to adopt any plan consistent with propriety that may bring on an event so highly interesting to me that it can bear no comparison."

Washington let Lincoln stay where he was. But he was having his worries in Gloucester, nonetheless. He had sent the Duc de Lauzun and his legion over there to serve under General George Weedon, and they were not exactly an ideal match. Lauzun was the most exotic flower of European nobility; Weedon had begun life as an innkeeper. Washington had offered to exempt Lauzun from taking any orders from the American, who was commanding only militia, but Lauzun insisted he was a good soldier and would obey the orders of any superior officer. What he thought of Weedon is evident in his memoirs, where he maintained that he was a good enough general—but that the sound of gunfire unnerved him. This was hardly true. Weedon had fought well at Brandywine and Germantown where the gunfire had been plentiful. Actually, Washington had cautioned him not to let the militia within range of Tarleton's cavalry; the dragoons had sent them fleeing too often, and now was not the time to let a rout, however minor, shake the morale of the army. Weedon had therefore encamped a good ten miles from the British lines. Tarleton, who was in command at Gloucester, having been shipped over the day Cornwallis withdrew from his outer lines, found this arrangement most satisfactory to him, since it gave him a lovely stretch of country in which to collect food for his men and forage for his horses.

Lauzun suggested moving the American line a little closer to the British camp; Weedon reacted with alarm. Nothing was done until Washington sent over an officer who was senior to both the Duke and Weedon: the Marquis de Choisy, who had arrived with Barras' transports. Since he could not

be inserted into the already arranged allied commands before Yorktown, it was most convenient to detach him to
Gloucester. Perhaps another motive was a description of him,
by the Duc de Lauzun, as "a good and brave man, ridicu-
lously violent, constantly in a passion, making scenes with
everybody and always without reason." Choisy immediately
decided on an advance to siege positions, and on the morning
of October third Lauzun and his legion led the way down a
lane toward Gloucester Point.

About four miles from their destination, they collided
with a large British foraging party guarded personally by the
vaunted Tarleton and his dragoons. It was an encounter
drenched in the stuff of historical romance. Both Lauzun and
Tarleton had uttered grandiloquent wishes to meet horse to
horse, saber to saber. In fact, according to Lauzun, as they
cantered down the lane, he saw a very pretty American girl
standing in the doorway of her farmhouse. He naturally
stopped to pay his respects, and she told him that Colonel
Tarleton had passed by only a few minutes before, and he
had asked her if she knew the whereabouts of the Duc de
Lauzun. "I long to shake hands with him," Tarleton had said.

Now he had his chance. Tarleton's dragoons rode across
the rear of the British foraging party, which was moving
slowly along, its wagons encumbered with Indian corn. Lauzun immediately charged, and in a moment there was a
ferocious melee on both sides of the little lane. Thirty-five
of Lauzun's legionnaires were armed with lances, and one of
these inadvertently prevented the dashing Duke and his English counterpart from meeting in single combat. Across a field
crowded with glittering sabers and cursing, sweating, bleeding horsemen, they spotted each other, and Tarleton, fearless
as always, tried to cut his way through to Lauzun, pistol in
his hand. Lauzun repaid him the compliment, but just as
they were about to meet, one of Lauzun's men sank his lance
into the horse of a nearby Tarleton trooper. The dying ani-

mal reared and plunged under Tarleton's steed, and the British hero went down in a wild tangle of horseflesh.

A shout of triumph broke from the French hussars; they thought Tarleton was wounded, and a rout was now in prospect. But Tarleton, detested as he might have been by Americans, had won the loyalty of his men. With utter disregard for their own safety, his troopers surrounded their fallen colonel and fought ferociously to prevent his capture. Within minutes, Tarleton was on horseback again, and both sides hastily regrouped for another charge. But Tarleton, finding his line in disarray, filed his men behind the light infantry company of the Twenty-third Royal Welsh Fusileers who had by now come around the wagon train and formed a line of battle.

Lauzun, careless of personal danger, charged anyway. A volley from the British infantrymen emptied a dozen of his saddles, and he soon found his men riding the other way. Now it was the French hero's turn to take advantage of infantry protection. A battalion of Virginia militia under Lieutenant Colonel John Francis Mercer had come up and they stood with muskets ready as the shaken French cavalry hastily retreated behind them to regroup.

Tarleton's cavalrymen were on their heels, and they cut off some stragglers. Lauzun, turning, saw one of his hussars surrounded by a half-dozen English dragoons. He charged single-handed into the unequal contest, and sent the English horsemen reeling. He brought his badly wounded hussar safely behind Mercer's militiamen and went back to the job of reforming his battered line. The little rescue was one more proof that Lauzun, the supposed court dandy, was a thorough soldier.

Tarleton, always contemptuous of American militia, charged the allied line before Lauzun had his horsemen reformed. But the British tiger abruptly discovered that these were no ordinary militiamen. Most, including Mercer, were veterans of the Continental Line, and they met the charge with a withering volley which broke Tarleton's men and sent them streaming back to their infantry once more. The foot soldiers advanced to support them, and the Virginians met them with a blast which killed their lieutenant and wounded several other men. Tarleton now decided it would be futile to waste men on such skirmishing. His wagon train of provisions was well on its way to the British lines, so he slowly pulled back, keeping his cavalry and infantry in a compact body which not even Lauzun was inclined to charge again.

Inside the camp at Gloucester, the firing made everyone think it was the signal for a general attack and every post was manned. Lieutenant Colonel Simcoe of the Queen's Rangers was down with the bilious fever which was afflicting so many of the British, but he had himself carried from his bed to the forward redoubts, and was even planning to mount a horse and go in Tarleton's support when the British column came trudging into sight. It was Tarleton's last visit to the countryside. The Americans followed him to within a half-mile of the Gloucester lines and began digging siege works and trenches to pen him in.

The Marquis de Choisy confessed he was amazed by the good conduct of the American militiamen, and Washington exuded a glow of local pride for his fellow Virginians. He also was careful to congratulate the Duc de Lauzun for the "judicious disposition and decisive Vigour with which he charged the Enemy." He called the affair a "brilliant success" and declared that the enemy had consisted of six hundred horse and foot, which had been "decisively repulsed" with a loss of fifty killed and wounded. Tarleton's version of his losses were one killed, twelve wounded.

Over in Yorktown, the allied army had laid aside most of its guns for shovels and picks. All during the first week in October, the regiments toiled on, completing the fortifications around the captured British redoubts. The British shelled them steadily and often with deadly effect. A single cannonball killed four men in the Pennsylvania Line. On October 2, Colonel Richard Butler noted in his diary that the British had fired 352 shots that day. Another diarist tells of a militiaman who got tired of digging and mounted the wall of his parapet where he did a mocking dance for the better part of an hour, while cannonballs whizzed around him. Why he was allowed to continue this mad sport is not explained but the farce ended tragically. A ball "put an end to his capers."

In spite of this evident danger, Washington spent a number of hours during the week reconnoitering in front of his lines. On the first of October, Lieutenant Feltman tells in his diary how a worried aide ordered a guard of fifty men from the Pennsylvania Line to march in front of Washington as a covering party, lest the enemy make a sortie and take him prisoner. All through the war, Washington's carelessness before shot and shell had driven his aides to distraction. During this reconnaissance, Feltman tells how the general, along with the French engineer Duportail and three men of the guard, advanced to within three hundred yards of the enemy's main works. This is within easy rifle range, and the British had crack riflemen in their ranks, notably the German Jagers. Colonel Philip Van Cortlandt of New York tells how one artillery shot came close enough to make most of the party retire behind a covering hill, but Washington, who had his field glass to his eye, did not even move his head.

Washington disregarded cannon almost as totally as did the dancing militiaman. On the third of October he was out again, at the Poplar Redoubt, one of the captured British positions, and the size of his group—the aides as well as spectators who seemed to accompany him with impunity—promptly drew the attention of the British artillerymen. A cannon ball plowed up the sand only a few feet away from them, throwing a shower of pebbles and dirt over the whole party. Chaplain Evans of the light infantry was one of those showered, and he was so alarmed he pointed out the debris on his clothes to the general before brushing it off. "Mr. Evans," Washington said with a smile, "you had better carry that home and show it to your wife and children."

While the generals were reconnoitering and planning, Knox and his artillerymen were frantically scouring the country for wagons and horses to pull the heavy guns over the sandy road from Trebell's Landing. Washington sent his own baggage wagons and asked all the general officers to send theirs as well. Other officers contributed horses, but more than a few of the metal monsters were dragged by back-breaking manpower. Thousands of other soldiers were kept busy filling gabions—wicker baskets used for the foundation of earthworks—and stripping trees to make fascines—bundles of thin sticks which would be placed in the walls of the redoubts to stiffen them against cannon fire.

Not until the fourth of October did any artillery reach the vicinity of the front lines. More than a few of the allied soldiers were itching to return some of the cannon shot the British had been firing at them, but there was no immediate attempt to put the batteries into action. This would have to wait for the opening of the first trench, or parallel, in the language of siege warfare. Nevertheless the optimism of those in the lines was high. On the thirtieth of September, Captain Davis of the Pennsylvania Line had bet his friend Lieutenant Feltman a beaver hat that Lord Cornwallis and his army would be prisoners of war by the next Sunday.

On the French side of the lines, the enlisted men were toiling at the same tasks: bringing up cannon and gathering the material for building siege-works. This was General Rochambeau's fifteenth siege, so things were more inclined to move efficiently on his wing. He too was worried about Cornwallis' opportunity to escape up the York River. His young German aide, Baron Ludwig von Closen, tells in his journal how each morning at dawn one of the aides had to go down to the river bank and report on the state of the English ships. This was dangerous business. They never made the visit without drawing a volley of musketry and sometimes cannon shot from the watchful Fusileers in their forward redoubt.

All these preparations, particularly the slow progress of the artillery, must have been agonizing to Washington. His original schedule had called for opening a parallel by October 1. He could have done so, but there was no point in making such an advance until he had heavy guns to man the batteries. So, as he had learned to do so often in the last six years, he waited.

Meanwhile, the routine of the army continued as usual. On October 2 a court martial met to consider the case of Captain Patrick Duffy of the Fourth Regiment of Artillery, accused of drawing his sword on Captain Jeremiah Ballard of the Second New Jersey Regiment and attempting to stab him, firing a pistol at him when unarmed, and also "for a most disgraceful breach of friendship in seizing from Lieutenant Blewer a loaded Pistol and snapping the same at him when attempting at Captain Duffy's own request an amicable settlement of his quarrel with Captain Ballard." Earlier in the same evening, according to Lieutenant Colonel John Stewart, Duffy had while thoroughly drunk rioted in the street, abused a French soldier who was passing innocently by, and "in a seditious and disorderly manner" threatened to arrest a French guard stationed at the hospital.

The court-martial found that the pistol Duffy had snapped at his friend Blewer was not loaded, but they recommended that he be discharged from the service anyway. On October 6, Washington approved the sentence.

As in every battle, deserters trickled between the two armies. It is understandable enough why the British and German soldiers in Cornwallis' army might desert. No man enjoys the sensation of being trapped. But it is hard to under-

stand why anyone from the French or Americans would desert to Cornwallis. Yet they did. In his diary on the second of
October Lieutenant William Feltman tells of seeing one with
his own eyes: "One of the Maryland soldiers deserted to the
enemy this afternoon from his post; my waiter was in pursuit
of him, but could not overtake him, and in his pursuing him
made him drop his arms and accoutrements, which he
brought off with him."

Back of the lines, the surgeons and commissaries were getting hospitals ready for the sick and wounded. Worrisome
Claude Blanchard was in his usual dither, because all the medicines and other necessities for his hospital were still on the
ships in the James River. He was also smarting over a semirebuke from Major General Chastellux, who saw the siege as
such a simple operation that he told Blanchard they would
not have "more than fifty sick or wounded." By September
28, the commissary had 300 sick enlisted men and ten officers
in his hospital, and was racing around trying to do something
for them, muttering: "fifty sick indeed." He also added that
the ten officers "were harder to please than all the rest."

While all these various departments of the 20,000-man
allied army were gathering their resources for the moment of
contact with the enemy, Washington did not lose sight of
other theaters of war. He wrote to Major General William
Heath on the Hudson, keeping him posted on every new
development in the siege. He did the same thing for Nathanael Greene who was fighting a separate war in South Carolina,
with practically no resources. On the sixth of October, he also
sent Greene a long memorandum which was so top secret
that he made the bearer, Lieutenant Colonel Lewis Morris
memorize it and then destroy it. In it he explained progress
thus far at Yorktown and why they could expect little help
from De Grasse elsewhere. He promised the fighting Quaker
all the men he could detach from Yorktown, the moment the

siege ended in victory—but all of these military matters fade beside the heart of the message, which shows how deeply thoughtful Washington could be.

> Colonel Morris will inform General Greene in the sincerest manner that there are but two motives which can possibly induce General W—— to take the command to the southward. One, the order of Congress to repair thither; the other, the French army going there. In the last case, Count Rochambeau would command if Genl. Washington did not go in person.
>
> General Washington wishes, not only from his personal regard to Genl. Greene but also from principles of generosity and justice to see him crowned with those Laurels which from his unparalleled exertions he so richly deserves.

Rare is the general who can find time to think so considerately of a subordinate when he himself is engaged in the thousand and one details of running his own army. But time for such thoughtfulness ended on the morning of October 6. The engineers reported to Washington that enough artillery and ammunition were in the front lines to fire a respectable barrage. It was all he wanted to know. That afternoon he wrote to the President of Congress: "We shall this night open trenches."

If optimism, ranging from cautious to glowing, was beginning to previal in the allied camp before Yorktown, an almost identical emotion persisted in British headquarters in New York. During the early weeks of September, while Washington and Rochambeau marched south, British confidence in the invincibility of their fleet was paramount. On the sixth of September, Captain Frederick MacKenzie notes in his diary a "report current in town that Admiral Graves had destroyed six French ships of the line in the Chesapeake, and won a shattering victory." This was based entirely on the flimsy experience of a few loyalists, who crossed over to Elizabeth, New Jersey, under a flag of truce and "were suddenly ordered off without being permitted to speak to their friends." This implied the "Rebels had received some unfavorable news."

On the tenth of September, the frigate *Lively* arrived from Plymouth, with the good news that Admiral Digby was en-route, with three ships of the line, and no less a personage than Prince William Henry, the King's third son, on board. One of the captains of the men-of-war was also worthy of note, for his name's sake: he was William Cornwallis, brother of the Earl.

On the thirteenth, another frigate came over the bar and dropped anchor off the battery. This was the *Pegasus*, from Admiral Graves's fleet. She brought only news of the first day's action off the Chesapeake, which was summed up as "nothing decisive happened, but that as the fleets continued in sight of each other, a general action was expected." The French fleet was reported as twenty-four sail of the line and everyone in New York assumed this total was the result of a junction between Barras and De Grasse. On the fourteenth, William Smith wrote in his dairy: "De Grasse got out of the Chesapeake before our fleet arrived and had been joined by Barras. That then they were twenty-four of the line and had left a Ship or Two Frigates in the Chesapeake."

The approach of Admiral Digby thus took on tremendous importance to the British. MacKenzie told his diary: "Should Admiral Digby arrive at this Critical period, we shall be fully equal to the French and we have every reason to hope that should a general engagement take place between the fleets, the abilities and courage of our Officers and men and their ardour to distinguish themselves under the eyes of the King's Son in so important a battle, on which it may be said the Sovereignty of the Seas and the fate of America depends, will ensure us that Victory over our Ancient and perfidious En-emy, which the justness of our cause so well deserves."

There was a widespread consciousness that "the most criti-cal period of the war" had been reached. "A week will de-cide perhaps the ruin or salvation of the British Empire," William Smith declared on August 31, after Graves and Hood had sailed for the Chesapeake. "Should the French gain such an advantage over our fleet as to enable them to continue their operations unmolested against Lord Cornwallis," Mac-Kenzie said, "our hopes in that quarter rest entirely on the firmness of him and his troops; on the contrary, should our fleet beat theirs, we have a fair prospect of ending the Rebellion and at the same time of giving a severe blow to the Military power of France by the destruction or Capture of their troops on this continent." A few days earlier, a report on the "firmness" of the army under Cornwallis had been encouraging. "The whole of both Garrisons, Gloucester and York, are in great spirits; and expecting an attack soon, are preparing to give the Enemy a proper reception."

Inside headquarters, Sir Henry Clinton himself remained amazingly sanguine. He had four thousand men aboard transports, ready to head seaward the moment he heard from Admiral Graves that the menace of French naval interference was removed. The small number reveals Clinton's continuing refusal to admit a supreme crisis was about to confront him. MacKenzie, who was on detached duty in the adjutant general's office, after studying the army's returns, remarked that it would have been possible to put 9,000 men in the field against Washington and Rochambeau's 7,000-man force while they marched through New Jersey with their flanks exposed. Yet Sir Henry was still loath to send more men to deal with the greatest threat to the victory he cherished so much, although he must have known that 4,000 men would still leave Cornwallis outnumbered by the allied army when it combined before Yorktown.

On September 14 dismaying news came in from Graves. His letter, written at sea, dolefully reported:

> The enemy have so great a naval force in the Chesapeake that they are absolute masters of its navigation. The French fleet at sea consists of twenty-four sail of the line (large ships)

and two frigates. We met them the 5th coming out of the
Chesapeake, and had a pretty sharp brush with their van and
part of their center; the rear on neither side was engaged.
They appear to have suffered, but not as much as our van.
We have been in sight of each other ever since; and for two
days they had the wind of us, but did not include to renew the
action. In this ticklish state of things, your Excellency will
see the little probability of anything getting into York River
but by night, and of the infinite risk to any supplies sent by
water. All that I can say is that every resistance the fleet can
make shall not be wanting; for we must either stand or fall
together.

Sir Henry's answer to this was calm and undismayed:

I can not but agree with you that there will be infinite risk
in sending supplies at present to York River unless you can
force the enemy's fleet. I do not, however, apprehend that his
Lordship is, or can be, in any immediate danger, as his numbers, including the sailors and marines of the King's ships
and the refugees who have joined him, may be computed at
8,000 and he can feed 10,000 at full allowance until the end
of October.

Clinton thus based his optimism solely on the amount of
food Cornwallis had. One might think that the Earl was running a restaurant, instead of facing an army which outnumbered him three to one and had all the French siege artillery
from Newport—which latter fact Clinton likewise knew by
this time. Sir Henry went blandly on to suggest to Admiral
Graves that it might be just as well to wait for Admiral Digby
to arrive, and also for two of Graves's men of war, the *Robust*
and the *Prudent,* which were being refitted in the New
York Navy Yard. Then, Clinton opined; "I shall hope you
may be able to force the Chesapeake and cover our landing.
For I must again repeat that I think nothing can relieve Lord
Cornwallis but a landing of troops in Chesapeake." Sir Henry

ended his letter with one of those paragraphs which only he could write so well; it is a masterpiece of little provisos and implications, which neatly roped Admiral Graves into sharing the responsibility for any attempt to relieve Cornwallis.

> Wherefore, sir, if you approve, I will instantly attend your summons whenever you determine on the attempt and think you can force the enemy into James River or up the Chesapeake Bay, and bring with me all the troops which can be spared from the defense of this post. And then sir, if you will be so good to land me on either York or Gloucester Neck, I will at all risks endeavor to effect a junction with Lord Cornwallis, provided you will continue in possession of the bay. . . .

Graves answered with renewed assurances that he and the fleet would do everything in their power to cooperate with the army and relieve Cornwallis. Meanwhile, Clinton was holding a council of war in Manhattan. He was a great believer in councils and committees. If he could show that a council agreed unanimously with a certain plan, or lack of plan, it seemed to lift the burden of decision from his shoulders.

The first council, on September 13, was attended by every general officer Clinton could find. At the head of the list was aging Lieutenant General Wilhelm von Knyphausen, commander of the German troops and an excellent soldier. Next came Major General (and Governor) James Robertson. He and Clinton were not friendly; in fact, Robertson's habitual gossiping had purportedly turned Lord George Germain against Sir Henry. Next came a group of young major generals: Stirling, a fighting Scot who had played a major role in the capture of Fort Washington in 1776, and was still recovering from a severe leg wound suffered at the battle of Springfield in New Jersey; John Campbell, another Scot, who had recently surrendered the British garrison at Pensacola to attacking Spaniards; James Paterson, the army's adjutant general, who had done nothing but staff work throughout the Revolution; Alexander Leslie, who had fought well beside Cornwallis in the South, and had just given up the command in Charleston because of ill health. After them came Brigadier Generals Benedict Arnold and thieving Samuel Birch, and finally, Commodore Edmund Affleck, commissioner of the port.

None of these men were close to Clinton. None had played a major role in the over-all direction of the war. Leslie and Campbell were in town more by accident than design. Knyphausen, being a foreigner, was used to being disregarded when decisions were made. Arnold, who had the energy and fighting instinct necessary to meet the crisis, was outranked, and had just returned from his New London foray, where Sir Henry and General Robertson, among others, thought the high casualties reflected on the turncoat's competence.

William Smith's opinion of Clinton's staff was low: "Our neighborhood has brought me to the knowledge of his Family—not a man of business or Enterprise among them. They are servile and study only to make use of their gen'l for their own interests. . . . Their Principal I understand gives himself to such gusts of passion that no Gent'l. of Spirit will long continue in his Family. I don't find any of the Generals to have his confidence. Arnold says they all complain. Elliot* and Gen'l Robertson are most attended to—the latter thinks meanly of him. . . . Poor Sir Henry!"

Everyone at the table must have been amazed when General Robertson opened the parley by making the most daring suggestion that could possibly be imagined. Five thousand men, he declared, should be immediately crammed aboard the only ship of the line available in New York, the *Robust,* and they should try to slip past the enemy fleet at

---

* Andrew Elliot, the Lt. Governor of New York—a civilian.

night and reinforce Cornwallis, who would then attack the enemy with his whole force. Robertson agreed that the failure of such a gamble would be disastrous, but if Cornwallis were wiped out, it would be equally disastrous. So why not, he argued, bet everything on a long chance, which would have the additional advantage of total surprise?

Clinton dismissed the idea curtly, and Robertson, unused to being a daredevil, let it drop, but the next morning he put the project more clearly in a letter to Clinton, who convened another council. Letters from Cornwallis and Rear Admiral Graves were read. Officers "lately arrived" from Virginia were examined. Clinton then put the following question to his assembled advisors:

> As the Admiral in his last letter says that the enemy being absolute masters of the navigation of the Chesapeake and having a naval superiority at sea, there is little probability of anything getting into York River but by night and infinite risk to any supplies sent by water, and as the army under Lord Cornwallis may be computed at eight thousand men and it appears from the returns that His Lordship has provisions at full allowance for ten thousand to the end of October, and it is the opinion of the officers lately arrived from Virginia that the post of York may be defended with its present garrison against twenty thousand assailants for at least three weeks, whether it is most advisable to commit a reinforcement of five or six thousand men to the hazards of the sea during our present naval inferiority, and endeavor to relieve Lord Cornwallis immediately at all risks, or to wait until we either receive more favorable accounts from Rear Admiral Graves, or the junction of Rear Admiral Digby's squadron affords a more certain prospect of success in the attempt?

If there is ever a contest for loaded questions, this one must compete for first prize. The members of the council "Unanimously resolved it will be most prudent to wait more favorable accounts from Rear Admiral Graves, or the arrival of Rear Admiral Digby." Thus Robertson's daring idea went down the drain, and he never mentioned it again.

While Clinton palavered, a feeling of profound uneasiness began to spread through the city. The month was slipping away, and nothing had been heard from Admiral Graves. Smith's diary has more and more denunciations against the laxity of the British generals. He lashes out at Robertson: "He is a Dotard & abandoned to Frivolity—He has Parties of Girls in the Fort Garden, in the Midst of his own Fears and the Anxieties of this Hour."

On September 16, MacKenzie wrote in his diary: "The anxiety of all ranks of people here at present is very great. Everything depends on the event of the Action which is likely to happen between the fleets. Should our fleet be defeated, the loss of the whole army under Lord Cornwallis is much to be dreaded. . . ." Two days later, the frigate *Fortunee* arrived from Graves's fleet, and the bad news spread through the worried town. The French had returned to the Chesapeake, and Graves was limping back to New York, much damaged. On the following day, the 4,000 men Clinton had held for three weeks on the cramped, unhealthy transports were ordered to disembark at Staten Island. MacKenzie noted: "All the shipwrights and Carpenters belonging to the Dock yard are now very busy in making yards and top Masts for the fleet: a good many of which will be wanted." Then he added, dolefully: "I fear the fate of the Army in Virginia will be determined before our fleet can get out of this harbour again, in a condition to force that of the Enemy."

On the twentieth, Assistant Adjutant MacKenzie allowed himself to lecture briefly on what he would do, if he were Sir Henry Clinton. He highly approved of the rumor that Clinton was considering an attack on Philadelphia. He had apparently seen a list of units drawn up by Clinton or a headquarters aide, listing 8,000 men who could take part in the expedition. MacKenzie summed up what might be called the common man's (or common sense) opinion on Clinton by writing: "Should he remain here for that time without undertaking something, he will be blamed by everyone let the matter end as it may; and it will be said that he remained an unconcerned spectator of the fate of that Army, with 11,000 fighting men equal to any enterprise, while the Enemy had nothing between the Hudson and the Chesapeake to oppose him."

This was written on September 20. Two days later MacKenzie made another entry, which is not directly pertinent but reveals a significant state of mind among the British general officers: he noted a "striking instance of the want of discipline in the British service." The troops slated for Cornwallis' relief had embarked on the sixth of September, and transports were allotted for the reception of the generals, but "no British General embarked with them; and tho' they landed yesterday on Staten Island, where there is now a body of above 6,000 men, no British General Officer is yet with them. Major General Paterson, tho' particularly appointed to command the British Grenadiers, has remained at Brooklyn ever since they embarked: Lord Lincoln, who commands the Brigade of British Infantry, has been in New York the whole time: and General Leslie is also here. None of them appear to have the least intention of going down to the troops. Major Generals Kospoth and Wurmb embarked with the Hessian troops, and have continued with them the whole time. What a contrast! Our Generals and Admirals don't seem to be in earnest about this business."

If MacKenzie was by now thoroughly alarmed, Clinton still was not. Even when the letters Cornwallis had written on the sixteenth and seventeenth arrived, reporting the true numbers of De Grasse's combined fleet—thirty-six ships of the line—Sir Henry wavered only slightly from his desperate optimism. "I must confess," he wrote in his memoirs, "that after I was thus fully apprised of the enemy's strength and informed by the Admiral of the crippled condition of the fleet, I should not have been greatly displeased to have heard that Lord Cornwallis had made his escape to Carolina with everything he could take with him."

In his letter of the seventeenth Cornwallis had advised Clinton to relieve him soon, or "be prepared to hear the worst." Sir Henry's interpretation of this phrase showed his state of mind perhaps better than anything else. On the night of the twenty-third, he wrote a long memorandum to himself, in which he maintained that the "worst" meant nothing more serious than retreat. He noted all the arguments which Cornwallis might make to himself to recommend such a move; Cornwallis knew the real naval odds, knew that Graves had retired to New York, knew that ships of the line could only come over the bar at Sandy Hook with the flood tide. Therefore, reasoned Clinton, he was planning to break out, fight his way across the Chickahominy, on to Richmond, and into North Carolina. "If his Lordship determines before the arrival of Washington, he may be saved although the Chesapeake is lost. . . . Tis better to lose it and save Lord Cornwallis than lose both."

This is not the thinking of a man in touch with reality. Two days later, on September 26, he gave this opinion to his once more assembled generals. It is not too hard to imagine the furtive looks passing from one man to another, the "ahems" and snufflings and shufflings, as each of them wondered if Sir Henry had lost his reason completely. They then voted unanimously that the expression "worst" meant something more serious than retreat.

Admiral Graves did not return to New York until September 24. He had arrived off Sandy Hook on September 19, but it took days to get the big ships over the difficult bar and up the long harbor to New York. At his first meeting with Sir Henry, the admiral was as optimistic as the British Commander in Chief. He vowed once more that nothing would be left undone to ready the fleet for sea as soon as possible, and saw no reason why they would be unable to break through De Grasse's ships at the mouth of the Chesapeake and land Clinton with his reinforcements. Graves said that De Grasse had taken a position where the strong tide would make it difficult for him to maneuver his ships at anchor so as to fire broadsides at ships approaching him head on; if the British chose the right moment, when there was a "leading wind and tide," they could slip past him with minimal damage. They would then anchor inshore, at the mouth of the York River, and debark the troops. The tide was not as strong in there, and they would be able to use springs on their cables, to come about and hurl broadsides at any French attempt to interfere.

It all sounded very logical, and Sir Samuel Hood, who probably knew better than anyone how risky it really was, warmly approved the idea and urged the construction of three or four fire ships, to throw the French into confusion at the crucial point of entry. But there were worries among the naval officers present; they agreed that the fleet might get into the Chesapeake, assuming it took De Grasse by surprise. But how was it going to get out, when surprise was out of the question? Weren't they risking not only the loss of Cornwallis and his army, Sir Henry and his reinforcement, but also the entire fleet? This would mean not only the loss of North America, but the immense treasures of the West Indies.

Sir Henry seemed to think that once the reinforcements landed, Washington would abandon his siege, and De Grasse would conveniently sail away to the West Indies. If neither of these things happened, he admitted it might be necessary to reembark the whole British army and attempt an escape by sea. In spite of these alarming doubts, the council of war unanimously agreed that relief must and would be sent to Cornwallis, and they unanimously approved of Sir Henry's writing to him with this assurance. Admiral Graves said that from returns made to him that morning, he thought the fleet would be ready to sail by October 5. Hood growled that his squadron could sail the next day, if necessary. Clinton promised to do everything in his power to expedite the fleet's preparations. He ordered the army departments to supply the King's ships with "lumber, boards, ammunition, howitzers . . . and the artificers of the ordnance were set about preparing the additional fire-ships for service." Whereupon Sir Henry wrote Cornwallis the letter which inspired the Earl to withdraw his troops from the outer defenses and retire into the inner works around York.

The lesser mortals in the city did not yet know the true size of the French fleet and were still frantically waiting for news of Admiral Digby. But some of the better informed were already beginning to worry about Admiral Graves. On the twenty-fourth of September, William Smith wrote to William Tryon, the last Royal Governor of New York: "Digby, Digby is the cry—if he arrives tomorrow Graves who has 10 ships refitting in our Harbour will not be ready to sail in some days, and every hour is precious to Lord Cornwallis tho' his provisions will hold out for 6 weeks. I wish it was clear that the Fleet will undertake to give him the intended Succours or if not we will make some activity in this part of the Continent counterbalance for our losses elsewhere, and the enemy's thirst for Peace be equal to our own. . . ." As a postscript to this letter he adds: "to our unspeakable joy Digby is at the Hook 4 of Clock P.M.—all well—the Presence of the Prince may supply our Deficiency."

For the next few days, a good portion of the city's time and attention was given over to the reception of the first member of the British Royal Family to visit America. To a student of history's ironies, he could not have come at a less propitious time. But the young Prince (the future King William IV) could hardly have sensed impending disaster in the enthusiastic and elaborate welcome he received. As he came ashore on the twenty-sixth of September, twenty-one guns boomed a salute. Clinton, all the general officers and distinguished citizens such as William Smith, greeted him at a house selected for his reception in Hanover Square. On the next day the Prince walked about the town with Sir Henry and his official family, followed by huge crowds "whose curiosity he had gratified all the Morning at the Window." He and Sir Henry reviewed the German regiment of Bunau, and watched the British Thirty-eighth Regiment march out of town to encamp in the fields near what is today Greenwich Village. That evening he and Sir Henry dined together and attended a concert of the army band. "The graceful appearance and manner of the Prince, with his liveliness and affability, gives universal satisfaction," MacKenzie noted.

Rivington's *Royal Gazette,* New York's loyalist newspaper, went even farther: "It is impossible to express the satisfaction felt by persons of all ranks from the ease, affability and condescension shown by this most pleasing and manly youth, when he appears abroad amongst the happy and approved loyal subjects of the good and gracious King, our best and firmest friend, the Majesty of England, his Royal Highness's sincerely beloved Father."

Up at Fish-kill on the Hudson, Samuel Loudon solemnly reprinted all this in his rebellious New York *Packet,* adding at the end: "(Whew. . . . w. . . . w!)"

On the twenty-eighth, the day that Washington's determined men were pushing through the woods and across the creeks of the Yorktown Peninsula toward Cornwallis' lines, the chief pre-occupation in New York was an address of welcome which was to be read to the Prince at an official reception that night. "I was called to the Governor's at 7," Smith says, "and settled a new draft of address wrote by General Robertson after some Conversation with Admiral Digby who was fearful of bringing the Prince into too much Notice for the King's inclination." Other members of Clinton's staff, the Lieutenant Governor, and various learned citizens and members of the Governor's council arrived. The address was read to them, and "no man objected." Two copies were then ordered, and one sent to the Prince. "At ten o'clock," Smith goes on, "we went with the Governor and were called up and introduced at the head of the stairs to Admiral Digby who brought us in to the Prince who had Sir Samuel Hood with him. The passage all through was lined with general and other officers of the Army and Navy waiting to be introduced."

General Robertson then advanced and read the address to the Prince, "but not having his spectacles got thro' with great difficulty," Smith noted acidly. The address was a flowery eulogy which assured the Prince that his "presence animates every loyal breast. The glow in our own persuades us you are formed to win every heart; a Rebellion that grew upon prejudice should sink at the approach of so fair a representation of our Royal Virtues." That night there was a state dinner, at which the Prince "drank down the left wing of the table," but Smith noted that the general atmosphere was anything but lively. "Few generals drank to him [the Prince] or others except those near them and there was no high toned conversation."

One reason for the depression may well have been the council of war held that afternoon, which was attended by Admiral Digby. He was Graves's senior and had been sent out to relieve him, but when he discovered the mare's-nest he was inheriting, he neatly sidestepped and said that he would not dream of superseding Admiral Graves when he was in the midst of such a difficult and complex operation. He would be happy to lend his advice, to sail with the fleet and fight his squadron, but no, no, my dear admiral, you have put this kettle of fish on the fire, and it is up to you to get it off.

Digby's maneuver would seem to have unsettled Graves more than a little. To have fought an indecisive battle against superior odds was not necessarily a blot on his reputation, but to lose the entire fleet would sink him in infamy forever. He began to wonder about the advisability of entering the Chesapeake and to have even more violent doubts about his ability to stay there, once the army landed. Digby bluntly remarked that the most that could be expected of the fleet was to put the troops on shore. From there, it was every service for itself. Sir Henry protested frantically that on the twenty-fourth, it had been decided by a unanimous vote that the army would be landed and the fleet would remain to protect it. Without that proviso, both Cornwallis and the reinforcements stood a good chance of going down the drain. Digby then demanded a clear statement from Sir Henry of what the army would do when it landed. It was always difficult to get a clear statement from Sir Henry, and now it was impossible. It would depend on circumstances, he said lamely. It was even possible that a withdrawal might be necessary. But he "supposed, of course, that there would be no more difficulty in getting off than in going in—of which, however, the Admiral's countenance seemed to express some doubt." Clinton meekly let the question drop, and proposed, instead, that the council let Cornwallis know that the date of sailing would be postponed, and he should be told to weigh the chances and act as he thought best.

The decision to postpone was made not merely in the hope that Cornwallis would be inspired to extricate himself somehow. It was also based on the harsh facts of repairing the damaged ships. On the twenty-seventh, the day before the conference, MacKenzie had noted in his diary the fear that "something decisive will take place against Lord Cornwallis before we can possibly be ready to go from hence. The officers of the Navy say they will be ready the 5th October; but when it is seen that the *Montague* has a Main Mast to get in, another Bowsprit to be fished, most of them either Yards or top Masts to get up, and several of them much to do about their rigging, I think I may venture to say they will not all be ready to go down to Sandy Hook by the 10th. After that we may allow three days before the ships are all fairly over the bar, and Seven days more before anything can be effected for the relief of Lord Cornwallis."

That same day, MacKenzie watched the departure of an "armed boat" with letters in cypher from Clinton to Cornwallis. Built like a whale boat, "quite open," it carried fourteen oars and four swivel cannon, besides small arms, and two sails. She had already made two successful runs between Yorktown and New York. On the last passage, she had been forced to anchor for sixty-two hours in open sea during a gale that would otherwise have driven her ashore.

On the thirtieth of September, while the reassured Cornwallis was withdrawing from his advanced positions in Yorktown, there was another council of war in New York. Graves opened it by informing Clinton that the fleet would not possibly be ready to sail before the twelfth of October. Clinton tried desperately to get some assurance from the admirals that they could get into the bay and out again "without risking an action that may probably be decisive against them." Naturally, the admirals could give him no assurance whatsoever, being unable to read De Grasse's mind. That night, Sir Henry wrote another memorandum to himself: "I see this in so serious a light, so horrible, that I dare not look at it."

The pessimism of Admirals Digby and Graves rapidly communicated itself to the fleet. On the first of October, the vigilant MacKenzie's hopes sank a little lower. "It appears very doubtful that the Navy will after all attempt or undertake anything towards the relief of Lord Cornwallis. The general conversation among them from the Captains downward is of the great superiority of the French fleet, the impossibility of destroying any of them by fireships, or forcing them in the position they have taken, and the certainty that they will come out immediately on the appearance of the British fleet, and attack it. They talk very freely of the conduct of the Admiral of the 5th of September, and appear more ready to censure the conduct of others than to refit their own ships. Several of the Captains spend more of their time on shore than they do on board, and appear as unconcerned about the matter as if they commanded Guard ships at Portsmouth. The *Montague* has not got either her Main or Mizen Masts in yet; and it seems agreed upon by most of them that the fleet cannot be ready for sea under ten days. If they cannot, they may as well stay for 10 months."

As if to show what might have been done, if genuine enthusiasm for the expedition animated the whole fleet, MacKenzie notes two captains, Lord Robert Manners of the *Resolution,* and Captain William Graves, the admiral's brother, commanding the *Bedford,* as men who "have set an example which should have been followed by many others. The former has not slept out of his ship once, and both their ships have been ready for some days."

On October 2, an arrangement for the distribution of the troops on board the men-of-war was released to the army. To make the best possible speed, there were to be no transports; the men would be carried aboard the ships of the line, about 350 men to a vessel. To supplement the fleet's fire power, there were to be six eight-inch howitzers put aboard six of the line of battle ships, to be manned by captains of the artillery.

On the third of October another whaleboat rowing twelve oars and armed with swivel guns left for Yorktown with Major Charles Cochrane in command. The Scottish major, who had volunteered for the dangerous mission, was an interesting figure. He had been one of the officers chosen by General Gage to patrol the roads outside Boston on the night of April 18, 1775, and intercept alarm-givers such as

Paul Revere. Major Pitcairn, the commander of the fateful expedition to Concord, had been Cochrane's father-in-law, and he had been with the veteran marine when those unpremeditated shots on Lexington green began six years of savage warfare. Cochrane had fought his way through all of it, distinguishing himself repeatedly. To win faster promotion, he had volunteered for Tarleton's legion, and quickly became his second in command, fighting with the tough dragoons through their countless skirmishes and battles in the South.

According to Cochrane's own testimony, he had originated the idea of mounting infantry on captured horses and letting them ride with cavalry to create a mobile striking force, which demoralized the enemy over a wide sweep of territory. In 1780 he had gone back to England with warm letters of commendation from Cornwallis to raise an amphibious legion of sailors and boatmen which would cooperate with the army in the river-entwined South. Cochrane had returned with his wife only a few days before the Yorktown crisis erupted, and leaped at the chance to rejoin his comrades.

Major Cochrane carried a letter from Sir Henry Clinton, which was interesting, in another sense of that word:

> My Lord:
>
> Your Lordship may be assured that I am doing everything in my power to relieve you by a direct move, and I have reason to hope from the assurances given me this day by Admiral Graves, that we may pass the bar by the 12th of October, if the winds permit, and no unforeseen accident happens; this, however, is subject to disappointment, wherefore, if I hear from you, your wishes will of course direct me, and I shall persist in my idea of a direct move, even to the middle of November, should it be your Lordship's opinion that you can hold out so long; but if, when I hear from you, you tell me that you cannot, and I am without hopes of arriving in time to succour you by a direct move, I will immediately make an attempt upon Philadelphia by land, giving you

notice, if possible, of my intention. If this should draw any part of Washington's force from you, it may possibly give you an opportunity of doing something to save your army; of which, however, you can be the best judge, from being upon the spot.

In his memoirs, Clinton makes a most revealing comment upon this letter. "Major Cochrane . . . was sent to his Lordship on the 3rd of October with a sketch of the plans we had formed for effecting the junction with him, accompanied by a *hint* for him to do what he could to save at least part of his army should he have the least reason to apprehend we could not arrive in time." In a moment of supreme crisis, Sir Henry was still incapable of giving a clear, understandable order. He could only give hints.

Sergeant Joseph Plumb Martin was a worried man. After six years as a private in the Continental Army of the United States of America, he had become a sergeant by volunteering for the sappers and miners. This was dangerous work —and on the rainy night of October 6, 1781, Sergeant Martin was acutely aware of it. He could almost feel sudden death reaching out to him through the dripping darkness, as he and a thousand other Americans dug furiously into the sandy earth of the York Peninsula. There were, it was true, some 2,500 men with loaded muskets crouched only a few yards away, ready to give these unarmed toilers their instant support. But how much help could the most willing soldier give, if the darkness suddenly turned into a nightmare of thundering cannon and crashing muskets?

It could happen. Invisible through the rainy murk, but starkly visible in the minds of Sergeant Martin and his fellow Americans, were 7,500 ominously silent English soldiers commanded by a man famous for his savage attacks.

Small wonder that Martin and his friends were alarmed, when the French engineers who were directing their labors suddenly ordered them to stop, and disappeared into the night. The men were left alone on the bare, open field, without a scrap of cover, under orders not to straggle a foot either to left or right. "We now began to be a little jealous of our safety," Martin said later, "being without arms and within forty rods of the British trenches."

Their uneasiness increased radically when out of the darkness strolled a lone figure wearing what seemed to be an overcoat. What in God's name was a civilian doing here, of all places? Was he a loyalist spy, counting heads to find out just how many men Cornwallis should order to the attack? Hands tightened on shovels and picks, as the visitor inquired for the engineers and asked what troops they were. They answered him in surly monosyllables, and were not at all impressed when he advised them to say nothing to the enemy if taken prisoner. "We were obliged to him for his kind advice," said Martin, "but we considered ourselves as standing in no great need of it. For we knew as well as he did that sappers and miners were allowed no quarter by the laws of warfare."

The stranger vanished, supposedly to find the engineers. The men waited, whispering nervously to each other in the rain, which now started to come down in a steady drizzle. A few minutes later, to their vast relief, the engineers returned, and the stranger with them. Martin, standing close by, could hear them talking, and his head snapped back when he heard one officer say: "Your Excellency . . ." It could only mean one thing.

The "civilian" was General George Washington.

"Had we dared," Martin said, "we would have cautioned him for exposing himself so carelessly to danger at such a time—and doubtless he would have taken it in good part if we had. . . ."

If Sergeant Martin and his friends did not appreciate the occasional drizzle in which they worked, George Washington undoubtedly said one of his infrequent prayers of thanksgiving for the cloudy sky. If the night of October 6 had been clear, there would have been a half moon illuminating the working men, making them an irresistible target for the British artillerymen.

The day had begun with Washington issuing no less than fifty-two rules and regulations for the conduct of the siege, most of them copied from a French military textbook. All morning and afternoon fatigue parties carried fascines and gabions along the many ravines intersecting the peninsula, and piled them as close as possible to the area where they would be used. The trench was laid out at a more than respectable distance from the British lines; the traditional distance was at least 1800 feet—out of the range of small arms, grape and canister fire, which could cause heavy casualties. But as Baron von Closen noted in his diary, "the reputation of Cornwallis and the strength of the garrison determined our generals to open the great trench at a distance of 2,880–3,200 feet from the fortifications, with the exception of the left, which was only 1,920 feet away."

The "great trench" ran from the head of Yorktown Creek, near the center of the peninsula, crossed the Hampton road at almost right angles, and then swung in a long arc to the high bank of the York River, where it came about 600 yards from the two advanced British redoubts, numbers nine and ten. The Yorktown Creek ravine made it unnecessary for the allies to dig their way across the entire peninsula. It hemmed Cornwallis in more effectively than any man-made ditch along almost the entire allied left flank.

The engineers were not especially happy at breaking ground so far from the main British lines. It meant still another parallel would have to be dug at three hundred yards on another night. But the allies had made a careful examination of the redoubts Cornwallis had abandoned, and they felt that the sandy soil of the peninsula made poor fortifications; it would not take too many days, they hoped, to cripple Yorktown's defenses sufficiently to permit the opening of the highly dangerous second parallel.

On the allied left, the two French regiments, the Bourbonnais and the Soissonnais, supplied a thousand diggers. At the same time the regiment of Touraine, under the leadership of General Saint-Simon, was to dig on the extreme left, before the Fusileers' redoubt, a "flying trench" or "sap" which was to support a battery of artillery with which the allies hoped to disrupt the English control of the York River. The American diggers were under the command of Generals Lincoln, Wayne and Clinton. At four P.M. they were paraded and marched to the front, where they waited, sheltered by a ravine. The French marched at five, and as soon as darkness fell, the French engineers began assigning detachments to their positions and laying out laths of pine wood end to end to mark the width and direction of the trench. The fascines and gabions were piled in front, and the dirt flung out of the trench on top of them, so that a parapet was automatically constructed, along with the ditch.

The darkness gave one man from the Touraine Regiment the chance he wanted. He deserted to the British and told them what he knew—that his regiment was moving forward that night against the Fusileer redoubt. He undoubtedly made it sound like an all-out attack; deserters usually tell a good story in the hope of getting a better reception. If the desertion was discovered, no one bothered to report it to the general officers. Washington and Rochambeau were both out in the darkness with their troops, checking personally on the details, urging the men to dig hard and fast. For over two hours there was no sound from the British lines.

At about nine, the watchdogs in the Fusileer redoubt began to bark. The woofs were taken up by other dogs along the whole British front. A moment later, with a tremendous crash, the British artillery opened every available gun on the men of Touraine. Lieutenant de la Loge of the French Royal Artillery was commanding a battery of guns immediately behind their lines; he was under orders to fire only to repel an enemy assault. He was never to enjoy this pleasure. A round shot tore off his right leg, and though he insisted on remaining in command for some time in spite of his wound, he was finally hurried to the rear, where he died a few hours later. Seven other French soldiers were wounded in this barrage, but the rest clung doggedly to their task, and kept on digging, without returning the fire. Ironically, the trench they were constructing was of minor importance and thanks to the deserter, the Touraine assignment diverted the British attention from the masses of men on the allied right, working in the open without an iota of cover. The few shots that were fired in their direction were aimed at the captured redoubts on the right and left of the Hampton road, now empty.

Joseph Plumb Martin tells of another diversion, created by the Americans deliberately to confuse the British artillery. Beyond a marsh on the far right of the British works, a number of men were ordered to build fires and move frequently back and forth in front of them, to give the impression of a large body of men assembling. This too inspired the British gunners to fire over the heads of the Americans entrenching, as Martin said, somewhat inaccurately, "literally under their noses."

The trench was no small task. Baron von Closen says it was 3,840 to 4,480 feet, and there were also four redoubts to be constructed, two supporting each flank. The digging men needed little urging to make the dirt fly. They knew what would happen if the dawn found them without sufficient cover. "The men employed that night eat no 'idle bread' (and I question if they eat any other)," Joseph Plumb Martin said. When the sun came up, the chagrined British found their opponents working securely behind a solid barricade of earthworks. The Americans had not lost a single man in the entire night's cannonade.

Behind the lines, while the first parallel was being dug, the medical men of both corps waited anxiously for the heavy casualties they feared might soon be coming their way. Commissary Blanchard wrote: "I trembled lest it should be murderous, for we had not the means to afford assistance." Dr. James Thacher of Massachusetts commandeered twenty drummers and fifers for a temporary hospital corps, and planned to march into the lines with the men. He gave one drummer, a mulatto, all his instruments, bandages and medicines, and told him not to lose sight of him for a moment. Almost the instant poor Thacher turned his head the fellow vanished in search of rum. The cursing doctor had to run a mile back to the American hospital and borrow fresh equipment from Dr. James Craik, who made him promise to treat Lafayette first if he should be wounded.

When Thacher got back he found that the troops had vanished into the darkness. He and his surgeon's mate, Dr. Aeneas Munson, did not have the faintest idea where they were going, but they tried to follow. After about half a mile a dozen white uniforms suddenly rose from the ground, and the two doctors had the uncomfortable sensation of bayonets tickling their throats. It was a French patrol, and they demanded the countersign for the day. The doctors stuttered out Pennsylvania, Jersey, but this was the American countersign, and it meant nothing to the French.

They stood there, eyeing each other warily, until an officer arrived who could speak English. He put the doctors back on the trail of the Americans, and they finally reached the lines, where they watched the men work. They were, Thacher proudly declared, "indefatigable."

Doctor Thacher's adventures with the French were not over, however. Toward the end of the long night, it began to rain heavily, and the weather turned very cold. Since his services were not needed, the doctor retired to a small brush hut nearby and lay down to doze. About a half hour later, his sleep was rudely interrupted by another white uniform in the door of the hut, this one with a sword in his hand, aimed at Thacher's chest. "Friend, friend?" the Frenchman said.

"Friend, *friend*," said the good doctor, scrambling as far away from the sword as he could get.

"Ah, *Monsieur* friend," said the Frenchman, who sheathed his sword and departed.

"It is doubtful whether he or myself was the most frightened," Thacher said.

At dawn, when the British gunners discovered the parallel's earthworks, they made the metal fly, but the working men were well-covered, and they paid little attention to it. It was more diverting than dangerous, and a British bulldog added to the sport by chasing the balls when they bounded off the American parapets. "Our officers wished to catch him and oblige him to carry a message from them into the town to his masters, but he looked too formidable for any of us to encounter," Sergeant Martin said.

By noon the trenches were pronounced ready for occupation and the formal opening of the siege. Lafayette's division was given the honor, and the light infantry regiment commanded by Lt. Colonel Alexander Hamilton led the way. He obeyed to the letter article twenty-five of the siege regulations: "All the troops either relieving or relieved will March with Drums beating, Colors flying." He also obeyed regulation twenty-six, which stipulated that the "standard bearers will plant their standards upon the Epaulments." Captain James Duncan of Hamilton's regiment looked forward to this formality with some uneasiness, because he was "posted in the center with the colors" and would have to mount the parapet, in clear view of the British gunners. He also thought they would be slaughtered while they marched to the trench, announcing their presence with their drums. But the French engineers had carefully laid out the trenches so that ravines on either side served as "covered ways"—the traditional method of approaching a trench. "We did not lose a man in relieving," Duncan noted, "Though the enemy fired much." Proudly, the young captain sprang to the parapet, and planted the regimental colors, with the motto: Manus Haec Inimica Tyrannis.

Then came a maneuver which was not in the general siege orders—and which only Alexander Hamilton would have conceived. With total aplomb, the twenty-six-year-old colonel ordered the entire regiment to mount the parapet, face the enemy, and there, to his bellowed orders, perform the entire manual of arms. The appalled Duncan was certain it was the end. But Hamilton knew his enemy. It was the kind of gesture which the English loved, and they would not dream of firing on such effrontery. It was in the swaggering tradition of the British Guards, who had been known in earlier wars to form in front of the French lines, announce who they were, and invite the French to fire first, before they charged. The agitated Captain Duncan, who did not share his colonel's huge ambitions, told his diary: "Although the enemy had been firing a little before, they did not now fire us a single shot. I suppose their astonishment at our conduct must have prevented them, for I can assign no other reason. Colonel Hamilton gave these orders, and although I esteem him one of the first officers in the American army, must beg leave in this instance to think he wantonly exposed the lives of his men."

The 1,500 American troops guarding the right wing trenches were supported by an equal number of armed men in ravines just behind them. The same precaution was followed on the French side. All during the day, a total of 800 men worked hard constructing artillery batteries and strengthening the redoubts. Sentries were stationed along the trenches at intervals, and they were ordered to give an instant warning if they saw a mortar shell being fired. This was for most of the Americans their first experience with these primitive but deadly forerunners of the high-explosive shell; from the moment they entered the trenches, the British began a steady shower of them. The eighteenth-century mortar shell was simply a hollow, cast iron sphere. It had a single hole where the powder was funneled in—not enough to pack too tightly, because the fuse must also be driven into it just before it was fired. The fuse was a wooden tube several inches long, with a powder composition tamped into its hole. The head of the fuse was hollowed out like a cup, and "mealed" or fine powder, moistened with alcohol, was pressed into the hollow to make a large igniting surface. An artilleryman could time the fuse by cutting it to specific lengths.

The mortar shells fired at Yorktown did not have the destructive force which shells of similar weight have today. The trenches were equipped with "blinds"—barrels filled with sand, usually—behind which the men took shelter when a shell landed in the trench. This was normally enough to protect the nearby occupants from the flying metal when a shell exploded. The sentries were forbidden to cry out a warning when a cannon was fired at them, because the ball would be on top of them before they could open their mouths, and this only caused confusion in the ranks of the working men. But the mortar shell was much easier to dodge. The projecting fuse gave it a tumbling flight, which might last as long as ten seconds, while the fuse sputtered smoke and fire. The irregular burning of the fuses often caused them to sputter for a minute or two after they hit. Sometimes the fuse would burn too fast, and then the shell would explode in mid-air.

About this time one mortar shell landed right in the middle of a breakfast feast the benevolent Baron von Steuben was giving his junior officers. There was only one thing to do, and everyone did it, fast. They dived head first into the swampy soil, and lay there until the shell exploded with a tremendous roar which covered the feasters with mud and dirt from head to foot, but did not injure one of them. As they staggered to their feet, the whole party burst out laughing at the muck on faces and epaulets and waistcoats. The Baron served rum all around, and they sat down like old soldiers to have another go at the breakfast.

Day and night during the seventh and eighth of October the fatigue parties worked on constructing gun platforms. Their digging was interspersed constantly with the sentry's cry: "A shell!" Whereupon everyone would drop flat in the trenches, and wait until the explosion sent fragments zinging through the air. So far not one American or French cannon had fired a single shot in answer to the British bombardment. This too was part of the protocol of a siege. Batteries did not open fire until enough of them had been completed to deliver a really destructive barrage. Otherwise, the garrison could concentrate all their guns on one or two batteries and knock them out before they could retaliate.

Gaspard de Gallatin, a young captain in the Royal Deux-Ponts Regiment, noted in his crisp journal the progress made on the batteries:

Condition of the batteries begun the night of the 7th-8th

American

On the right, joining the river, one battery of six cannon and four howitzers. Near the first French redoubt, a battery of five cannon.

French

No. 1. A big battery composed of four 16 pounders, 2 mortars of 12 inches, 4 mortars of 8 inches, 2 howitzers of 8 inches, a

little behind the parallel to the left of the Hampton Road.
No. 2. A battery of four 24 pounders, also behind the parallel
and to the right of the ravine on which its rests.
No. 3. One of three 24 pounders, in the direction of and behind the extremity of the parallel.
No. 4. One of three 24 pounders, to the left of the ravine on
which the parallel rests.

The twelve cannon in battery number one soon earned it
the title of "The Grand French Battery." On the eighth the
French set up still another battery, number five, consisting of
seven mortars, in front of the parallel on the right. On the
morning of the ninth of October, teams of oxen dragged the
big guns forward over the sandy soil, and the artillerymen
wrestled them into position, ignoring the British fire.

Lieutenant William Feltman of the Pennsylvania Line was
in the trenches on the morning of the ninth, and he watched
the British artillery firing from a field piece which they had
advanced in front of the Nelson house. Just after the piece
fired and the usual cloud of smoke billowed around it, one of
the cannoneers darted forward, and ignoring the shouts of his
officers, began legging it for the American lines. He made it
unscathed and was cordially received by Feltman's men.

"He informed us," Feltman says, "that Cornwallis had
given out orders to them not to be afraid of the Americans,
that they had not any heavy pieces of ordnance except a few
pieces of field artillery. He also informed the soldiery and inhabitants that the French fleet was inferior to him and were
afraid to attack him; that they came to this place to procure
a quantity of tobacco, and if they could not be supplied here
that the fleet would set sail in eight or ten days at the furthest,
and leave the continent. Such are my Lord's addresses to his
soldiery, but they have more sense than to believe his weak
expressions."

On the seventh of October, Lieutenant Feltman won his
beaver hat from Captain Davis. Cornwallis was still far from

being a prisoner. The ebullient lieutenant then bet the captain a pair of silk stockings that His Lordship would not be in American hands "by this day, two weeks." He might not have made the bet if the allied artillery had gone into action that day. Until the heavy guns went to work, there must have been strong feelings of frustration among the working soldiers; day and night they had been digging and ducking, and the British fortifications still stood there, bristling with cannon and those long, menacing spears of pine variously called "fraising" or abatis, designed to impale anyone rash enough to charge them.

But at three P.M. on the ninth of October, this frustration ended. Washington gave the French battery on the far left permission to open fire. Some of the Americans felt a little chagrined at losing this honor, but the French had completed their battery first, and deserved the privilege of opening. The first shots boomed down on the British ships in the harbor, notably the frigate *Guadaloupe*, which had been lying offshore and had given the French considerable annoyance from her cannon. A few rounds forced her to slip her cables and drift with the current into midstream, until she worked her way out of range on the Gloucester side of the river.

For the Americans, however, the big excitement was the firing of battery number one with its ten cannon—three 24 pounders, three 18 pounders, two eight inch howitzers and two ten-and-a-half inch mortars fixed upon carriages invented by Henry Knox, which enabled them to fire their shells on a horizontal line into the enemy's walls, where, it was hoped, the explosive shells would increase the rate of destruction. At five o'clock the American standards were run up above the battery, and according to Colonel Richard Butler and Dr. James Thacher, General Washington himself put the match to the touchhole and sent the first twenty-four-pound ball whistling through Yorktown. Colonel Philip Van Cortlandt of the Second New York Regiment later recalled how he "could distinctly hear the ball strike from house to house."

That opening shot was only the beginning. Both French and Americans began pouring mortar shells and round shot into the town, the Americans aiming at the majestic Nelson house, which was Cornwallis' headquarters, as well as other houses which were thought to contain British officers. Then they switched to firing *en ricochet*—a technique which sent the balls skipping across the ground and up against the British gun embrasures. The enemy cannon were, in the ritual of the siege, the first target of the allied guns. The idea was to knock them out as totally as possible or at least reduce their fire to the point where they would be unable to interrupt the further progress of the siege. Washington noted in his diary that the French and the American batteries fired "both with good effect as they compelled the Enemy to withdraw from their ambruzures [sic] the pieces which had previously kept up a constant firing."

Washington ordered the batteries to pound away all night to prevent the British from repairing their damaged batteries. Lieutenant Ebenezer Denny was in the trenches, and he thought the scene viewed from the allied side was now grand. "A number of shells from the works of both parties passing high in the air and descending in a curve each with a long train of fire, exhibited a brilliant spectacle." These were mortar shells, their fuses sputtering like fireworks in the darkness. The round shot was continued too, ball after ball tearing into the soft sandy earth of the British parapets or humming through the town.

On the morning of the tenth, the French Grand Battery went into action, along with a battery of four 16 pounders, and the Americans opened another battery of four more 18 pounders, and a third of two mortars. This brought the number of cannon in action to at least forty-six. Since the average gun could fire about 100 rounds a day, this meant there were approximately forty-six hundred shells and round shot pouring into the few thousand square yards of Virginia territory still under the control of the soldiers of George III. "The whole of the batteries kept up an incessant fire," Washington noted in his diary, "the Cannon at the Ambruzures of the enemy with a view to destroy them, the shells into the Enemy's works, where by the information of deserters they did much execution." The Nelson house was soon a battered ruin, its windows knocked out, gaping holes torn in its roof, its noble chimneys heaps of scattered brick.

About noon a flag of truce appeared on the American ramparts, and the guns on both sides fell silent. A messenger disappeared into the British works. After about a half hour, out of the town gates hobbled an old man, whom many in the trenches recognized instantly. It was Thomas Nelson, known to most Virginians as "Secretary Nelson." Although the old man was neutral, his two sons were ardent patriots and were serving in the American trenches with the Virginia militia. Appalled at the destruction the allied artillery was wreaking on their father's house, they had persuaded Washington to send the messenger into town, asking Cornwallis to let the old man go unmolested. General Chastellux tells how he happened to be near one of the sons while the armies waited for Cornwallis' answer. "After the flag was sent to demand his father, he kept his eyes fixed upon the gate of the town, by which it was to come out, and seemed to expect his own sentence in the answer."

"Lord Cornwallis had too much humanity to refuse a request so just," Chastellux tells us, and quickly granted Nelson permission to depart. The Earl even looked the other way while a Negro servant wrapped the family silver in a blanket and smuggled it along.

The Secretary was suffering from a severe attack of gout, and had to be carried most of the way to Washington's tent, where he was seated on a chair. American officers crowded around him, anxious to get the first real information on what the British were thinking and saying inside Yorktown. Nelson reported that Majors Cochrane and Gordon had arrived from New York in a whale boat, bringing the good news that Admiral Digby now had thirty sail of the line and was resolved to relieve the garrison by an attack on the French fleet, and that reinforcements commanded by Sir Henry Clinton were also to be embarked.

The Secretary also reported that the American bombardment had already been ferociously effective. There was little shelter inside Yorktown, and Cornwallis and his chief officers were "burrowed in the ground" in a grotto at the foot of the Secretary's garden, others were living in caves hollowed out of the riverbank. On the Gloucester side, he had heard that Tarleton and Simcoe had been forced to kill over 1,000 horses for lack of fodder, and that both men were ill and inactive. The Secretary himself had had a narrow escape; a Negro servant was killed by a cannon ball while standing beside him in his living room.

The moment the Secretary was safe in the American lines, down came the flag of truce, and the guns began booming again. No doubt it was around this time that Governor Thomas Nelson endeared himself to Lafayette, who was in one of the American batteries watching the men fire. Lafayette had, in his enthusiasm, suspected the Governor of lack of zeal during the campaign before Washington arrived. Now Nelson noted that the Secretary's house was effectively ruined as a British command post but there were a number of other houses which British officers were undoubtedly using. "Fire on that one over there," he said, pointing to a fine red brick dwelling several hundred yards behind the Secretary's house.

"Whose house is that?" Lafayette asked.

"Mine," the Governor said.

Later in the afternoon, there was some excitement on the French side of the lines. Six flatboats loaded with British troops suddenly appeared in the river, heading upstream toward the Gloucester side. It was apparently an attempt to out-flank Choisy and Lauzun on that side of the river, or at least to feel out how strong would be the opposition to a move up the river by daylight. The opposition proved to be very strong. Choisy opened a vigorous cannonade from his side of the river, and the big French battery commanded by the Touraine Regiment sent dozens of shells and shot cascading around the boats.

Panic struck the soldiers of one boat, and they rowed madly for the nearest shore, leaped out, and ran helter-skelter down the beach to the British lines on the Gloucester side, leaving their boat behind them. The other five boats, soaked by near misses and shaken by spouting explosions of mortar shells, rowed hastily back to York.

This movement by water inspired the French gunners in the battery by the river to open a furious bombardment on the British ships off Yorktown. They sank two small vessels. That night the French gunners returned to the attack on the ships, this time with hot-shot—balls heated to an almost molten state, then fired from the cannon while still glowing. About nine o'clock, several of these struck the frigate *Charon* and two other ships, and they instantly began to burn. For well over an hour the three ships made a unique spectacle. The *Charon* blazed from the water's edge to her trucks. John Laurens watching from the American lines, noted in his diary that "it was allowable to enjoy this magnificent nocturnal scene, as the vessels had previously been abandoned by their crews."

During the night of the eleventh, the French opened three more batteries, each consisting of three 24 pounders. In the morning they joined in what Colonel David Cobb of Washington's staff called "most noble music," pounding away at the British gun positions. Meanwhile, the British towed most of their remaining ships out of cannon range, to the Gloucester side of the river.

The maneuvers on the water, and the concern Cornwallis showed for his vessels awoke once more Washington's anxiety about an enemy escape upriver. During the day he was delighted to find waiting for him at his headquarters tent two naval officers, the Chevalier de Grandchain and Captain d'Avilier, sent by Admiral de Grasse to reconnoiter the state of the river and give their opinion of the advisability of stationing ships above the town.

Washington noted with satisfaction that after they made their reconnaisance, they "seemed favourably disposed to adopt the measure which had been strongly urged of bringing ships above the Town and made representations accordingly to Count De Grasse." The same day he found time to write De Grasse another letter, urging him to send the ships, and promising him pilots and anything else he might need. As for the fire ships, "the batteries of our first parallel incommode the transports so much that I do not think the preparation of fire ships could be carried on, besides they appear by corroborating reports to be deficient in means for construction engines of this kind, and at all events I am persuaded that the frigates may take such a position as will effectually secure them from danger."

In answer to this De Grasse admitted that he had nothing to fear from British cannon while passing York. But he still worried about the fire ships, "the construction of which appears easier to me than to your Excellency, since there wants but some fascines to make a perfect fire ship." But he agreed to send the men of war, if Washington agreed to furnish him with a number of rowing boats to protect against the fire ships. Washington could only take a deep breath, and struggle to control his substantial temper. Of course he would be willing to supply rowing boats. But it would take two days to get the answer to De Grasse, and two more days to get his answer back and God knows how many more days to get the ships up the river. In the meantime, Charles Cornwallis had an ideal opportunity to dash for safety any dark night he chose.

While the allied artillery had been flinging its destructive missiles into the British camp, the French and American fatigue troops had been digging steadily, day and night, all along the line. First they would zig, then they would zag, then they would zig again, each twist carrying them a few more feet outside the main trench, closer to the British lines. On the eleventh, they were at some points within 360 yards of the enemy parapets. This was the point of no return. To go any further would be to invite a sortie which could slaughter them before support could reach them from the allied lines. It was time to open the second parallel.

This was always the crucial moment in a siege. Usually the enemy sortied to prevent the parallel's completion. Once it was finished, the big guns would be moved into it, and they would open fire at 300 yards—point blank range for a skilled cannoneer. They would be able to pound the British positions into rubble. The Americans were keenly aware of this. Adjutant General Edward Hand wrote a friend: "As soon as our batteries on the second parallel are completed, I think they will begin to squeak."

Everyone expected a British sortie at any moment. At about four o'clock, Baron de Viomenil, the crusty French general who was Rochambeau's second in command, took charge of the line just to the left of the American sector. Baron von Steuben's division was in the trenches, and Steuben, like Lafayette, was still determined to prove to the French that the Americans were every inch the soldiers that the French professionals considered themselves. It was well known that Viomenil tended to look down, just a little, on the military pretensions of these rebellious colonials.

Steuben was busy directing the preparations for opening the second parallel, which was to be undertaken by his men as soon as darkness fell. Fascines and gabions were stacked in the trenches so thickly the men could barely move. The Baron was barking orders in his heavy Prussian accent when an aide arrived from Viomenil. The Frenchman wished Baron von Steuben to know that he suspected the British would sortie sometime that night. He wanted to assure the Baron that if they came against the American line, the French would gladly send 500 to 800 of their men to strengthen Steuben's far left, which seemed to Viomenil numerically weak on an uninvited inspection tour he had just made.

The implication was obvious, and Steuben rose superbly to the occasion. He sent his compliments to Baron de Viomenil, and his thanks for the offer. But he did not think he would be attacked. If he was mistaken, he had no doubt of his ability to hold his line without reinforcement, until support arrived. At the same time, he wished Baron de Viomenil to know that if the sortie should be against the *French* sector, the Baron could rely on the prompt assistance of 800 fighting Americans, in two columns.

As the startled French aide digested this message, Anthony Wayne, who had been listening to the whole exchange, reminded Steuben that they only had 1,000 men in the whole division.

"That is my calculation too," said the Baron, with a twinkle in his eyes. "But if it should happen, I should, on my own responsibility, leave 200 men to defend the battery and with the remaining 800 attack forthwith in two columns." Viomenil's aide, listened, goggle-eyed at such military daring, thanked Steuben once more, and departed. When the Frenchman was safely out of earshot, Steuben admitted to Wayne and the other American officers around him that he had been stretching the truth a little, "for the honor of our country." Wayne shook the Baron's hand and turned to the others, saying: "Gentlemen, now it is our duty to make good the exaggeration of Baron Steuben, and support him just as if he had double the number of troops he has."

The eleventh of October ended with almost all the British guns silent. The few that fired were listless and ineffectual. Count William de Deux-Ponts noted in his diary, "all our guns have been well aimed; several parapets can already be seen damaged. . . . He fires not scarcely six guns an hour, while heretofore he has kept up a rather steady fire, and well directed."

As soon as darkness fell, the workers and their covering parties from both armies crept forward, in total silence, and once more the French engineers laid out the line of the trench. Lieutenant Feltman, who had eighty-two men in his command, told how every second man of the detachment carried a fascine and every man a shovel, spade or grubbing hoe. "Within an hour," Feltman says, "we had ourselves completely covered, so we disregarded their cannonading." For most of the night, the British seemed to have had no idea that the Americans were there, but in the French sector, they heard some noise, or had some information, for they opened up a terrific bombardment on the Gâtinais and Royal Deux-Ponts. The French artillery returned the compliment, and the night was filled with thunder and the fiery tails of mortar shells. Many of the French shots went over the American section of the line, and in the darkness some fell short. "We were in the center of two fires, from the enemy and our own," Feltman noted wryly, "but the latter was very dangerous. We had two men killed and one badly wounded from the French batteries, and a number of shells bursted in the air above our heads, which was very dangerous to us."

The French, William de Deux-Ponts noted in his diary, were disturbed several times during the night by volleys of musket fire, which caused everyone to rush to their guns. But each time it was only a skirmish between patrols, and "it is to this all the outside attempts of the enemy are confined." The second parallel approached, at some points, within 200 yards of the British gun emplacements. But it did not completely hem in the British left down to the river bank, as the first parallel had done. The allies were prevented from doing this by the position of British redoubts nine and ten, which were advanced about 200 yards in front of the main British line, directly in the path of the second parallel. According to Baron von Closen, the diggers stopped 768 feet from these redoubts. The engineers there had the fatigue parties throw up an *épaulement,* or shoulder, a large breastwork which could hold a considerable number of men.

In the morning of the twelfth, when the British saw the allies had advanced a giant step nearer Yorktown, their guns awoke from their brief slumber. Shots and shells rained on the American and French lines all morning, and casualties were unusually heavy. The mortar shells, particularly, could now be dropped with almost pinpoint accuracy over the protective earthworks, and since they were fired from positions in the British rear, it was difficult for the allied artillery to knock them out. The French lost seven men killed, twelve wounded, during the day. A shell dropped in the middle of a Virginia militia company and killed and wounded a large but unreported number.

Not even the generals were immune. Baron von Steuben and Anthony Wayne were in the second parallel trench toward the end of the day when a shell came crashing to earth only a few feet away from them. Without a moment's hesitation Steuben dived for the bottom of the trench, and Wayne did likewise, landing on top of Steuben. After a few moments of fizzling, the shell exploded with its usual crash, and the Baron looked over his shoulder at Wayne. "I always knew you were brave, General," he said, "but I did not know you were perfect in every point of duty; you cover your General's retreat in the best manner possible."

The siege was full of similar narrow escapes and strange fatalities. Sergeant Martin tells of sitting on the side of the trench one morning when some New York troops were marching in to relieve. One of their sergeants stepped up to the breastwork to look around. At that moment the British threw a small mortar shell which landed outside the works. The sergeant paused, and turned to look at it. An instant later, a cannon shot whizzed past his head, terribly close, but without touching him. The poor fellow toppled back into the trench, dead. "I put my hand on his forehead," Martin says, "and found his skull was shattered all in pieces and the blood flowing from his nose and mouth, but not a particle of skin was broken."

A man never knew when a mortar shell would come tumbling down on top of him. Captain James Duncan heard a sentry call "a shell" one midnight and an instant later found it sputtering in the middle of the trench, less than two feet away. Everyone dove for cover, and "though the explosion was very sudden and the trench as full of men as it could contain," not a single man was killed, and only two were slightly wounded.

But aside from the sudden increase in their artillery fire, the British did nothing to stop the allied construction of the fatal second parallel. It was hard to believe. Wayne was among those who admired Cornwallis as a general, and he was convinced that the Earl would never surrender without at least one bloody sortie. Aide Jonathan Trumbull, Jr., with the optimism of the young, wrote in his diary: "If no more effectual opposition is experienced, the town must soon be too hot for his Lordship and his troops." But Washington, pondering the scene on the twelfth, refused to take such a cheerful view: "Lord Cornwallis' conduct," he wrote in his diary, "has hitherto been passive beyond conception; he either has not the means of defence, or he intends to reserve his strength until we approach very near him." Which was the right answer? Washington, always the realist, had to admit that he simply did not know.

At five o'clock on October 9, the officers of the Seventy-sixth Regiment were sitting down to dinner with Commissary General Perkins of the British army. They were undoubtedly looking forward to the meal. The commissary general, even during a siege, usually manages to eat better than most men in the army. But this was a feast which never reached the table. Before a dish could be touched, the American artillery fired its opening barrage. One can easily visualize the scene. The commissary at the head of the generously laden table, perhaps reaching for his wine, his hand freezing as it touches the glass, the startled looks on the faces of the other officers, as the crash of heavy guns shakes the floor beneath them.

Why no one inside Yorktown was not better prepared for this event is something of a mystery. Perhaps everyone, including Cornwallis, really did believe the allies had nothing but light field artillery to fire at the British defenses. Still, the evidence of their own eyes must have contradicted this assumption. The Americans dragged their heavy cannon into position only 600 yards from the British lines, and references made to it later in the siege accurately described its weight and numbers. Perhaps it was the traditional *sang-froid* of the professional soldier which inspired them to ignore the coming holocaust.

Whatever it was, it was a fatal mistake for the members of that dinner party. One of the first twenty-four pound balls tore through their wooden house and screamed down the table, striking the commissary general in the body and killing him instantly. On entering, it struck and severely wounded the old Highland officer who wanted to meet General Washington so badly, and slightly wounded two other officers. Seldom has the gruesome underground of war so brutally intruded on the civilities by which men try to make it bearable. The mind recoils from the blood-drenched image of that wrecked dining room, with its dead and wounded men lying among the shattered crockery.

The English enlisted men seemed equally unprepared for the bombardment. Until it opened, they were all living placidly in tents, within the narrow compound created by the trenches and redoubts. Ten minutes of fire from the allied guns convinced them they were nothing less than perfect targets, and a frantic rush to the trenches followed. Stephan Popp, the Anspach soldier, betrays his panic by wildly overestimating the weight of the allied mortars: "The heavy fire forced us to throw our tents in the ditches. The enemy threw bombs, one hundred, one hundred and fifty, two hundred pounders. . . . A person could hardly stand the bombardment out of the town."

Johann Doehla agreed with his compatriot on the intensity of the allied bombardment. "One could not avoid the horri-

bly many cannon balls whether inside or outside the city." He
tells how his regiment's sutler was killed instantly by a cannon
ball while working in a small wooden house he was using for
an office. Later on the same day (October 10) a grenadier had
his leg torn off by a bomb. Doehla says some of the cannon
balls flew all the way across the river to the Gloucester side
and damaged ships there.

Yorktown's civilians were even more unprepared and had
less immediate places of refuge than the troops in the trenches.
Corporal Popp tells how "the people fled to the waterside and
hid in hastily contrived shelters on the banks. Still they did
not entirely escape, for many of them were fatally injured
through the ricocheting of the bombs and howitzers, had
arms or legs broken, or were killed. The houses of the resi-
dents were completely shot to pieces."

By now there were very few civilians left in Yorktown. On
the fourth of October, Cornwallis had decided to "turn out
every nonessential mouth," in order to make sure his supplies
held out until Clinton arrived. Many of these were Negroes
who had fled from their masters on the promise of British
freedom. Ruthlessly now their liberators, faced with capture
themselves, went back on their grandiose promises. A shock-
ing proportion of these hapless victims of the siege were ill
with dysentery, smallpox and malaria. Terrified to return to
their masters, they wandered in the woods around the allied
camp, starving to death when they did not die of disease. The
indignant Americans were convinced that the British had
sent them out to propagate smallpox in the allied army. Fortunately, Washington had only the militia to worry about; he
had long since insisted every member of the Continental Line
must be inoculated against smallpox when he enlisted.

The bombardment's fury apparently came as a shock to
Cornwallis too. His decision to retreat to the inner works was
a tacit admission that he placed his reliance for salvation totally on the prospect of relief which Sir Henry Clinton prom-

ised him. On the third of October, he had allowed himself some mild optimism in a letter to Clinton: "From the time the enemy has given us, and the uncommon exertions of the troops, our works are in a better state of defence than we had reason to hope." But he added to this a more realistic post-script: "I can see no means of forming a junction with me but by York River, and I do not think that any diversion would be of use to us. . . ."

Cornwallis had to abandon the Nelson house hastily when the guns opened on it. He moved into an underground dug-out behind the house, more or less as the Secretary described it to the Americans on his escape. Right up until the day the bombardment began, he kept his men working on the town's entrenchments. They dug lines of communication between the different redoubts and the hornwork, and as late as the seventh of October were throwing up "traverses" to bolster the fortifications. Doehla's diary tells us how hard the men worked. In a single day he shoveled on three four-hour shifts in the trenches. "Constantly day and night 2,000 men from our troops must work on entrenchments," he says on Oc-tober 1.

But Washington had shrewdly predicted his opponent's chief embarrassment in a prolonged siege: he was short of ammunition. To impede the progress of a besieging army effectively, the besieged must be able to expend prodigies of shot and shell. On the fourth of October Lieutenant James, in his journal, noted that "we kept up as heavy a fire on them as our want of ammunition would allow." James, who was com-manding a battery on the British right, was in a position to know about such a problem.

Meanwhile the Americans played one of their favorite games on the British—the sort of trick that invariably infuri-ated them, because it did not seem to be the sort of thing "gentlemen" did in a war. On the eighth a deserter gave the Americans precise knowledge of the strength and position of the British pickets outside the trenches, and at midnight they attacked with a strong patrol which drove the pickets inside the works. Then, about an hour later, while the British were still manning the works with every available man, American voices came out of the darkness, asking permission to surrender. Two lieutenants who were commanding in the sector got up on top of the parapet to show them the way in. Instantly, shots rang out, and the two officers toppled back into the trenches dead.

Each night during the siege the British stationed pickets outside their ramparts, in no man's land. The enlisted men hated the assignment. Johann Doehla gives a vivid picture of it during the night of October 5. "I went on duty at a detached picket which was outside our lines. It was dangerous on this picket post; one had either to sit or lie the two hours one stood post, so that he could not be seen against the starry sky from the enemy's outposts, which often stood scarcely 5–600 paces distant from us. When it was quiet one could hear every relieving of watch and patrols; and now French, now English or German calling out: 'Who's there?' 'Friend.' . . . Throughout the night the location of the post is altered in order that the enemy might observe the less. Everything must proceed quietly. One dares call out neither to sentry nor patrol except to give only the agreed signal. Nor does one dare smoke tobacco nor make a fire. The men call it the 'lost post' with all justice."

The firing of the frigate *Charon* and the other ships seems to have struck the British with peculiar poignancy. Seeing their ships ablaze emphasized acutely the trap closing around them. For Lieutenant James, manning his guns on the parapets, the sight of the *Charon* burning was especially painful. "From our being quartered at the guns in front of the army," he says, "that timely assistance could not be given her which was necessary to extinguish the fire . . . the loss of our things in the *Charon* are so very trivial when compared to the more distressing scenes of the garrison, that I shall say no more on this head, but that we saw with infinite concern one of the finest ships in the navy of her rate totally destroyed on this day."

The tenth of October was ominous in a more significant way inside Yorktown. By evening British battery number five, commanded by the first lieutenant of the *Charon,* was totally silenced by the allied counterfire. The lieutenant and his men were obliged to "quit" the battery, James says, "the shot and shell having dismounted his guns and tore up his platform." That night the full fury of the allied artillery poured down on the hapless British from dusk to dawn. Sleep was impossible. There was constant skirmishing outside the works, and according to James the Hessians twice panicked and retreated from the trenches.

Not every unit suffered equally from the hail of allied shot and bombs. The Hessian Regiment de Bose, for instance, was in the second line of defense, considerably behind the trenches. But this made them a prime target for mortar shells which could be dumped into their midst with impunity. Scarcely an hour passed without one of them being killed or wounded. But the most heavily battered unit was the British light infantry, who were manning the "hornwork"—the foremost line of the British defense. Both the French and the American artillery worked them over, and they suffered horribly. Before the siege was over, they were to lose four lieutenants, five sergeants and seventy-five rank and file—the heaviest casualties of Yorktown.

"I now want words," Lieutenant James wrote in his journal for October 11, "to express the dreadful situation of the garrison. . . . The enemy on this evening began their second parallel, having advanced three hundred yards nearer to us; their fire continued then incessant from heavy artillery and mortars, and we opened fresh embrasures to flank the enemy's works, keeping up a constant fire with all the howitzers and small mortars then in the garrison. Upwards of a thousand shells was thrown into the works this night, and every spot became alike dangerous. The noise and thundering of the cannon, the distressing cries of the wounded, and the lamentable sufferings of the inhabitants, whose dwellings were chiefly in flames, added to the restless fatigues of the duty, must inevitably fill every mind with pity and compassion who are possessed of any feelings for their fellow creatures."

Doehla gives an equally vivid description of the eleventh of October, when the bombardment reached new heights of fury on both sides. "Stupendous cannonading," he says. "During these 24 hours, 3,600 shot were counted from the enemy, which they fired at the town, our line and at the ships in the harbour. These ships were miserably ruined and shot to pieces. Also the bombs and cannon balls hit many inhabitants and Negroes of the city, and marines, soldiers and sailors. One saw men lying nearly everywhere who were mortally wounded and whose heads, arms and legs had been shot off. Also one saw wounded continually dragged and carried down by the water. Likewise on watch and on post in the lines, on trench and work details, they were wounded by the terribly heavy fire; and soldiers and sailors were always digging in the sand by the water. I saw with astonishment . . . how cannon balls of 24 and more pounds flew over our whole line and the city into the river, where they often struck through 1 and 2 ships; some even went clear across the river to Gloucester, where they even injured some soldiers on the beach. I saw bombs fall into the water and lie there for 5, 6, 8 and more minutes and then still explode. . . . The fragments and pieces of the bombs flew back again and fell on the houses and buildings where they . . . robbed many a brave soldier of his life or struck off an arm or a leg. I myself had a piece of an exploded bomb in my hands which weighed more than 30 pounds and was over 3 inches thick."

Yet there was still no thought of quitting. "Amidst all this dire destruction," James says, "no murmuring was heard, no wish to give up the town while the most distant hope was in view of being relieved. On the contrary, this very distinguished little army, taking example from their chief, went through the business of the siege with a perfect undaunted resolution and hourly discovered proofs of their attachment to the general, who had so often led them to the field with success."

Cornwallis was famous for the unhesitating way he shared the sufferings of his men. On his march through the South, he had slept in the open with them and eaten the same meager rations. Now he was constantly in the trenches, studying the allied lines or directing the construction of a battery to replace one that had been knocked out. With such a general, it is almost a pleasure to volunteer for the post of danger, and this is what young Lieutenant James did on the morning of the twelfth. The sailors from the transports had been manning the batteries in the hornwork, but that day they quit it as a bad job. The allied fire concentrated on any battery that dared to oppose them, and working the guns was, if the choice had to be made, the most dangerous duty inside Yorktown. Moreover, the hornwork, because of its position, drew fire from both sides of the allied line, which made it doubly harrowing to defend. James volunteered for the job because, as he admits frankly in his journal, he was "desirous of recommending myself to his Lordship."

Only someone used to the point blank artillery duels of naval warfare could have endured what James went through in the next eight hours. By now at least sixty-two allied guns were in action, and there were few British batteries left in condition to oppose them. So when Lieutenant James, his midshipman and thirty-six seamen opened up with their battery of six guns, almost every cannon in the allied lines answered him. "Fifty-two minutes after my arrival in the hornwork, the

enemy silenced the three left guns by closing the embrasures,"
James says, "shortly after which they dismounted a twelve
pounder, knocked off the muzzles of two eighteens, and for
the last hour and a half left me with one eighteen pounder
with a part of its muzzle also shot away."

The carnage among James's men was even more horrifying.
In eight hours, he had nine men killed and twenty-seven
wounded, eight of whom died before they could be moved;
every man that came with him in the morning was a casualty
by nightfall, and an awful casualty at that. "Most of the
wounded," James says tersely, "had lost an arm or a leg, and
some both."

At six o'clock in the evening the first lieutenant of the
Charon arrived to relieve James, and as they greeted each
other a mortar shell burst between them, severely bruising
James in the face and right leg and wounding the midshipman who had been on the firing line with him. "In short,"
James says, "myself and the midshipman, both wounded,
were the only two that returned out of thirty-six, having stood
a close cannonade with the enemy for eight hours, who had
ninety-seven pieces of heavy cannon playing on us all that
time." We can forgive James for exaggerating the allied artillery a little. Undoubtedly it had seemed like ninety-seven
while he and his desperate band of sailors stood there on the
exposed parapet with the cannon balls hissing around them.
"I quitted the works about a quarter after six," he says
proudly, "having received the thanks of Lord Cornwallis, who
was in the redoubt during the greatest part of the time."

By now, Major Cochrane had arrived in his whaleboat,
bearing Sir Henry Clinton's message that the relieving fleet
could not sail until the twelfth of October, if then. Cornwallis
hailed the major's gallantry for his daring voyage and honored him by an immediate appointment to his staff as an aide.
But individual feats of heroism were not enough, and Cornwallis knew it. The impact of the allied cannonade can be

seen in the Earl's answer to Clinton's letter, which he wrote on October 11:

> Cochrane arrived yesterday. I have only to repeat what I said in my letter of the 3rd, that nothing but a direct move to York River, which includes a successful naval action, can save me. On the evening of the 9th the enemy opened their batteries, and have since continued firing without intermission with about forty pieces of cannon, mostly heavy and sixteen mortars from eight to sixteen inches. We have lost about seventy men, and many of our works are seriously damaged. With such works, on disadvantageous ground, against so powerful an attack, we cannot hope to make a very long resistance.
> P.S. Since my letter was written we have lost ninety men.
> Oct. 12, 7 P.M. Last night the enemy made their second parallel within 300 yards. We continue to lose men very fast.

Soon after Cochrane's arrival, Cornwallis received some unsolicited advice from his senior officers. According to Banastre Tarleton, they came to him and told him he should "evacuate the miserable works of York Town where every hour of day and night was an hour of watching and danger to the officer and soldier, where every gun was dismounted as soon as shown. . . . To abandon fortifications that were not tenable and adopt a design which at this juncture had every probability of success was equally honorable and judicious."

"Every line of Clinton's letter," it was pointed out, "described circumstances which might delay his presence and expressed anxiety for the situation of Earl Cornwallis and it concluded by requiring his Lordship's opinion respecting a diversion that he could make to cover the retreat of British forces from York and Gloucester."

Tarleton believed that a retreat under cover of darkness to the Gloucester side, and a breakout from there could attain a headstart "of one hundred miles distance . . . by rapid marches" before the allied army could move in pursuit. Cornwallis listened politely to this suggestion, and then returned a quiet no. If Sir Henry Clinton wanted him to evacuate the post, he should have given him an order. As things now stood, admitting all the circumstances Sir Henry had mentioned which might delay him, the commander in chief was still coming south to relieve Cornwallis, and until that plan was explicitly abandoned, Charles Cornwallis did not feel free to move.

Back in New York, Sir Henry Clinton still waited wearily for the fleet, and meanwhile continued to hold endless councils of war. Clinton and his generals were extremely agitated by a letter they received from Admiral Graves on the sixth of October, in which he suggested that Sir Henry and his men would be better situated if they followed the fleet in transports, protected by frigates, while the fighting ships sailed ahead to engage the enemy fleet. This would, of course, have eliminated Graves's obligation to force a landing in the Chesapeake, and permitted him to fight the same kind of tentative battle he had fought on September 5.

Sir Henry wrote back in warm terms, reminding him of the resolutions of the first council of war, in which everyone agreed that an attempt must be made to force a junction with Lord Cornwallis, no matter what the risk. Graves had indeed approved this idea, but there is more than a little evidence that he was playing the politician when he gave his assent.

On October 7, Admiral Graves called a naval council of war on board his flagship, the *London*. Admirals Digby, Hood and Drake and Captains Reynolds and Cornwallis were invited, and scarcely had they seated themselves in Graves's stateroom when the admiral announced that he wished to propose a question: "Whether it was practicable to relieve Lord Cornwallis in the Chesapeake?" Since they had agreed on September 24 that it was practicable, this reversal must have shocked his listeners. We have Sir Samuel Hood's word that it certainly had this effect on him. In a "private" letter to a friend at the Admiralty, he says: "This astonished me exceedingly, as it seemed plainly to indicate a design of having difficulties started against attempting what the generals and admirals had most unanimously agreed to, and given under their hands on the 24th of last month."

It would seem that Graves was trying to build up a counterbalance of naval opinion, with which he could defend himself, if the mouth of the Chesapeake looked particularly ominous when they came near it. Perhaps he was even considering a total refusal to make the effort. This would seem to be unlikely, since Sir Henry had his assent in writing, and would be able to (literally) hang him with it. But from his twisting and turning, it would seem obvious that Admiral Graves would have gladly traded a peerage for permission to drop the idea of charging into the bay under the guns of De Grasse's fleet.

If he was hoping for support from his fellow sailors, he did not get it. This was largely because of Sir Samuel Hood, who exploded the instant Graves presented his question. "It occasioned my replying," Hood wrote, "that it appeared to me a very unnecessary and improper question as it had already been maturely discussed and determined upon to be attempted with all the expedition possible; that my opinion had been very strong and pointed (which I was ready to give in writing with my name to it) that an attempt under every risk should be made to force a junction with the troops the Commander in Chief embarks in his Majesty's fleet with the army under General Earl Cornwallis at York." This opinion, which Hood undoubtedly delivered with all the savagery he could muster, silenced anyone else present who might have been inclined to side with Graves.

Hood then poured a little salt into the wound by also recommending that the moment the troops were landed, "admitting that junction to be made without much loss and provisions landed, I was also of the opinion that the first favourable opportunity should be embraced for attacking the French fleet." This was something Graves was even less inclined to do, with the French outnumbering him by eleven ships. But Hood was speaking in the great tradition of the British navy, and again, no one, including Graves, dared to contradict him. Hood says that he made this recommendation, "though I own to you that I think very meanly of the ability of our present commanding officer."

"It would," he says, "in my humble opinion, have been a most fortunate event if Mr. Graves had gone off to Jamaica upon Mr. Digby's arrival as commander in chief. . . . I know he [Graves] is a *cunning* man, he may be a good theoretical man, but he is certainly a bad practical one, and most clearly proved himself on the 5th of last month to be unequal to the conducting of a great squadron."

Hood's opinion of his brother officers was rarely complimentary, but in his estimate of Graves, his selection of "cunning" would seem to hit rather closely to the mark. The twelfth—the latest of the admiral's announced deadlines, began to appear as ephemeral as the fifth. The seemingly endless repairs to the six or seven damaged ships went methodically onward. On the seventh of October, the same day that Graves called his abortive conference with Hood and the other officers, a British frigate brought in a most valuable prize—an American ship of twenty guns, loaded with masts, yards and other supplies for the French fleet in the Chesapeake. This was conclusive evidence that the French had not escaped unscathed from the battle on September 5—and were in no position to repair their ships while on guard duty at the mouth of the Chesapeake.

A more impetuous admiral might have decided that he would therefore leave some of his damaged ships behind, betting that the French damage would equal his own; but

Graves was hypnotized by the numbers of the enemy fleet, and was convinced he dare not sail without every available ship in perfect fighting shape.

Meanwhile the city abounded with rumors about York-town. The British avidly read American papers smuggled from Philadelphia, which gave as little accurate information as the most imaginative rumor passer in New York. One paper told how Cornwallis had been forced to abandon Glouces-ter. Another report announced that the allies under the command of Lafayette had attacked on September 25, and had been repulsed with a loss of 600 men. Captain Frederick Mac-Kenzie pooh-poohed this possibility. But he noted another with more seriousness: a rumor that two French ships of the line had gone up the York River and had been seriously damaged by British artillery in the passage. The sending of two ships up the river would have pleased General Washing-ton if it were true; but the rumor only showed how desperately the British tried to wish away the superior numbers of De Grasse's fleet.

On the ninth, the day the allied guns opened on Cornwallis, there arrived in New York what superstitious observers might have declared a bad omen: a number of British and German officers captured at Saratoga with Burgoyne and now finally exchanged. About 200 exchanged enlisted men came with them. They had been held prisoners in Connecticut. Only about 400 soldiers of that army were still in American hands. The 5,000 man American army bagged at Charleston in 1780 had given the British ample manpower for exchanges.

The same day came a small reminder that the Americans were still active around New York. A band of Connecticut partisans slipped across the Sound and surprised a loyalist post at Smithtown, Long Island, killing four men and taking twenty prisoners.

On the tenth, MacKenzie noted with satisfaction that "almost every article of the provisions and ammunition to be car-

ried by the ships of war is now on board them, and it is determined that on the 12th the troops are to embark on board
the transports formerly allotted them and are to go from them
on board the Men of War, as soon as the latter get down to
Sandy Hook." Then, more dolefully, he reported that "the
Invincible still wants her fore Mast in, and the *Intrepid* her
Mizen Mast."

On the twelfth, Prince William Henry went down to Staten
Island to see the troops embark. The army managed to put on
a good show for the royal visitor. They marched by him,
MacKenzie said, "in subdivisions two deep in open order, and
Slow time. The officers and Colors saluted, and the Drummers
beat a March. . . . His Highness was much pleased with the
appearance of so fine a body of men, and asked a great many
questions respecting the different corps and companies, and
the officers commanding each. After the whole had passed, he
went to the beach and was very particular in observing the
manner of embarking the men, and placing them in the
boats, and seemed highly pleased with the troops (particularly the British Grenadiers) who were in high spirits." The
Prince was accompanied by his mentor, Admiral Digby, and
several officers of the navy, who may well have had their own
thoughts on the embarkation.

What these thoughts were can be glimpsed from an entry in
William Smith's diary for October 13. It begins, "General
Robertson is in a rage . . ." and goes on to tell how Robertson was denouncing Graves all over New York for attempting
to persuade his officers to resolve against entering the Chesapeake. "Sir Samuel Hood is now in town," the diary continues,
"disheartened by Graves's delay. . . . Last night Commodore
Affleck talked against the expedition like a midshipman.
. . . General Robertson calls Graves dastardly."

By this time another whaleboat from Yorktown had arrived, with Cornwallis' letter of the third of October. This
was still in a cheerful tone. Not a shot had been fired at him.

The first parallel had not yet been opened. The hopes of one and all in New York immediately soared. A new rumor, that the allies had attacked one of the advanced redoubts and had been beaten back with a loss of 180 killed, began to circulate.

Inside army headquarters, the generals were discussing suppositions that were almost as insubstantial as the rumors. On October 8, at a council of war, Generals Knyphausen, Leslie, Robertson and Parsons studied a map while Sir Henry Clinton submitted to their judgment what they might and might not do once they "entered the Chesapeake." A junction with Lord Cornwallis was considered the "first object." But if that were not possible, what then? Sir Henry thought they could enter the James River, where there were three possible landing sites—Newport News, Mulberry Island and James City Island. He preferred Newport News, because it was farthest from the main body of the allied army, and thus less vulnerable to armed interference.

Why Sir Henry thought he could get into the James River if at the same time he was unable to get into the York River no one bothered to ask. Instead they went on to discuss possible routes of retreat, should there be a "misfortune" in attacking the enemy army. They decided to fall back on Portsmouth, where they would await wagons, saddles and other supplies, which would be promptly shipped from New York by General Robertson. Thus equipped to invade the country, they would sally forth again. All these ideas were "unanimously approved" by the listening generals, and General Robertson was advised to have everything ready to be embarked and sent to the army in the Chesapeake "when required."

There is an air of unreality to it all, even now, reading these discussions in the matter-of-fact prose of the aide who wrote the minutes. The generals would seem to have sensed it, for all through October, no one disagreed with Sir Henry's ideas. They were all unanimously approved, much in the way friends agree with and humor the wishes of a dying man. On October 10, when the full fury of the allied artillery began pounding Cornwallis, another council of war went over the whole question of where to land again, and the generals agreed once more to do what Sir Henry suggested.

> Upon a question put by the Commander in Chief where will it be best to land the troops in case it should be found absolutely impracticable to effect the junction by York River . . . and in consequence determined to go up the James River—and we should not hear from Lord Cornwallis? RESOLVED —at Newport News.

They then resolved to send three alternate plans to Cornwallis. First was the landing at Newport News. The troops were then to advance along the James River road "to some favorable position in communication with that River, where they will wait until information arrives from Lord Cornwallis or circumstances may make it proper for them to cooperate with his Lordship in effecting a junction of the two armies; which it is at present the opinion of the general officers will be best done without his lines in preference to an attempt of doing it within."

The second plan was a junction with Cornwallis by a combined move, Clinton's army moving up the James River to Jamestown, and his Lordship's up the York River to either Queen's Creek or Cappahosick Ferry, and the two meeting each other as near Williamsburg as they can, "thereby putting themselves in a Situation to attack the Enemy, should it be thought advisable."

The third plan was to "save as great a part of Lord Cornwallis' corps as possible" by bringing them off in boats at Jamestown. This was to be managed by making a feint at attacking the allied army from Newport News or Mulberry Island, and while the allies wheeled to meet it, Cornwallis was to embark every man he could move in boats, go up the York River to Queen's Creek or Cappahosick Ferry, and then march across the top of the peninsula to Jamestown.

The generals directed that these three plans be sent to Cornwallis immediately. Then Sir Henry added a supremely ironic postscript: "His Lordship to be at the same time acquainted that the above is the opinion of the General officers in case they do not hear from his Lordship. But if they should receive other ideas from him, they will of course be governed by them."

On the fourteenth of October, little more than four hundred yards separated the allies from confronting Cornwallis with their completed second parallel. But those four hundred yards ran across the left wing of Cornwallis' front, and squarely in the middle of them were the two advanced British redoubts, numbers nine and ten. On the British right, the Fusileers still held out in their star redoubt. Capturing this fiercely held fortress did not especially interest Washington and Rochambeau, because it offered no tactical advantage. But from redoubts nine and ten, allied artillery could sweep the whole British camp.

For several days, it had been obvious to everyone in the French and American army that these redoubts would have to be taken by storm. The impatient Baron de Viomenil had been urging Rochambeau to let him attack them even before the parallel was dug. Rochambeau had disagreed, but now he gave orders to cease firing, and taking only his son with him, he climbed out of the trench and went slowly down a gulley to the nearest redoubt's outer works. His aides watched this performance with great anxiety, but the English did not fire a shot at them.

Back came the portly French general, shaking his head solemnly. "The outer works and the palisades are still intact," he said. "We shall have to double our fire to break them and knock down the parapet. We shall see tomorrow if the pear is ripe."

Both the American and French artillery spent the rest of the day pounding the two redoubts, while on the left, Saint-Simon's battery maintained almost as fierce a fire on the Fusileer redoubt. This was the first stage of the allied strategy. By giving both ends of the British line equal punishment, they kept Cornwallis guessing.

The artillery did the job well, pounding the abatis of both redoubts until many of the deadly shafts were shattered and drooping. By two P.M. the engineers reported to Washington that they considered the British positions so heavily damaged that a successful assault could be made. Washington immediately ordered Lafayette to prepare 400 of the light infantry for the task. For the Americans, Washington chose the redoubt number ten, the one just above the river bank. He assigned to the French the redoubt number nine, and gave Rochambeau the freedom to choose whomever he wished from among his own troops.

The rumor of the attack raced through all ranks of both armies and caused some unexpected repercussions. Among the Americans, Alexander Hamilton protested violently when he heard that Lafayette had entrusted the leadership of the assault to the Chevalier de Gimat, his former aide, who had come to America with him in 1778. Hamilton argued eloquently that he was senior colonel to Gimat, and moreover, it was his tour of duty in the lines, and therefore Lafayette could not rightfully supersede him. Lafayette explained, rather lamely, that Washington had already approved the arrangements, and it was now too late to change them.

Hamilton scoffed at this excuse. Ignoring his bitter quarrel with Washington, he sat down and wrote the commander in chief a fervent letter, demanding the assignment for himself. Washington once more proved that he was above revenge; he conferred with Lafayette and discovered that Hamilton was right about the tour of duty and was indeed senior to Gimat in his commission. He ordered Lafayette to give Hamilton the command. Gimat was mollified by placing him in command of the battalion of light infantry which would have the honor of heading the attack.

Someone has remarked that Alexander Hamilton was a great man who never failed to seek first the interests of Alexander Hamilton, and Washington was a greater man because he could put first the interests of other men. This may be true. But this was no parade ground honor for which Hamilton was fighting. It was the privilege of leading a frontal attack on entrenched veterans, who had been hoping and praying for two weeks that such an attack would be ventured. Leading in the eighteenth century was taken literally. It meant the position at the head of the column. Hamilton may have been looking out for Alexander Hamilton when he asked for this assignment, but he thereby proved that Alexander Hamilton was no ordinary man.

Moreover the young West Indian had a good reason for avoiding the post of danger. He had been married less than a year, and his wife Betsy was expecting their first child. How thoroughly in love he was can be glimpsed from a letter he wrote on October 12.

> I wrote you two days since, my Dear Betsy, but as I am informed by one of the Gentlemen at Headquarters that there

is an opportunity for Philadelphia, I embrace it with that pleasure which I always feel in communicating with you. You complain of me, my love, for not writing to you more frequently, but have I not greater reason to complain of you? Since I left Kings Ferry, I have received three letters from you, that is three in seven weeks. You have no occupations to prevent your writing; I am constantly employed. Yet I am sure I have written to you during that period more than twenty letters. Don't imagine that this neglect will go unpunished. I hope to see you in three or four weeks from this time, and you may then expect to be called to severe account. I know you rely upon your power over me. You expect that your usual blandishments will have the usual charm. You think you have only to smile and caress and you will disarm my resentment; but you are mistaken. The crime is of too serious a nature to be forgiven; except with one atonement which I am sure it will not be easy for you to make. This is to love me better than ever. If upon deliberate examination you shall find this impossible, I may compound for one substitute. You shall engage shortly to present me with *a boy*. You will ask me if a girl will not answer the purpose. By no means. I fear, with all the mother's charms she may inherit the caprices of her father, and then she will enslave, tantalize and plague one half the sex, out of pure regard to which I protest against a daughter. So far from extenuating your offence, this would be an aggravation of it.

In an instant my feelings are changed. My heart disposed to gayety is at once melted into tenderness. The idea of a smiling infant in my Betsy's arms calls up all the father in me. In imagination I embrace the mother and embrace the child a thousand times. I can scarce refrain from shedding tears of joy. But I must not indulge these sensations; they are unfit for the boisterous scenes of war and whenever they intrude themselves make me but half a soldier.

Certainly the man who could write this letter was no mere egotist. Hamilton would never have won Washington's friendship and admiration with only restless ambition to recommend him. As a young man, Washington himself had been befriended and supported by older men, and he never forgot it. Throughout the war he had made a practice of choosing exceptionally talented and dedicated young men as his aides. Now in this crisis he was calling upon three of them; Hamilton was the assault commander, Lafayette was the commanding general; and John Laurens was given eighty picked men who were to circle redoubt number ten in the darkness and attack it from the rear.

Before the afternoon was over, another young man visited Washington in his tent. Almost forgotten now, the Marquis de La Rouërie was considered by Parisians of his day far more exciting than the Marquis de Lafayette. In Paris Lafayette had been rather dull; only when he reached America did he begin to glitter. La Rouërie was a sensation from the moment he appeared on the Boulevards—as witty as he was handsome, with flashing eyes, superb manners, and a ready sword. Shortly after he became a lieutenant in the Royal Guards, he fell hopelessly in love with the beautiful Mlle. de Beaumesnil, star of the Paris Opera. Unfortunately, the lady was having a love affair with the young Marquis' uncle and patron, and so refused his offer of marriage. The Marquis promptly forsook the world, and joined a Trappist monastery. His uncle was so impressed that he gave up Mlle. de Beaumesnil and persuaded her to change her mind about his nephew, who promptly vaulted from his monk's cell to Mademoiselle's boudoir.

Rouërie's passion for the beauteous Beaumesnil was the talk of Paris. But his impetuous temper destroyed his bliss. He got into a duel with Comte de Bourbon Busset, the King's cousin, and wounded him so badly he almost died. The King was furious and swore he would have Rouërie hanged. The swordsman fled to Switzerland; then the American Revolution broke out, and he found it irresistible. On his voyage to America, his ship was attacked by an English frigate, and he had to swim ashore with nothing but the clothes on his back. Nevertheless Congress welcomed his offer to raise at his own expense a "legion" of horse and foot. He spent 2,400 pounds of his own money on this project. He even temporarily renounced his title, because nobility did not suit a Republican officer, and was known to Americans by his family name, Armand.

At the battle of Camden, Rouërie had seen Cornwallis and Tarleton wipe out his legion, which he had recruited largely from German mercenaries captured with Burgoyne's army. Undaunted, he borrowed money and raised another legion. He therefore had a score to settle with Cornwallis, and he wanted Washington's permission to go along with the assaulting party. It would not hurt, he argued, to have a few more veteran officers at the head of the column, to steady the troops. Washington agreed.

A half-hour before the main attack, Saint-Simon's men were to stage a feint attack on the Fusileers' redoubt, to draw British attention in the opposite direction. Orders were sent to Baron de Choisy to make a feint attack on the British lines in Gloucester at the same moment. Toward the end of the afternoon Washington rode over to the French side of the siege lines and conferred with Baron de Viomenil. The commander in chief learned, no doubt with a certain pleasure, that there were more than a few Hamiltons in the French camp. The Baron was being besieged by at least a dozen young officers for permission to participate in the attack.

The honor of leading the French assault had been given to Lieutenant Colonel William de Deux-Ponts. In his journal the young Count recalls how he received the command: "On the 14th of October . . . at the assembly of the regiment . . . for duty in the trenches, the Baron de Viomenil ordered me to come to him on our arrival at the beginning of the trenches. I carried out his order. He separated the grenadiers and chasseurs of the two regiments and gave me command of the battalion that he had just formed, telling me that he thought he gave me by that proof of his esteem and confidence."

Deux-Ponts appreciated such esteem and assured the Baron that he was ready to attack immediately. Later that afternoon Viomenil and Baron de L'Estrade, lieutenant colonel of the Regiment of Gâtinais, who was to be Deux-Ponts' second in command, went with the young assault commander to the end of the second parallel. They took with them two sergeants of the grenadiers of the Gâtinais Regiment, "men as brave as they were intelligent," who were told to reconnoiter in minute detail the path they would have to follow in the attack that night. De L'Estrade was an experienced officer, and the eager Deux-Ponts was worldly-wise enough to realize that the older man was coming along to "make up for the blunders which I might commit."

The reconnaissance completed, the general ordered Deux-Ponts to form his battalion and proceed to "that part of the trenches nearest to which we ought to come out." The grenadiers and chasseurs he led were the picked troops from his own regiment, and the Regiment of Gâtinais; they were about 400 in number. Deux-Ponts told them matter-of-factly where they were going and what they were about to do. He saw no need to "excite their courage." They would have been insulted by oratory.

"We then started into the trenches," Deux-Ponts says. "We passed by many troops, either of the trenches, of workmen, or of the auxiliary grenadiers and chasseurs. Everybody wished me success and glory, and expressed regrets at not being able to go with me. That moment seemed very sweet, and was very elevating to the soul and animating to the courage." The young Count stopped to say goodbye to his brother, Count Christian, the regiment's colonel, and the older man "gave me marks of a tenderness which penetrated to the bottom of my heart."

As the grenadiers and chasseurs of the Gâtinais Regiment filed into the trenches, they heard a voice calling to them. *"Auvergne, Auvergne sans tache."* It was General Rochambeau himself, making a personal appeal to this section of his old regiment, which he had led on more than one bloody battlefield. "My children," he said, "I have great need of you tonight. I trust you will not forget that we have served together in the brave Regiment of Auvergne, surnamed *Auvergne sans tache*—the spotless."

Deeply moved, the men cried out to the general that if he would restore their ancient and honored name to them, "they would do everything to deserve it." They apparently detested the name Gâtinais which had been foisted on them when the regiment had been divided into two sections, some years before, and yearned for the royal *Auvergne,* which the bureaucrats had taken away from them. "We will fight like lions until the last man is killed." they swore, as Rochambeau remembered it in his memoirs. The general, deeply moved himself, instantly vowed that if they kept their promise, he would go to the King himself and regain their old name for them.

At the head of the trench, Deux-Ponts was joined by some uninvited volunteers. The Chevalier de Lameth had begged Rochambeau to let him participate in the assault. Rochambeau had sternly refused, but the young firebrand went anyway. With him were Comte Charles de Damas, and Comte de Vauban who had been sent by Rochambeau as an observer but now insisted on joining the ranks of the assaulters. "I tried to turn them back," Deux-Ponts says, "but they would not pay heed to the protest which I made— which would have withdrawn them from the field of glory and of honor." The protest was undoubtedly a feeble one, since Deux-Ponts understood all too well how they felt.

Washington, meanwhile, satisfied with the French dispositions, rode back to his waiting Americans. The 400 men in their ragged shirts and ruined shoes did not look like the equals of the superbly equipped, brightly uniformed French grenadiers and chasseurs he had just left. But he had complete confidence in their fighting ability. More than a few had seen five years of war. They were professionals now, lean, tough and confident. Usually Washington was not the sort of general who gave speeches. But he gave a short one to these men. He urged them to be firm, and brave; the success of the attack on both redoubts depended on them.

The speech is a good indication of the tension Washington felt. Both attacks had to succeed, or both failed. If the British possessed one of the forward redoubts, they could easily pour troops into it, and take back the captured one by assault before the allies could possibly support it. Reinforcements would have to run a terrible gauntlet of fire from the forewarned British gunners on the inner parapets. If the attack was once repulsed and the allied intention was known, the British would cram every possible man into the redoubts, and make a further attack impossible. The siege could be delayed for three or four precious days.

Among Washington's most attentive listeners was young Stephen Olney, a captain of a Rhode Island company in the light infantry battalion. He was slated to be at the head of one attacking column. "I thought then," he said, "that his Excellency's knees rather shook, but I have since doubted whether it was not mine."

As darkness fell, Baron de Viomenil began once more to worry about the ability of the American troops. He was probably the author of the French opinion that the attack should be made entirely by French troops, with the Americans coming behind only to mop up. Washington had firmly declined this suggestion as humiliating to American honor. Now the Baron approached Lafayette and reiterated his doubts about the Americans. Lafayette almost exploded; the one thing he could not bear was French condescension toward his men. But he kept his temper and replied coolly: "We are young soldiers and have only one way in these cases. That is to unload our guns and march right in with our bayonets."

The Marquis then proceeded to give Hamilton and his men the boasted order: every musket was to be emptied. Viomenil was reduced to silence. He went back to his grenadiers and chasseurs. The twilight thickened. The waiting Americans fingered their bayonets, and talked broodingly of the slaughter of the defenseless militiamen at New London. The news had reached the army only a few days before. More than a few of the battle-tough New Englanders swore they were going to get their revenge before the night was over.

About seven-thirty—just when darkness became complete—there was a popping of small arms fire on the extreme left of the allied line, soon punctuated by the crash of cannon. Saint-Simon's men were making their feint on the Fusileers' redoubt. Over in Gloucester, too far away to be heard, there was similar firing, but according to the Duc de Lauzun the attack was no feint. The impetuous Choisy, seconded by the even more impetuous Lauzun, had decided to make a genuine assault on the far less formidable Gloucester defenses, hoping to carry the place by storm. It would have been a remarkable feat and certainly have earned both noblemen enduring military fame. But they relied for one of their assaulting columns on American militiamen, and at the first volley from the defenders, the untrained civilians threw down their guns and ran for their lives. The maneuver was therefore promptly reduced to the feint which had been originally intended.

Exactly at eight o'clock, the guns from the French Grand Battery gave the tensely awaited signal, six mortar shells fired in rapid succession. Sergeant Joseph Plumb Martin was in the front ranks of the American attackers, armed with an axe. As a sapper, it was his job to cut a path through the forbidding abatis to permit the troops to storm the redoubt itself. "The two brilliant planets, Jupiter and Venus, were in close contact in the western hemisphere," Martin says, and he was so tense that more than once he almost sprang to his feet, thinking they were blazing mortar shells signalling the attack. Then the guns fired, and the words *up, up,* were barked through the ranks. "Our watchword was Rochambeau," Martin said, "a good watchword, for being pronounced Ro-Sham-Bow, it sounded, when pronounced quick, like Rush-on-boys."

With Hamilton leading the way, the light infantrymen moved into the darkness. They quickly divided into two columns, Hamilton heading one and the deposed Colonel Gimat leading the other. With Gimat was the Marquis de La Rouërie. Olney found himself only a few steps behind the two Frenchmen. "The column marched in silence, with guns unloaded and in good order," Olney says. "Many no doubt thinking that less than one-quarter of a mile would finish the journey of life with them. On the march I had a chance to whisper to several of my men (whom I doubted) and told them that I had full confidence that they would act the part of brave soldiers, let what would come; and if their guns should be shot away, not to retreat, but take the first man's gun that might be killed."

Halfway to the redoubt, the column was halted, and one man was detached from each company for the "forlorn hope." These were to be the first men over the wall; they were most likely to meet desperate enemy resistance and were expected to clear away any unexpected obstructions for the main body of attackers on their heels. The best and bravest men were usually selected. "My men all seemed ready to go," Olney says proudly. The column moved forward once more, the pioneers in front, the forlorn hope next, then Gimat, Rouërie and six or eight officer volunteers. In a few minutes they reached the outer abatis work of redoubt number ten without being detected. To their momentary dismay, however, they found the abatis had been only slightly damaged by the artillery fire. It still bristled up at them, a forest of menacing spears in the night. In the same instant, a sentry challenged them from the redoubt. He naturally got no answer. A moment later the darkness exploded, as, in Olney's words, "the enemy fired a full volley of musketry."

"At this our men broke silence and huzzaed," Olney says, "and as the order for silence seemed broken by everyone, I huzzaed with all my power, saying how frightened they are, they fire right into the air." This was not entirely true. Several men, including Colonel Gimat, were hit in the first volley. The Frenchman received a painful wound in the foot, and had to be carried out of the battle. The sappers now began hacking away at the abatis. "This seemed tedious work in the dark within three rods of the enemy," Olney decided. Most of the other Americans made the same decision. Screaming like Indians, they surged past bewildered Sergeant Martin and the other sappers, crawled and twisted through and around the pointed stakes, and poured down on the redoubt, howling, "Rush on boys, Rush on boys, the fort's our own!" The British reply was another volley of musketry. But gunfire was by no means the only problem. Inside the first line of abatis were huge holes, torn up by the allied mortar shells, "sufficient to bury an ox in," says Joseph Plumb Martin. Rushing on toward the redoubt, now that his axework was no longer needed, Martin saw men disappearing all around him. "I thought the British were killing us off at a great rate," he says. "At length one of the holes happening to pick me up, I found out the mystery of the huge slaughter."

Now the Americans were in the trench just underneath the British breastwork. Martin recognized an old friend from the light infantry here, "hitching himself down into the trench. I knew him by the light of the enemy's musketry, it was so vivid." Captain Olney was one of the first into the trench. The redoubt was protected by a palisade, a series of stakes driven into the ground and sharpened at the top to make climbing impossible. But Olney found an opening ripped by a cannon ball, stepped through it and sprang up on the parapet, calling out, "Captain Olney's company form here." He instantly found himself dueling for his life with six bayonets. "I parried as well as I could with my espontoon," he says. But the blade of this now forgotten officer's weapon (a sort of spear) broke off, and "their bayonets slipped along the handle of my espontoon and scaled my fingers." One bayonet found Olney's thigh, another pierced his abdomen just above the hip. A third redcoat fired at him point blank, and the captain thought his arm was torn off by a terrific impact. By the light of the musket he made a desperate thrust at his assailant with the remains of his espontoon and caught him in the forehead. At this point the forlorn Olney was joined by two of his men, John Strange and Benjamin Bennet, who had decided that Lafayette's bravado about empty muskets was sheer idiocy, and had stopped to load their guns in the ditch. They sprang up beside Olney and fired at his attackers, who promptly either ran away or surrendered.

Farther down the line, Hamilton had trouble getting up on the parapet, until he ordered two men nearby to give him a boost. Behind him the trench was now crammed with light infantrymen, all but standing on each other's shoulders in their fury to get inside the redoubt. The British flung primitive hand grenades among them, but the crackling and popping of these weapons, designed more to frighten than to wound, were totally ignored. Martin thought they were cartridge papers on fire. The sappers and miners informed their commanding officer, Captain James Gilliland, that they were going inside too, even if they only had axes to defend themselves. Gilliland tried to stop them, but they ignored him. "We will go," they shouted. "Then go to the d——l," he shouted back, and went with them.

Martin tried to fight his way through an entrance he and several other sappers had chopped in the palisades, but it was so crowded it was impossible. He therefore chose another place, where a few of the stakes had been blown away by artillery fire. "While passing, a man at my side received a ball in the head, and fell under my feet, crying out bitterly." No one stopped to help the luckless victim. There was still hot work to be done inside the fort.

Bayonet to bayonet now, the British and Germans fought it out with the Americans in the tumultuous darkness. Men writhed on the ground, clutching their ripped bellies, German oaths and British curses resounded against the growing howl of American triumph. Some of the British had already decided that the game was over. By the light of the musket Olney had had fired in his face, he had seen that one side of the redoubt was bare of defenders. But the Americans who were supposed to be attacking it never arrived. The running British had slammed into them in the darkness, bayoneted a few and sent the rest fleeing, convinced that they had been caught in a counterattack. "I asked one of the others how he did not get into the redoubt," Olney recalled later. "He said the enemy pricked them off with their bayonets." A number of other British leaped over the wall on the river side, slid down the almost perpendicular bank, and legged it into the safety of the town.

Soon Americans were pouring over the walls from every direction. When Major Campbell, the British commander of the redoubt, saw John Laurens and his eighty men swarm in from the rear he realized that further resistance was useless and surrendered to the dashing South Carolinian. Campbell had had only sixty men to oppose his 400 attackers, and he had himself been wounded in the opening shots. The remaining

Hessian and British soldiers flung down their muskets and begged for quarter. It was all over in five minutes.

There were nine Americans dead and twenty-five wounded. This plus the terrific tension of the assault drove one New Hampshire captain slightly mad, and he lunged at the British commander, his bayonet raised, swearing he was going to avenge the slaughter committed by Benedict Arnold's raiders in New London. But Hamilton sprang in front of his captive, and sternly told the New Englander that not a single surrendered soldier was to be touched.

There were more important things to do. The prisoners and wounded had to be moved out and reinforcements moved in against an expected British counterattack. This did not prevent one of Olney's men, a wild Irishman named Charles McAfferty, from finding a British bottle of wine and inviting his captain to have a drink. Olney, who was in severe pain from his wounds, curtly refused. "Who but an Irishman or an Englishman would have thought of such a thing?" he asks.

Lafayette, meanwhile, was waiting in the first parallel trench. The moment he knew that the redoubt was captured, he sent his division inspector, Major William Barber, to Baron de Viomenil to let him know that redoubt number ten was in American hands—and did the French general need any help in carrying number nine? Later Lafayette admitted to "unspeakable satisfaction" at being able to send this message to the haughty Baron. Viomenil's answer was resounding enough: The French were not yet masters of redoubt number nine but they soon would be. As he left the French command post, the gallant Barber was wounded in the side by a cannon ball, but he ignored the wound and carried the message back to Lafayette, no small feat because by now the entire British garrison was alerted, and the air was full of flying shells, shot and musketry.

The French, true to their professional training, had

waited for their sappers to cut away the abatis before storming redoubt number nine. This left them standing in the
open while the defenders, 120 veteran troops of the Hessian
Regiment de Bose, poured volley after volley of musketry
into them. They took it like the veterans they were, although men fell in droves. "Before starting," Comte de Deux-
Ponts said, "I had ordered that no one should fire before
reaching the crest of the parapet of the redoubt; and when established upon the parapet, that no one should jump into the
works before receiving the orders to do so." Deux-Ponts and
his men found the abatis "strong and well preserved" twenty-
five paces from their objective, and it was no small job to get
through it.

But within five minutes they were in the ditch, and the
eight carpenters in their van were hacking breaches in the
palisades, while the more impetuous grenadiers and chasseurs fought their way up as best they could. In this furious
melee, a touch of humor intruded. The veteran Lieutenant Colonel L'Estrade, sent along to make sure young Deux-
Ponts made no mistakes, was one of the first men up the
British parapet. Just as he planted both feet on top, a soldier behind him reached up and not recognizing the colonel
in the darkness, grabbed him by his coat-tails and sent him
flying back down into the ditch. "About two hundred men
passed over his body," Rochambeau's aide, Cromot du Bourg
says, before the unlucky veteran managed to stagger to his
feet and fight his way up the wall again.

The fiery young Chevalier de Lameth was one of the first
up the wall, but he received a full volley from the defenders
and toppled back into the ditch, both knees shattered. After
him came Captain de Sireuil, who crumpled with a shattered
leg, which was to prove fatal. Lieutenant de Sillegue of the
chasseurs turned to help Deux-Ponts to the top, and dropped
with a fatal wound just as the colonel reached his side.
But now Deux-Ponts found the parapet "becoming manned

visibly," and the desperate Hessians fell back to "a kind of entrenchment of barrels" no doubt erected for protection against shell fragments. Firing down from the parapet at this mass of men, "all our shots told," Deux-Ponts says grimly.

The Count was on the point of ordering a bayonet charge when the defenders threw down their guns and asked for quarter. *"Vive le Roi!"* shouted Deux-Ponts, and the men around him took up the cry, and soon it was echoed by all the French troops waiting in the trenches. "The enemy replied by a general discharge of artillery and musketry," Deux-Ponts says. "I never saw a sight more beautiful or more majestic." Apparently the British thought a general storm was about to take place, and fired what was called a "roulade," rolling fire down their whole line, designed to catch attackers as they moved out of their trenches.

But the allies were more than satisfied. They had no intention of making any more attacks that night. On the contrary, they fully expected the British to counterattack in a desperate effort to retake the lost redoubts. The French had suffered 114 casualties—46 dead and 68 wounded—and reinforcements were rushed into the redoubt to bolster the now triumphant attackers. While the British filled the air with metal, Deux-Ponts was working feverishly to get his wounded out of the redoubt and back to the hospital. A nervous sentry, facing the British lines, thought he saw movement in the darkness. He cried an alarm, and Deux-Ponts rushed to the parapet to peer after the fellow's pointing finger. At that moment a cannon ball ricochetted off the parapet, flinging sand and stones in Deux-Ponts' eyes, blinding and stunning him. He had to be led to an ambulance, and for several days there was serious concern for his sight and hearing.

Generals Washington, Knox and Lincoln were in the lines, standing in what was described as an exposed spot. When the nervous British began firing their roulade, Washington's aide, Colonel David Cobb, begged him to retire to a safer position. This time the tense Washington did not take the warning with such good humor. "If you are afraid, Colonel Cobb," he snapped, "you may retire."

A quarter of an hour after the two redoubts were secured, firing broke out again on the far left where the first French feint was made. Monsieur de Custine, colonel of the Soissonnais Regiment, had completely scrambled the timing of the operation and thought that the feint was to be made at eight-thirty. The reason, Baron von Closen learned from a friend in the regiment, was the inebriated condition of the colonel before, during and after the orders were given. The feint was much too boldly conducted, considering the aroused state of the British defenders, and they answered the fire with volleys of grape shot, which left nine Soissonnais grenadiers casualties.

From their captives, the French learned that British Major McPherson, the commanding officer of redoubt nine, had ignominiously retreated with thirty men the moment the firing began, thus ruining all hopes of a successful defense. The allies had expected the British to resist to the last man, and were rather startled to find themselves in possession of seventy-three prisoners, including six officers.

The moment the redoubt was secured, the men of the Pennsylvania Line, who had been waiting in reserve under the command of Colonel Richard Butler, flung aside their guns and seized picks and shovels, and began digging their way down the trench toward the victors, to complete the second parallel. The British poured a devastating fire on the diggers, and on the men in the redoubts, but most of the shells went over their heads. The French in their section of the second parallel were not so lucky; there a British battery found the range with terrible effect, killing twenty-seven men and sending 109 wounded streaming back to the hospital. By the end of the night distraught Commissary Blanchard had a total of 500 sick and wounded on his hands—and not nearly enough medicines or supplies to give them adequate care.

In their official reports all the commanding officers were generous with their commendations. Viomenil, who, because he outranked Lafayette, considered himself the officer in command, said the American infantry had conducted themselves "like grenadiers accustomed to difficult things," and declared the Marquis himself had acted with "as much intrepidity as intelligence." Rochambeau gave the assaulting troops two days extra pay as a reward for their valor, and to the axe-swinging carpenters, who had taken even greater risks, he added two louis each. Moreover, Baron de Viomenil showed he was by no means a total snob by having breakfast the next morning with two French sergeants who had especially distinguished themselves in the attack.

The British artillery fire died out toward morning, and Colonel Richard Butler tells how the allies decided to find out whether the British were holding back or running short of ammunition. Orders were passed up and down the trenches to stage an alarm and see what kind of response they got. Guns were fired, a shout went up, and all the preliminary signs of a general attack were made—but the British response was, according to Butler, "faint."

By dawn the sweating Pennsylvanians had dug their way down to the two redoubts, and the American second parallel was now complete. Early that morning (the fifteenth) Washington visited the trenches, which were now close enough for riflemen to exchange fire. Balls whistled menacingly around them, and as usual, Washington ignored them and his aides worried. The general conferred with his engineers and decided where to build two artillery batteries, which would be connected to the captured redoubts, and before the day was over the artillerymen had managed to drag two howitzers into position inside the former British bastions.

The importance of these two redoubts, once they were armed with allied cannon, would be incalculable. "From them," Washington wrote the President of Congress, "we shall enfilade the enemy's whole line and I am in hopes we shall be able to command the communication from York to Gloucester." They could pour round shot and shell down all the British forward trenches in the hornwork, making it impossible for any man to live in them. It was the prelude to the general assault, the climax of every siege.

The men who had captured the redoubts were relieved by the New York Brigade early the following morning. They swung down the main trench with drums beating and flags flying. The British entertained them with music of their own: a furious bombardment of mortar shells. Baron von Steuben, who was in command, regretfully had to order the flags to be furled and the drums to be silenced. Henceforth this bit of bravado was abandoned. The allies were now too close to the British guns for showy heroics.

Later that day, Hamilton returned to the captured redoubt and became embroiled in an argument with Henry Knox, who was supervising the construction of the new batteries. No doubt considerably emboldened by his feat of the evening before, the young colonel began complaining to General Knox about Washington's order to sound a warning when a shell was fired and take cover until it landed and exploded. Hamilton felt it was demeaning, unsoldierly, even cowardly to have officers and men constantly diving into holes. The military thing to do, he argued, was ignore the enemy's fire, just as a soldier does when he is racing to a frontal assault.

Knox disagreed. He thought the general's order was eminently sensible, and designed to save the lives of the men. Supporting the lame side of the argument, he was getting a bad time from the far more eloquent Hamilton when the cry of a sentry interrupted them: "A shell!" Moments later two fizzling British mortar shells landed smack in the center of the redoubt. That was the end of the argument, as both Hamilton and Knox dived for the protection of some blinds a few feet away. They arrived simultaneously, and Hamilton, seizing the well-padded Knox, spun him around so that the artilleryman's bulk was between the shell-scorner and the still sputtering bomb. With a squawk of rage, the burly Knox sent Hamilton flying off his back and out from behind the blinds toward the still hissing shells. Hamilton scrambled back and a minute later the shells went off, showering the redoubt with fragments, but fortunately wounding no one.

"Now," said Knox, "now what do you think, Mr. Hamilton, about crying shell? But let me tell you not to make a breastwork of me again!"

Above and around these individual figures, the grim business of the siege went on. The allied cannon continued to slam home shot and shell by the thousands. Now there was not a single British cannon able to answer. Only the mortars, sheltered from the direct fire of the allied batteries, kept up their answering fire. The French guns in particular were so well zeroed in that the gunners were able to hit the same embrasure on the British walls six out of seven shots in a row.

More guns had been dragged into position. The Americans now had a "grand battery" consisting of twelve 24's and 18's, plus four mortars and two howitzers. "The whole peninsula," Dr. Thacher noted in his journal, "trembles under the incessant thunder of our infernal machines." At five P.M. on the fifteenth, the mortars which had been dragged into the captured redoubts opened fire, dropping their deadly bombs almost literally down the necks of the British troops in the enfiladed trenches. On the next day they would be joined by a full battery of cannon. Close to 100 guns would be in action then, capable of flinging ten thousand rounds a day into the British positions. The moment was approaching, faster than anyone expected, when the enemy, with all his guns silent and his walls breached by the artillery, would be stormed. Another day, two at the most, would bring the signal, and the waves of French and American infantry would pour out of their trenches for the final furious dash across the two hundred yards that separated them from York, town. Unless, from the empty ocean, there should sail the re-lieving fleet, with a fresh army led by Sir Henry Clinton. Or unless Charles Cornwallis, in what seemed to be his last ex-tremity, had a final card to play.

In New York, it began to look as if Sir Henry Clinton might yet appear with his fresh army. By evening on the twelfth of October the troops were all on board the men-of-war. With any kind of decent weather, they could make the passage from New York to the Chesapeake in four days. But the gods of lightning seemed to be conspiring against Sir Henry even more effectively than Admiral Graves. The thirteenth of October was a fine warm fall day, until about noon, when out of the western sky came a huge black cloud.

With almost no warning, a tremendous storm broke over New York harbor. The wind, which had been a mild southwest breeze, shifted to north, northwest, and for an hour and a half almost blew the town away. Thunder crashed, lightning seared the sky, and rain mixed with hail pelted men and ships. Sailors and soldiers out in small boats, running errands from the men-of-war, vanished as if a giant hand had dragged them into the depths. The wind tore at the sails and rigging of the great ships, and anchor cables groaned and screamed as the wind strained them to the snapping point. Then through the roar of the storm came the dismaying crunch of ship against ship. The *Alcide* had snapped her cable, and smashed into the *Shrewsbury*, carrying away her bowsprit and springing her own foreyard.

The next day, with a fresh west wind, the fleet could have —and should have—sailed for Yorktown. But Admiral Graves would not dream of putting to sea with even one of his ships in slightly damaged condition. Adjutant MacKenzie notes mournfully in his journal for the fourteenth of October: "it is feared that the accident which happened to the *Shrewsbury* yesterday will detain them a day or two longer." MacKenzie also thought that it was idiocy to put the troops on board transports and then transfer them to the men-of-war on the other side of Sandy Hook. "The troops are in perfect readiness to be put on board the Ships of War; and I am of opinion they should be embarked immediately, for as some little time is necessary to fix themselves in the places allotted them on board, and to embark such trifling baggage and stores as the officers are allowed to take with them, it will be done in less time, and with least trouble to all parties, while the ships are in harbour."

But saving time seemed to be the last thing that concerned Admiral Graves. On the fifteenth of October, the entire fleet waited off Staten Island while the *Shrewsbury* was fitted with a new bowsprit. On the sixteenth, some ships of the line tried to move from the upper river to Staten Island, but the wind was against them, and they had to anchor again. While swinging at anchor, the *Centaur* went aground on Robins Reef— and stayed there even during the high tide.

Ships of the line colliding, running aground in a harbor

which the British navy had used for five years—it was all a little too dream-like, and arouses the suspicion that more than a few of these captains, and possibly the admiral, were taking active steps to make sure there would be no need to force the entrance of Chesapeake Bay. Of course, such accidents can be explained equally well by the cumbersome nature of the old square riggers and the almost forgotten extent to which the age of sail was at the mercy of wind and tide. Still, MacKenzie's diary has an entry on the sixteenth of October which reawakens the puzzle of the ever-lengthening delay. "If the Navy are not a little more active," he writes hotly, "they will not get sight of the Capes of Virginia before the end of this Month, and then it will be too late. They do not seem to be hearty in the business, or to think that the saving of that Army is an object of such material consequence. One of the captains has exposed himself so much as to say that the loss of two line-of-battle ships in effecting the Relief of that Army, is of much more consequence than the loss of it. . . ."

The adjutant's distress was caused by the arrival of a whaleboat from Yorktown on the morning of the sixteenth. It had left York on the twelfth, three days after the allied bombardment had begun, and the news it brought was grim. One hundred men were dead, the works were damaged considerably, and Cornwallis was in "daily expectation" of the relieving fleet. "Without them, he has no great hopes of withstanding the great force collected against him."

If things were gloomy in New York, they were close to despair in Yorktown. The loss of the two forward redoubts made everyone feel that the last link in the chain of destruction was now forged. Stephan Popp has nothing but gloom, doom and exaggerations in his diary for October 14. He tells how a Hessian soldier who had been defending the redoubts and escaped when they were carried, was torn into three pieces by the barrage of grapeshot the British artillerymen fired the moment the redoubts changed hands. The howls of the charging Americans terrified the young Anspacher, and he estimated the attackers at four thousand. Lieutenant James, unused to the clatter of land warfare, went even farther and declared the enemy "stormed from left to right" with seventeen thousand men. "In the commotion," Popp says, "many people deserted."

There is some evidence that the British garrison was close to mutiny. Every day Johann Doehla's diary records new desertions; his own regiment had by now lost almost fifty men. A deserter told the Americans of one British regiment refusing to do their duty in the lines until Lord Cornwallis gave them an extra ration of wine and promised them that the fleet would relieve them soon. But there is considerable doubt that the Earl himself believed this was still a tenable hope.

On October 15 he wrote another letter to Sir Henry Clinton, which was a frank statement of impending collapse:

> Sir,
>
> Last evening the enemy carried my two advanced redoubts on the left by storm, and during the night have included them in the second parallel, which they are at present busy in perfecting. My situation here becomes very critical; we dare not show a gun to their old batteries, and I expect their new ones will open tomorrow morning. Experience has shown that our fresh earthern works do not resist their powerful artillery, so that we shall soon be exposed to an assault in ruined works, in a bad position, and with weakened numbers. The safety of the place is therefore so precarious that I cannot recommend that the fleet and army should run great risk in endeavoring to save us.

He wrote this in cipher, and sent it out by whaleboat that night. But Charles Cornwallis was not the kind of general who gave up without striking a blow. At a midnight conference he and his officers decided to attempt a sortie to spike some of the allied cannon in the second parallel batteries and possibly gain control of some portions of the trench itself, from which they could enfilade other allied batteries and silence them before they spoke.

Lieutenant Colonel Robert Abercromby was ordered to assemble 350 men. The grenadiers from the Foot Guards, the light infantry company of the Eightieth Regiment, and a large detachment of the light infantry brigade under the command of Major Armstrong, were chosen. They were ordered to rely solely on the bayonet, and to concentrate more on spiking enemy cannon than on fighting opposing troops.

It was desperation—but it was also necessity. If the cannon of the second parallel opened at dawn, they could well make the British defenses untenable before the end of the day. To disrupt them at least, to destroy them at most, would gain precious time for that fleet which every man still believed would somehow appear over the distant horizon. At three A.M. the picked troops filed into the British hornwork, Abercromby at their head. They chose their point of attack carefully: just at the junction of the French and American sections of the trenches, which they suspected might not be as carefully guarded as some other points in the allied line. More important, there were two batteries of artillery within easy striking distance of this junction, an American one on the left and a French one on the right.

Grimly the men crept into the darkness, and without a single sentry challenging them, slipped over the barricade and into the main trench of the second parallel. Fumbling along in the blackness, they came to the French redoubt, which was guarded by an officer and fifty men of the Agenais Regiment. Incredibly, most of them were asleep, and when a sentry challenged them, the British pretended to be an American relief detachment. Then, with a furious rush, they were into the redoubt bayoneting the hapless Agenais and sending the survivors running for their lives. The British made no attempt to pursue, but turned immediately to the job of spiking the cannon.

The detachment of light infantry under Major Armstrong at the same moment approached the American battery, which was occupied by only 100 Virginia militiamen on fatigue duty under Colonel Henry Skipwith. They did not even have their guns with them, but had carefully stacked them outside the redoubt. A sentry had sharp ears, however, and had challenged the approaching British:

"What troops?"

"French," was the reply, and they moved confidently forward. Then, at the moment of contact, Armstrong howled, "Push on my brave boys and skin the bastards!"

Colonel Skipwith immediately ordered his men to get out of the redoubt as fast as they could and find their guns. By this time the British were over the parapet, but they wasted no time on the fleeing militiamen. It was the cannon they were after, and they rammed their bayonets into the touch-holes to spike them. This was all they had time to do, because into both redoubts aroused French grenadiers under Lafayette's brother-in-law, the Vicomte de Noailles, were pouring by the dozen, crying, *"Vive le Roi!"*

A fierce bayonet fight followed in the murky dawn, with no quarter asked or given. The darkness rang with British cheers and French shouts, cries of anguish and roars of defiance. One British sergeant of the Guards won special admiration from the French for his refusal to retreat, even when it became apparent that the reinforcements far outnumbered the invaders and put them in danger of being cut off. The sergeant finally fell with a dozen French bayonets in his body, while behind him the rest of the sortie streamed back to the British lines, carrying an Agenais officer with them.

Colonel Richard Butler admired the "secrecy and spirit" with which the British had executed the sortie, but Washington in his diary dismissed it as "small and ineffectual . . . of little consequence to either party." They were both right. The British had had no time to do a really efficient spiking job on the cannon. To render a gun useless, a metal wedge must be rammed into its touchhole (where the powder which ignites the charge is inserted) so tightly that not even a blacksmith can get it out without melting down the entire cannon. Merely jamming in their bayonets and breaking off the points was the best the raiders could do in both the French and American batteries.

Engineers and artillerymen were immediately ordered to work at clearing the guns, which had not been moved into position. They worked with angry efficiency all morning, and by noon, when the emplacements were ready to take the cannon, every gun was back in condition. So, with a roar made even more monstrous now by proximity, the allied bombardment began plastering the British lines with redoubled power. Johann Doehla says that one battery of fourteen guns was so close to the hornwork "that one could nearly throw stones into it." Stephan Popp said it was worse than any fire they had received yet. It seemed to him "as though the heavens should split." Everyone expected the final storm "to finish us off" would take place at any moment.

There was no place left in York now where a man was safe; even in the hospitals the sick and wounded, which by now numbered almost two thousand, were being decimated by the rain of steel; in the middle of the morning they were moved in boats to the Gloucester side of the river. Around the same time there occurred a grisly incident, that must have shaken Cornwallis badly and accentuated the agony which his men were enduring.

The Earl and Major Cochrane, the officer who had brought Sir Henry Clinton's last message into Yorktown via whaleboat and who had stayed in camp to serve Cornwallis as an aide, came into the hornwork at the height of the allied cannonade. Cochrane had a professional soldier's interest in artillery fire, and he wanted to see how firing *en ricochet* looked. Cornwallis, who had seen too much of it in the last few days, expressed little or no interest in the subject, but Cochrane proceeded to stand up on a firing platform so that he could peer over the British wall and watch the allied balls skip across the ground. At that very moment a shot hissed low over the parapet and Major Cochrane's long adventure in America was over. A headless monstrosity toppled backward into the trench at Cornwallis' feet.

That afternoon, Stephan Popp noted that the enemy firing was "almost unendurable." Worse, the young German could see the allied fatigue parties building a huge battery of ten mortars and 24-pound cannons on the right flank of the British line. When they opened up at second parallel range, no one would be able to move out of the holes they had dug.

Cornwallis did not need Cochrane's grisly corpse to tell him that the situation of his army was now impossible. The sortie had failed. Was there anything else a general could do? Yes, if that general were Charles Cornwallis: fight his way out.

He would take that advice his senior officers had extended a week ago. Clinton's orders, or lack of orders, his asinine hints and queries and suggestions, no longer mattered. He had written his farewell letter to Sir Henry, telling him not to bother to come with his mythical reinforcements, because the British Army of Virginia was no longer an organization which could give these reinforcements material help. There were simply not enough soldiers left to make the kind of bold move on which Sir Henry's schemes depended. But now Charles Cornwallis was his own man once more, and he did the thing which came to him instinctively.

The weak link in Washington's entrapping chain was across the river in Gloucester. There was only Lauzun's legion, really; the other units—the 750 French marines, the

Virginia militia under Weedon—could be more or less dismissed. In his dugout during the afternoon of the sixteenth of October, Cornwallis huddled with his officers, working out a plan to smash their way to freedom from Gloucester.

As soon as darkness fell, the British regiments were to be carefully and quietly withdrawn from their positions in the front lines and ferried across the river. A careful count of the available boats and the number of men still in fighting condition made it clear that the entire army could make it across in three trips. Tarleton was ordered to prepare his legion and gather every horse still alive. Thanks to the cooperation of a loyalist on the Gloucester side, Colonel Simcoe knew a secret path down which he could lead his rangers to fall on Lauzun's legion from behind.

The attack was to be made precisely at dawn. At that very moment the whole British army would surge from the Gloucester works and sweep before it the French marines and the American militia. Trapped between two forces, Lauzun's legion would either be annihilated or scattered. They would seize the Duke's horses and mount as many men as possible, putting two on a horse, and begin a march down the peninsula into Maryland, commandeering horses and food from every farm they passed. Their eventual goal would be New York; but they would act as circumstances advised, perhaps striking out for the coast in the hopes of finding the British relieving fleet, or if their search for food and horses proved successful, continuing through Maryland and Delaware all the way to the mouth of the Delaware River, where they could easily make contact with headquarters in New York.

In Yorktown were to be left all the convalescent and sick, together with the sailors from the fleet. They were to man the ramparts through the night and into the dawn. The moment the army escaped from Gloucester, Lieutenant Colonel Johnston was to run up a white flag and surrender. Cornwallis even wrote a letter, commending his sick and wounded to Washington's mercy.

It was by no means an impossible plan. The American cavalryman Light Horse Harry Lee, who was at Yorktown and was himself a veteran of the kind of forced march warfare Cornwallis was contemplating, wrote in his memoirs: "This bold conception bespoke the hero, and was worthy of its author. Nor can it justly be deemed so desperate as was generally conceived." Cornwallis realized that Washington would have to guard simultaneously against two possibilities, that the British might swing in a wide arc and march through western Virginia into North Carolina, or that they would continue north toward New York. "Washington could not possibly in time seize the northern and the southern route; and without availing himself of horses, he could never overtake his foe," concluded Lee.

Horses were by no means immediately available. If Washington collected all the horses in the allied camp and in the neighborhood, Lee estimated, the allies could have mounted four thousand men in four days. This would have left Washington barely equal to Cornwallis' retreating army. If the allies gambled on Cornwallis taking the northern route, they could, of course, have easily placed most of their army on De Grasse's ships, assuming the admiral was willing (a large assumption), and sailed to the head of Chesapeake Bay to bar Cornwallis from the Delaware. But this would mean that they would also have to expect the presence of Sir Henry Clinton and his army, who could quickly reach those same shores of the Delaware by sea. Moreover, the British would have the far more advantageous strategic position. They would have two armies moving toward each other in a straight line, while Washington would be pursuing with his larger army, and the army of the north under General Heath would probably be following Clinton's rear. The British then would have the delicious sport of beating the allies *en détail*. "Washington," Lee says, "would not have risked such a game."

But would not the Earl expect to meet a violent opposition from the countryside through which he passed? Lee scoffs at this notion. Cornwallis would be preceded by the most fearsome cavalry leader in the war, Banastre Tarleton, capable of sweeping aside any puny force of volunteers a local militia organization could hope to raise. Moreover, Lee points out, the sections of Maryland and Pennsylvania through which Cornwallis was to pass, "had been ever considered affected with an ardent attachment to the British government." Most of Pennsylvania was Quaker, hence "averse to war" and incapable of opposing a professsional army.

Finally, suppose that Washington and Rochambeau decided to mount their men and pursue. This would mean a pitched battle—something Cornwallis was a genius at fighting. He would be outnumbered, true. But "victory gave him safety," Lee says, "and victory was not impossible." At Guilford Court House, Cornwallis had been outnumbered at least two to one, yet he had forced Greene from the field. "Who then," says the admiring Light Horse Harry Lee, "comparing his Lordship's present condition with the worst that could befall him in the execution of his heroic decision, can withhold his admiration of a determination so bold and wise?"

While darkness descended on the broad river and the little town, and the allied guns continued to thunder, the breakout operation began. Stephan Popp's regiment supplied 300 men who relieved the British light infantry in the hornwork—not without a shudder, to be sure, because no soldier cared for duty in that exposed position. The British veterans filed down to the water's edge in absolute silence and boarded sixteen big heavy flat boats manned by sailors of the navy. In a few moments they were joined by the Foot Guards and the better part of the Twenty-third Royal Welsh Fusileers. Cornwallis was sending his best troops first, so that they would have a chance to get some rest during the latter part of the night.

On the Gloucester side, Tarleton describes the tense atmosphere of preparation: "The guards of cavalry and infantry were immediately augmented and many officers were advanced as sentries to prevent any intelligence being conveyed to the enemy. The spare horses of the garrison were ordered to parade for the benefit of the infantry and the necessary artillery and wagons were prepared."

It took at least two hours to make the trip back and forth across the river. All the other soldiers could do was wait, while the shot whistled around them and the mortar shells tumbled brilliantly through the night. Sleep, young Popp says, "was something they had forgotten for a long time." Finally, at about midnight, the cumbersome boats loomed out of the river's blackness, and the second contingent embarked. There is no record of what troops these were. Probably the rest of the Royal Welsh, and the remaining British regiments. The German regiments Cornwallis would be inclined to take last, because they were to his mind the most expendable.

So far not a hint of awareness had come from the allied camp or from the river. There were no patrol boats on the river and not a sound outside the Gloucester camp. On the bank of the silent stream, Cornwallis must have watched his men of the second detachment pull away with grim satisfaction. Perhaps there was a chance of rescuing glory from certain catastrophe. Glory that would be his alone, that would make Sir Henry Clinton look like the idiot that he was.

But ten minutes after the boats had vanished into the night, the first scattering rain began to fall. Within seconds it was a driving, pelting storm. Thunder from above joined the manmade thunder from the allied lines. Lightning streaked the river, giving the men on the shore an occasional glimpse of the soldiers and sailors in the boats, struggling to control the pitching, rocking craft in the rising wind. Within five minutes there was a full gale blowing, almost as violent, from the descriptions in various diaries, as the storm which had disrupted the fleet in New York.

Shivering in the bitter wind, soaked to the skin, the exhausted soldiers and sailors found it impossible to make any headway. All the boats turned back to the York shore. Driven by the wind they were forced to land well over a mile below the town. Two became completely lost in the darkness and were blown four or five miles down the river, where alert sentries aboard the French men-of-war at the mouth of the York spotted them at dawn and captured them. Not until two o'clock in the morning, Banastre Tarleton says, did the weather begin "to moderate." The cavalryman was waiting on the Gloucester shore, ready and eager to begin the gamble which he had urged ten days before. But out of the darkness now appeared one lone boat, carrying orders which were a numbing sound in Tarleton's ears. The Guards and light infantry were to return to York as soon as possible.

Wearily, Cornwallis had computed the hours it would take to get the second detachment reassembled and over to Gloucester, the boats back again to York for the third detachment, and over to Gloucester again. They were too many. The storm, like an angry monster, had devoured the precious darkness they needed. There was nothing to do but return to the grim business of the siege once more.

There must have been no smiles on the faces of those light infantrymen and Guards as they piled into the boats again and began the trip back to York. These were the men who had marched through half the South with Cornwallis, fighting pitched battles against desperate odds, always winning. They were not the sort of soldiers who enjoyed a siege, especially the kind to which they were returning at York, where they had to take the enemy's blows without being able to hit back. But they were soldiers, and they had their orders.

Dawn caught the last boats out on the river. Now began the worst ordeal of all. Both the French battery which had burned the *Charon* and the other ships and the American battery in the captured redoubts could sweep the river with their guns, and they opened up on the men in the boats. It was a grisly target practice, with the huge mortar shells sending up great fountains of water as they exploded and the even more deadly shot whizzing all around. The official report says that the troops suffered "a few casualties" on the return to York—a pale mockery of the cost in blood and terror to the weary men huddled in the boats.

In the first light of morning, the allied guns opened up in full chorus on the British lines. Now the thunder was close enough literally to shake the town itself. During the night all the guns from the first parallel batteries had been shifted to batteries in the second parallel. From both flanks and from the center 100 cannon bellowed and belched metal on the cowering confusion of regiments and companies that had once been the British Army of Virginia. Everywhere along the line, walls were being torn apart by the impact of the point-blank firing. There was not a single British cannon left in position to reply. The British could do nothing now but suffer, numbly.

About seven o'clock, Cornwallis and General Charles O'Hara appeared in the hornwork and morosely studied the sweep and scope of the allied fire. Then Cornwallis called a council of war. Captain George Rochfort of the artillery reported that their ammunition was exhausted. They had only about 100 mortar shells left. The sick and wounded multiplied by the hour. Mournfully Cornwallis, who had certainly had no sleep that night, turned to his fellow officers, and asked their advice. What shall we do, gentlemen? Fight to the last man?

The answer was unanimous. Every officer there told Charles Cornwallis he must do something he had never before done in his life: surrender. These brave men under his command had done all he had asked of them and more. By the end of the day, perhaps, the works that were then offering them some slight protection would be so crumbled that they would be totally exposed to the fire of the allied artillery. Exhausted and heartsick as they were, their ranks thinned by wounds and fever, they could not possibly withstand the assault that was certain to come within the next twenty-four hours from veteran troops who now outnumbered them almost five to one.

Slowly, Cornwallis nodded his assent. He turned to an aide, and dictated an historic letter:

> Sir, I propose a cessation of hostilities for twenty-four hours, and that two officers may be appointed by each side to meet at Mr. Moore's house to settle terms for the surrender of the posts at York and Gloucester
>
> I have the honour to be &c.
>
> Cornwallis

About nine o'clock on the morning of October 17, Lieutenant Ebenezer Denny was on duty in the American lines. By now trench duty had become rather routine and even a little boring to the infantrymen. They just sat there, while the artillerymen did the real work. There was some amusement in watching the French gunners firing *en ricochet,* or trying to figure out whether a particular mortar shell had hit home. But mostly it was dull and somewhat deafening.

Suddenly atop the ruined parapet in the center of the British works appeared a small redcoated figure, beating vigorously on a drum. "Had we not seen . . . the red coat when he first mounted," Denny says, "he might have beat till doomsday. The constant firing was too much for the sound of a single drum." A moment later a British officer waving a white handkerchief appeared outside the hornwork and began walking toward the American lines. The drummerboy climbed down the wall and accompanied him.

Where there had been thunder and trembling earth, now there was suddenly, unbelievably, silence. Every allied gun ceased firing and in the still morning there was only the sound of the drummerboy beating what the French call a *chamade* on his instrument. "I thought I never heard a drum equal to it," Denny says, "the most delightful music to us all." An American officer ran from the trenches to meet the Briton halfway. The American took the white handkerchief and tied it around the Briton's eyes; then he sent the drummerboy back to the British lines and escorted the Englishman into the American trenches, where Cornwallis' note was handed over.

A messenger was instantly summoned, and dispatched with the note to General Washington's tent. The commander in chief had not yet visited the lines that morning. He was busy writing letters to a variety of people. One was to John Blair, rector of William and Mary College, who was worried about how long the army was going to use his buildings for a hospital. With the usual courtesy he showed civilians, Washington apologized for the imposition, but explained that his sick and wounded were increasing so fast that he was going to have to take over some adjoining buildings as well. "I flatter myself," he wrote, "that the good people of this part of the country will the more readily submit to a partial and temporary inconvenience when they have reason to hope that the close of our present operations will place them in a state of quiet and security, which I trust will be lasting."

Washington then turned to one of his favorite correspondents, Admiral de Grasse, and began assuring him that "sixteen flat boats" would be ready to protect his ships from fire rafts whenever the admiral and the wind agreed on sending them up the river. Washington had just finished the first paragraph of the letter when the messenger came racing up to his tent with Cornwallis' note. Washington calmly finished the letter to De Grasse, telling him of Cornwallis' offer, and suggesting that the admiral himself come ashore to take part in the surrender parley.

He then conferred with his aides on an answer to Cornwallis. Once his young assistants understood the general's wishes, Jonathan Trumbull, Jr., drafted the following reply:

> My Lord: I have had the Honor of receiving your Lordship's Letter of this Date.
>
> An Ardent Desire to spare the further Effusion of Blood, will readily incline me to listen to such Terms for the Surrender of your Posts and Garrisons of York and Gloucester, as are admissible.
>
> I wish previously to the meeting of Commissioners, that your Lordship's proposals in writing may be sent to the American Lines: for which Purpose a cessation of Hostilities during two Hours from the Delivery of this letter will be granted.
>
> I have the Honor, etc.

While Washington and his aides pondered this letter, the allied cannon began thundering in the distance once more. Firing had recommenced the moment the British officer and his flag of truce had returned to the Yorktown lines. John Laurens suggested changing the word "cessation" to "suspension" and Washington agreed. He then decided the reply was adequate, and signed it. By now it was about two o'clock in the afternoon.

At about the same time, up in New York, the British fleet was at last putting to sea. It was a clear, pleasant day, with a fine wind out of the northwest. The starting signal had been made early that morning, but the men-of-war were incredibly slow in getting under way, and Admiral Graves repeatedly signaled them to make all possible speed. Earlier in the morning, he had sent a message to Sir Henry Clinton to explain the fleet's conduct: "I would not give you unnecessary alarm," he wrote, "and meant to have sent you an officer at eight o'clock, when I should have explained to Your Excellency that all this show of signals and topsails were no other than so many spurs to push forward the lazy and supine. And I am sorry to find that difficulties go on increasing, and that nothing can turn the current but being actually at sea."

This bit of sunny optimism was in strange contrast to the letter the admiral had written to the Admiralty the day before—a letter which Sir Henry Clinton did not, of course, ever see. After several pages of routine business about captured ships and appointments of new commanding officers, Graves finally got around to discussing the situation which was costing Great Britain half a continent.

> A dispatch from Lord Cornwallis . . . gives us but little prospect of being able to effect a relief. . . . The enemy having collected all their Naval strength between the Horse Shoe and York Spit plainly pointed out that they had little to apprehend from an attempt in James River. Lord Cornwallis' letter confirms that opinion, and I am inclined to believe that with the advantage of position and numbers, they think there is as little to apprehend from an attempt to force York River.
>
> The excessive want of stores and provisions and the immense repairs wanted for a crazy and shattr'd Squadron, with many cross accidents which have interven'd, has thrown back the equipment of the Squadron to a great distance. They are not quite ready— They are now very short of bread, and all the ovens will not keep up the daily consumption. Several Ships have parted their cables, others broke their anchors, and three been on shore; that I see no end to disappointments . . .

His signals fluttering, Admiral Graves scolded his fleet down the Hudson River and past Staten Island to the narrows. By evening all except three ships of the line, the *Montague,* the *Europe* and the *Shrewsbury,* were anchored off Sandy Hook. The three battleships were still in the Hudson River when night fell.

Down at Yorktown, the big guns had ceased firing at two o'clock, when the American messenger returned his answer to Cornwallis' opening letter. The two armies confronted each other across the unaccustomed silence, while Cornwallis pondered Washington's offer. In the hornwork, Stephan Popp watched the British light infantry begin to slash their tents and ruin their equipment, and he realized for the first time that surrender was close. In the American lines, men with good memories suddenly remembered that it was October 17—the same day on which General Burgoyne had surrendered at Saratoga four years before. It was, Sergeant Joseph Plumb Martin noted, "a rather unlucky day for the British."

Cornwallis found Washington's insistence on a presentation of written terms within two hours a rather severe demand. The twenty-four hours he had asked would, of course, have given the relieving fleet another day to make its appearance—and negotiations could be broken off immediately if it by some miracle should come over the horizon. There was more than a little resentment in Cornwallis' reply, which arrived at the American lines at four-thirty:

> Sir: I have this moment been honoured with your Excellency's letter, dated this day.
>
> The time limited for sending my answer will not admit of entering into the detail of articles; but the basis of my proposals will be, that the garrisons of York and Gloucester shall be prisoners of war, with the customary honours. And, for the conveniency of the individuals which I have the honour to command, that the British shall be sent to Britain and the Germans to Germany under engagement not to serve against

France, America or their allies until released or regularly exchanged. That all arms and public stores shall be delivered up to you; but that the usual indulgence of side arms to officers, and of retaining private property shall be granted to officers and soldiers, and that the interest of several individuals in civil capacities and connected with us shall be attended to.

If your Excellency thinks that a continuance of the suspension of hostilities will be necessary to transmit your answer, I shall have no objection to the hour that you may propose.

The last statement was a rather left handed way of saying that it would be nice if the cannon remained silent, certainly something the British wanted far more than the allies. In an apparently verbal exchange with the British bearer of this letter (there is no record in writing), Washington agreed to a "suspension" for the night.

At about seven o'clock, the British disturbed this temporary peace with a ghastly accident. The artillery commander had ordered the cannoneers to spend the night filling mortar and howitzer shells with powder, in case hostilities began again the next day. The artillerymen, meanwhile, had somehow gotten their hands on some brandy and were thoroughly drunk when they went to the powder magazine. Someone was careless with the lantern or candle inside the magazine and suddenly with an enormous explosion, the powder magazine and thirteen soldiers went skyward. One of the victims was from Popp's regiment, an Anspach grenadier who was guarding the magazine. "Of him only a coat plait and a piece of his pocket braid were found," Popp wrote. "Of the others we found only pieces of bodies and limbs."

Thereafter, authentic peace descended on Yorktown. It was the first night since the cannon opened fire eight days before that men on both sides of the lines could sleep without wondering if a mortar shell or a cannon ball were not going to tear them apart before they awoke. Even the heavens seemed to reflect the sudden peace. In his diary St. George Tucker wrote: "A solemn stillness prevailed—the night was remarkably clear & the sky decorated with ten thousand stars—numberless Meteors gleaming thro' the Atmosphere afforded a pleasing resemblance to the Bombs which had exhibited a noble Firework the night before, but happily divested of all their Horror."

At dawn a strange sound came drifting out of the British lines—at first harsh and unfamiliar to French and American ears—but then pleasing, even touching. The Scottish bagpipers, no doubt from the Seventy-sixth Regiment, were serenading the enemy. Not to be outdone, the Royal Deux-Ponts Regimental Band answered them through the grey stillness. Then the sun rose slowly over the battlefield, revealing an astonishing scene. From one end of the allied lines to the other the parapets were crowded with men and officers, and on the British side the ramparts were equally full. No one spoke. Both armies simply stared at each other and the silent battlefield, as if they were seeing it for the first time. Behind the British, Yorktown was a scene of utter desolation. Secretary Nelson's house sagged in the rosy light, one of its noble corners broken off, and huge holes gaping in the roof and walls. Behind it other fine houses were equally battered and forlorn. From the bluff's edge hundreds of people were visible on the beach below, and in the river the masts and yards of the sunken ships could be seen. Over on the Gloucester side, the frigate *Guadaloupe* lay at a giddy angle, her decks awash. The British had apparently scuttled her during the night.

During the same night, Washington and his aides had labored over a letter which would stipulate in some detail their ideas on surrender terms. They flatly rejected Cornwallis' request to send his army back to Europe. This was the controversial concession that General Burgoyne had wrung from

General Horatio Gates at Saratoga, but Congress had wisely, if somewhat dishonorably, managed to avoid fulfilling it. In the world war which this Revolution had become, troops sent back to Europe merely released troops there to come across the ocean and fight in their places. Otherwise, Washington's ideas did not differ radically from Cornwallis' opening proposals.

> My Lord: To avoid unnecessary Discussions and delays I shall at Once, in Answer to your Lordship's letter of Yesterday, declare the general basis upon which a Definitive Treaty and Capitulation must take place. The Garrisons of York and Gloucester, including the Seamen, as you propose, will be received Prisoners of War. The Condition annexed, of sending the British and German Troops to the parts of Europe to which they respectively belong, is inadmissible. Instead of this they will be marched to such parts of the country as can most conveniently provide for their Subsistence; and the Benevolent Treatment of Prisoners, which is invariably observed by the Americans, will be extended to them. The same Honors will be granted to the Surrendering Army as were granted to the Garrison of Charlestown. The Shipping and Boats in the two Harbours with all their Guns, Stores, Tackling, Furniture and Apparel, shall be delivered in their present State to an Officer of the Navy, appointed to take possession of them.
>
> The Artillery, Arms, Accoutrements, Military Chest and Public Stores of every Denomination shall be delivered unimpaired to the Heads of Departments to which they respectively belong.
>
> The Officers will be indulged in retaining their Side Arms, and the Officers and Soldiers may preserve their Baggage and Effects, with this Reserve, that property taken in the Country, will be reclaimed. With Regard to the Individuals in civil Capacities, whose Interests Your Lordship wishes may be attended to, until they are more particularly described, nothing definitive can be settled.

I have to add, that I expect the Sick and Wounded will be supplied with their own Hospital Stores, and be attended by British Surgeons, particularly charged with the Care of them.

Your Lordship will be pleased to signify your Determination either to accept or reject the Proposals now offered in the Course of Two Hours from the Delivery of this letter, that Commissioners may be appointed to digest the Articles of Capitulation, or a Renewal of Hostilities may take place.

Once more, Washington gave Cornwallis only two hours to make up his mind. The American was determined not to let the British use negotiation to delay a siege that was balanced on such a delicate timetable. Washington admitted that the surrender offer was coming "at an earlier period than my most sanguine hopes had led me to expect." Timothy Pickering wrote excitedly to his wife that the "event was unexpected." But the Americans were still taking no chances.

If Washington had known how far away the British fleet was when he sent his answer to Cornwallis, he might have been a little more lenient about time. On the eighteenth of October, another fine day with a moderate wind, the remaining men-of-war finally left the Hudson River and went through the Narrows toward the sea. Down at Sandy Hook, the day was spent laboriously transferring the troops from the transports to the men-of-war. Only four ships, including the *Barfleur* of Sir Samuel Hood, went over the bar and actually reached the open sea.

In Yorktown, Cornwallis pondered Washington's terms. Knowing the uproar Burgoyne's agreement with Gates had caused, the Earl could not have had much hope of winning the transfer of the troops to Europe. There was nothing else that he found particularly objectionable. Protection of British sympathizers within the Yorktown lines was left an open question, but Cornwallis undoubtedly reasoned he would be even less able to protect them if the place was taken by storm.

He would, moreover, be able to press this question intensely when the negotiations began.

While the morning ebbed and Cornwallis pondered, two French frigates and a schooner came up the York River and dropped anchor just off the town. These were the ships that Washington and the admiral had argued about so long and so fruitlessly. They were finally arriving, now that they were no longer needed. The schooner brought Admiral de Barras, with a message that Admiral de Grasse was down with an asthma attack and to his deep regret could not take part in the surrender negotiations. Barras was to act as his representative.

Around noon Cornwallis' reply came forth from the lines under the usual flag of truce.

> Sir: I agree to open a treaty of capitulation upon the basis of the garrisons of York and Gloucester including seamen, being prisoners of war, without annexing the condition of their being sent to Europe; but I expect to receive compensation in the articles of capitulation for the surrender of Gloucester in its present state of defence. I shall in particular, desire that the *Bonetta* sloop of war may be left entirely at my disposal from the hour that the capitulation is signed, to receive an Aid-de-camp to carry my dispatches to Sir Henry Clinton. Such soldiers as I may think proper to send as passengers in her, to be manned with fifty men of her own crew, and to be permitted to sail without examination, when my dispatches are ready; engaging, on my part, that the ship shall be brought back and delivered to you if she escapes the dangers of the sea, that the crew and soldiers shall be accounted for in future exchanges, that she shall carry off no officer without your consent, nor public property of any kind; and I shall likewise desire that the traders and inhabitants may preserve their property, and that no person may be punished or molested for having joined the British troops.
>
> If you choose to proceed to negociation on these grounds, I shall appoint two field officers of my army to meet two offi-

cers from you at any time and place that you think proper, to digest the articles of capitulation.

The sloop *Bonetta* was Cornwallis' escape hatch, if the negotiations over the loyalists collapsed. He planned to cram aboard it every one it could carry and thus get them out of reach of American vengeance. Fortunately Washington was not a vengeful man. Though he undoubtedly recognized Cornwallis' intentions, he agreed to negotiations "on these grounds." Messengers hurried back and forth between the British and American lines, agreeing on Cornwallis' original choice for the conference, the Augustine Moore house, half a mile behind the American first parallel. Washington appointed Colonel John Laurens as his representative, and asked Rochambeau to choose a French officer to accompany him. He chose Vicomte de Noailles. Cornwallis appointed his aide, Major Alexander Ross, and Lieutenant Colonel Thomas Dundas. Over on the Gloucester side, the Americans appointed the Duc de Lauzun to discuss details with his personal antagonist, Banastre Tarleton. The Duke advanced to the parley waving a white lace handkerchief, thus maintaining the well-established tradition, to quote a fellow Frenchman, "that the Duc De Lauzun never acted like anyone else would in the same circumstances."

The Moore house is still standing at Yorktown. It is not hard for a modern visitor to picture the scene, on that afternoon of October 18, 1781. John Laurens in his worn buff and blue uniform and Noailles in gorgeous white and gold waited in the garden of the simple frame house for the arrival of the British commissioners. Finally the two redcoated officers appeared out of the trenches of the first parallel and walked slowly toward them through the Fall sunshine.

It must have been an especially mortifying day for young Major Ross, who had attached himself so closely to Cornwallis' rising star. If anyone could be accused of having influenced the disaster that was befalling England, Ross must certainly be put high on the list, as the man who stoked the controversy between Clinton and Cornwallis and talked the Earl out of the decision to attack Lafayette in September. The stolid Scot Dundas had no such personal involvement. Not too surprisingly, therefore, it was Ross and Laurens who did most of the talking. With that consummate tact which had governed French conduct since they landed, the Vicomte de Noailles remained subordinate to the American's leadership.

Since the basic issues had been more or less decided before the commissioners met, most people thought they would accomplish the negotiations in a few hours. Washington ordered an American and a French detachment, each of 200 men, to be ready to occupy British defenses on the main roads into Yorktown, and thus control all exit and entry. The men were prepared to move by mid-afternoon, but there was still no sign of the commissioners with the surrender articles. Colonel Richard Butler, who was in command of the American detachment, noted in his diary: "after the troops were ready to march, they were ordered to remain on their arms."

Ross and Laurens had vast difficulty in agreeing on details. The British major haggled over everything, but the argument was particularly intense over the fate of American deserters who had enlisted in the British army. Ross insisted that they be guaranteed protection, and Laurens insisted with equal fervor that he had no power to do such a thing. Ross was, of course, only continuing the argument that Cornwallis had begun, but he still tried to wring the concession from the allies, betting on their eagerness to have the British in their hands before relief arrived. This was the technique Burgoyne had employed at Saratoga, with considerable success. Laurens finally agreed to put the loyalist clause into the articles of capitulation, but he undoubtedly warned Ross that he was sure General Washington would not approve it. Even this much was a victory for Ross, and he accepted.

A more vitriolic argument broke out over the military details of how the defeated army would march out. According to the accepted etiquette of siege warfare, if a commander surrendered a fortress before the place was taken by storm, and he had put up a vigorous defense, he was allowed to march out with "the honors of war." This meant he was fully armed against insult and kept all his regimental and national flags flying boldly. His bands, by some curious logic, were permitted to play one of the victorious army's national songs. Saluting the enemy with his own music was a way of saying that though defeated, the vanquished were not humiliated beyond exchanging a gentlemanly compliment with the victors.

Laurens absolutely refused to permit the British this consolation. In this he knew he was warmly supported by Lafayette, who supposedly had urged the idea before the negotiations began. But Laurens needed no urging. He had been captured at Charleston in 1780, and there the British had imposed these conditions on the defeated Americans under Benjamin Lincoln, although they too had put up a gallant defense.

Ross protested violently against this modest revenge. "This is a harsh article," he said.

"Which article?" asked Laurens.

"The troops shall march out with colors cased and drums beating a British or a German march."

"Yes, sir," replied Laurens, "it is a harsh article."

"Then, Colonel Laurens, if that is your opinion, why is it here?"

With superb formality, Laurens answered: "Your question, Major Ross, compels an observation which I would have gladly suppressed. You seem to forget, sir, that I was a capitulant at Charleston, where General Lincoln, after a brave defense of six weeks in open trenches by a very inconsiderable garrison against the British army and fleet . . . and when your lines of approach were within pistol shot of our field works, was refused any other terms for his gallant garrison than marching out with colors cased and drums *not* beating a German or a British march."

"But," said Major Ross, "My Lord Cornwallis did not command at Charleston."

"There, sir," said Laurens, "you extort another declaration. It is not the individual that is here considered. It is the nation. This remains an article, or I cease to be a commissioner."

Ross then switched his attack and demanded the honors of war for the garrison of Gloucester, at least. After all, he argued, they had not even been assaulted; scarcely a shot had been fired at them. Laurens maintained that it was all one garrison. They finally settled for permitting the Gloucester cavalry to ride out with drawn swords and blaring trumpets, while the infantry would march out with colors cased.

Over these and other points, the negotiations dragged on into the evening. Meanwhile in the American lines, there was another kind of crisis. When Lafayette arrived with his division to relieve Baron von Steuben, the crusty old Prussian refused to move an inch. He maintained that according to the protocol of sieges, those who were in the trenches when the enemy opened negotiations had the privilege of remaining in them until the final surrender, and thus the honor of occupying the enemy's defenses. Actually, Lafayette had been in command of the trenches when the first British overture was made, the day before. But he had had no previous experience in sieges, and did not know what he was giving up when he relinquished his command to the Baron. Lafayette was more than a little annoyed, since he did not particularly like Steuben in the first place, but when he appealed to

Washington, the commander in chief found in favor of the drillmaster.

Not until close to midnight did the weary Laurens and Noailles return to Washington's tent with the articles of capitulation, and even then they were only in the form of a rough draft. They had agreed to extend the truce until nine o'clock in the morning of the nineteenth, while they conferred with Washington about some of the contested points. Once again, therefore, both armies enjoyed a peaceful night.

By morning, the articles were in final form, and were presented to Washington for his approval or rejection. The general sat in his tent, his aides around him, and read the clauses one by one. Under each one he wrote his decision.

Disallowing a few very minor points, he granted them all except two. Article Ten, which claimed the inviolability of Americans who had joined the British army, received a firm negative, as Laurens had predicted. "This article cannot be assented to," Washington wrote, "being altogether of civil resort." He also objected to the demand that medicines for the British sick and wounded must come from American hospitals. "The hospital stores now in York and Gloucester shall be delivered for the use of the British sick and wounded. Passports will be granted for procuring them further supplies from New York as occasion may require. . . ."

Having penned these notes on the original copy of the Articles, Washington now had the whole document copied. A messenger was summoned, and ordered to bring one copy to the British commander. With the Articles went another note, advising Cornwallis that Washington expected to have everything signed by eleven o'clock, and that the garrison was expected to march out at two o'clock for the formal surrender ceremonies. Washington then had breakfast, and rode out to the captured British redoubt number ten, where Rochambeau and Admiral Barras were waiting for him, along with a swelling crowd of other ranking officers. They waited patiently and with perfect decorum, while inside Yorktown Cornwallis and his staff studied the final terms.

At about the same hour, off Sandy Hook, the British rescue fleet was finally at sea in a body, and under way to Yorktown. For some reason known only to himself, Sir Henry Clinton was lifted up that morning by another tremendous burst of optimism. He wrote a letter to a friend in England, assuring him (and himself) that Cornwallis' defenses were in perfect order and his position impregnable.

> He must be saved or— . . . I understand nothing of sea matters, you know, but my oracle, Sir Samuel Hood, seems to think that if they meet us at sea, we have everything to hope from our better sailing—and I could add, from the superior abilities of all our naval chiefs. The stake is great. . . . The two services start in perfect good humour with each other, and determined to do their best.

More than once, while Cornwallis and his staff were pondering Washington's terms, their eyes must have turned longingly to the broad river, and beyond it, to the open bay, hoping the impossible would happen, that on the horizon would be the masts of the British fleet. But there was never more than the empty sky, and the masts of the French men-of-war riding at anchor in the mouth of the York. It was hopeless, hopeless, and there was nothing to do but swallow hard and sign. At about eleven o'clock, Cornwallis put his signature at the bottom of the long piece of paper, and Captain Thomas Symonds signed underneath him for the British navy.

The papers were then delivered to redoubt number ten where the American Commander in Chief wrote "G. Washington" for the United States. For the French, there was "Le Comte de Rochambeau" and Barras: "Le Comte de Barras en mon nom & celui du Comte de Grasse." No trumpets blared, no shouts of victory were heard. It was all matter-of-fact. But Washington, with that quiet realism which was in many ways more dramatic than histrionics, ordered an aide to place above the allied signatures the line: "Done in the trenches before Yorktown in Virginia, October 19, 1781."

The waiting troops were now ordered to move forward and occupy the two British redoubts. Baron von Steuben marched at the head of the American detachment, which was from the Pennsylvania Line. To his immense pride, young Lieutenant Ebenezer Denny had been given the regimental standard, which he was to plant on the British parapet. But the Baron, who had spent two days in the trenches waiting for the honor of occupying the posts, was not going to let a lieutenant perform the final flourish. As Denny mounted the parapet, Steuben snatched the flag out of his hand, and personally shoved the point of the staff into the ground. Colonel Richard Butler, the commander of Denny's regiment, almost exploded when he saw this pre-emption. He and Steuben exchanged some extremely warm words, and friends on both sides were worried that there might be a duel before the argument ended.

The French grenadiers occupied their redoubt, directly on the river bank, without acrimony. The situation looked so peaceful that Washington had reduced the detachments to 100 men each. They were under orders to let no soldier or civilian out of Yorktown and no one from the allied army or countryside in. Young Denny was repelled by the scene inside Yorktown. "Never was in so filthy a place—some handsome houses, but prodigiously shattered. Negroes lie about sick and dying, in every stage of the small pox. Vast heaps of shot and shells which came from our works."

In the midst of this carnage, the British prepared for the surrender ceremonies. It was spit and polish all the way. Boots were shined, gaiters were whitened, fresh uniforms were broken out of knapsacks. In their last moments of existence as an army, Cornwallis' men were determined to look the part. The public stores were even opened, and any soldier who was dissatisfied with the fit or appearance of his present uniform had full permission to draw a new one. The commissary department also freely dispensed its supplies of rum, preferring to see it go down British throats rather than pass into American hands.

The surrender field was a meadow about a half-mile down the Williamsburg road from the Yorktown defenses. The road no longer exists, but a large portion of the field is still preserved. At about one P.M. the allied troops filed out of their camps on either side of the field, and rank upon rank lined up along the road. The French had put on their best white uniforms, and their officers were aglitter with plumes and gold braid. The Americans had polished their guns and boots and repaired their tattered uniforms as much as possible. They stationed the Continentals in the front ranks, and put the militia, with their sloppy civilian clothes and ways, in the rear. Washington and his staff, all on horseback, took

their positions at the head of the American ranks, and opposite them were Rochambeau and his staff, also on horseback. The allied army thus formed two lines which
stretched from the second parallel to where the generals
waited. On both sides of the lines was a great crowd of civilians on foot and in wagons and chaises.

They waited in silence broken only by the playing of the
French bands. Then they ceased, and in the distance was the
lugubrious beat of drums, pounding a slow march, and band
instruments playing a mournful tune. The British were
coming. At their head rode a superb-looking officer in full
dress, followed by an equally well-uniformed staff. Was it
Cornwallis? No, the dark, ruddy Irish face, the magnificent
teeth identified General Charles O'Hara. Cornwallis had
found, at the last moment, he could not endure the mortification of the surrender, and had given the task to his deputy.
Now they were within the twin rows of the allied army, and
Americans began to recognize the tune which the British
band was playing. It was an old English air, to which innumerable songs and ballads had been written. One was
called *When the King Enjoys his Own Again*. But a far
more popular version was *The World Turn'd Upside Down*.

It was an accurate description. The man who had been
called the last courtier was riding now to surrender in the last
formal siege in history. Soldiers of the world's most powerful
king were surrendering to ragged rebels who had defied that
sovereign in the name of a new idea, the liberty of free men.
But to the British it was surrender, not to an idea, but to
colonials whom they had scorned and denounced, and Cornwallis was not the only one who found it mortifying. For the
first few minutes, as they went past, rank on rank, every English soldier had his eyes riveted to the right, at the French,
trying to blot out, by a physical gesture, the existence of the
Americans on the other side of the road.

Lafayette noticed this immediately and did not like it. He

snapped an order and a moment later the American band exploded with a swoop of drums and a squeal of fifes into their old favorite, *Yankee Doodle*. As if on a string, every British head was jerked by the sound in the other direction, and they stared, against their will, into the impassive faces of their ex-subjects.

At the head of the British column, meanwhile, General O'Hara asked Comte Mathieu Dumas to point out General Rochambeau for him. The young aide did so, and O'Hara spurred his horse toward the general. Dumas realized, almost too late, that O'Hara was going to try to surrender formally to the French, not the Americans, and according to his memoirs, he raced after O'Hara and placed his horse between him and Rochambeau. At the same moment, Rochambeau, perceiving O'Hara's intention, raised his hand and shook his head, and directed O'Hara across the road to Washington.

There, with a glittering, if somewhat embarrassed smile, O'Hara explained that Lord Cornwallis was indisposed, and he was acting in his place. Washington coolly directed O'Hara to receive his orders from General Benjamin Lincoln, the American second in command. As commander in chief, Washington had no intention of dealing with a subordinate. He thus proved he could play the protocol game as well as the English. Lincoln told O'Hara that the troops were to march ahead to an open field, in which a detachment of French hussars had formed a circle. There they were to deposit their arms, about face, and march back to their cantonments in Yorktown.

O'Hara passed these orders on to his army, and the final surrender began. The utmost decorum was observed by both French and American soldiers. Every man seemed to realize, as the ceremony progressed, the poignancy in the affair, as well as the importance. Now that these British soldiers were enemies no longer, everyone, even Americans who had cause to hate them thoroughly, found a strange sympathy running through their thoughts and feelings. Light Horse Harry Lee, who watched the redcoated regiments file past, perhaps put it best. "Valiant troops," he wrote in his memoirs, "(were) yielding up their arms after fighting in defence of a cause dear to them (because the cause of their country) under a leader who, throughout the war, in every grade and in every situation to which he had been called, appeared the Hector of his host. Battle after battle had he fought; climate after climate had he endured; towns had yielded to his mandate, posts were abandoned at his approach; armies were conquered by his prowess. . . . But even he, in the midst of his splendid career, found his conqueror."

In spite of his admiration for Cornwallis, Lee felt he had made a mistake in not leading out his troops. He surrendered to "sensations which his great character should have stifled. He had been unfortunate, not from any false step or deficiency of exertion on his part, but from the infatuated policy of his superior, and the united power of his enemy, brought to bear on him alone. There was nothing with which he could reproach himself; there was nothing with which he could reproach his brave and faithful army: why not then appear at its head in the day of misfortune as he had always done in the day of triumph?"

In spite of these generous thoughts from his conquerors, Lord Cornwallis chose to stay home. General O'Hara, having received his orders from General Lincoln, led his men past Washington to the open field, where the French hussars formed the fateful circle. Rank upon rank, they passed through, and as each platoon arrived, the sergeant barked the bitter order: "Ground arms!" Dr. Thacher thought that in most cases the order was given "sullenly,"—which is not surprising. In the beginning, many of the men flung their muskets to the ground with all their strength, hoping to damage them. But General Lincoln gave prompt orders to stop this practice.

The sight of the army abandoning its weapons was too much for more than a few of the officers. Some, mostly English, swore terrible oaths. (Lt. Colonel Abercromby is said to have bitten his sword in impotent anguish.) Others, mostly Scots, wept openly. Only the Germans seemed to have performed the operation with stolid dignity. American observers were struck by the precision and polish with which the Germans marched out. The English were unable to match it; several American observers noticed many of the redcoats were thoroughly drunk and marched "most irregularly." Colonel von Seybothen of the Bayreuth Regiment, however, was unable to retain his dignity, and his cheeks were wet with tears when he gave the commands: "Present Arms! Lay Down Arms! Put off Swords and cartridge boxes." A Scot in the Seventy-sixth gave his musket the sort of embrace a man usually reserves for a sweetheart, and threw it down with the words, "May you never get so good a master!"

On the French side, Admiral Barras contributed a moment of humor. Rochambeau and his staff were concerned about the problem of putting the admiral on horseback. As a sailor, he had no skills in this area. But the admiral stiffly insisted on taking his place beside the French general staff, and vowed he would remain in the saddle "for twenty-four hours" if necessary, to see the last English soldier march out. Still the young French aides watched him nervously—it was obvious that the admiral was not really enjoying his uneasy perch. Suddenly his horse stretched and answered a call of nature. Hearing the rush of water, the admiral panicked and exclaimed: "Good Heavens, I think my horse is sinking!"

In the circle formed by the hussars, the British muskets were by now a huge brown and silver pile. The last German platoon laid down their guns in good order, wheeled and marched away. Then twenty-eight British captains advanced, with the cased colors of the captured regiments. Formed to receive them was a line of twenty-eight American sergeants, commanded by eighteen-year-old Ensign Wilson, the youngest officer in the Continental army. Handing over the colors was the last and most painful acknowledgment of defeat. But when the British captains saw that their recipients were sergeants, they balked angrily. They were not going to hand their beloved colors to anyone but officers. The sergeants, they protested violently, were an insult. Things lingered for a moment in this state of impasse and then Alexander Hamilton rode up to find out why the two lines of men were standing there staring at each other. The English captain in charge explained his chagrin, and Hamilton quietly agreed with him. He therefore ordered Ensign Wilson to accept the colors from the captains, one by one, and pass them to the sergeants.

It was all over at Yorktown by three o'clock. On the Gloucester side, the smaller ceremony was just beginning. Tarleton's cavalry rode out with their sabres drawn, their trumpets defiantly braying, as the articles of surrender had agreed. The infantry, led by Lieutenant Colonel John Simcoe's Queen's Rangers, marched with colors cased, their drums beating an unidentified English march.

In all this pageantry and poignancy, there was only one discordant note. Jacky Custis watched the surrender ceremony from a carriage not far from the Hussar's circle. Jacky's cheeks were flushed, his eyes unnaturally bright; he should not have been there, and Dr. James Craik, knowing how deeply Washington was attached to the boy, had done his best to keep him in bed. Jacky had the same "bilious fever" which had already struck down hundreds of American and British soldiers. But Craik had been unable to resist Jacky's charm; the young man had insisted that he wanted to see the ceremony, and talked Craik into procuring him a carriage. Immediately afterward Jacky was taken to the home of relatives, at nearby Eltham, and put to bed.

Washington was told that his stepson was seriously ill. But he hardly had time to do more than send a message to Martha and Eleanor Custis. There were a hundred military obligations and problems crowding in on him.

The British officers were now officially gentlemen in distress, and both the Americans and the French hastened to extend them every courtesy. Washington invited General O'Hara to dinner that night, and the French entertained other English officers who were amazed by the way their ancient enemies received them. "The Americans," says Captain Samuel Graham, "behaved with great delicacy and forebearance while the French, by what motive actuated I will not pretend to say, were profuse in their protestations of sympathy. When I visited their lines immediately after our parade had been dismissed, I was overwhelmed with the civility of my late enemies."

When they were alone, Americans found it difficult to restrain their joy. One American colonel wrote that night in the camp: "I noticed that the officers and soldiers could scarcely talk for laughing and they could scarcely walk for jumping and dancing and singing as they went about." At dinner, in Washington's tent, General O'Hara amazed everyone with his *sang-froid*. He could not have been more at ease if he had been entertaining a captive Washington. Other British officers were equally debonair, and the French aide, Cromot du Bourg, confessed on the twentieth, when Rochambeau gave a dinner for General O'Hara, that he "could not imagine that the day after such a catastrophe as had happened to them they could forget it."

For the enlisted men, the hours after the surrender were not quite so charming. Lieutenant Denny, on guard duty in York, was appalled at the lack of discipline in the defeated army. They had apparently filled their canteens with all the rum they could carry, and the night was one long orgy of brawling and shouting and cursing and singing. Three times they tried to break into the public stores, and were repulsed by the American sentries. During one of these altercations, one drunken British soldier seized a bayonet and killed an American with it. The redcoat probably became the last casualty of Yorktown a few moments later.

Considering the number of men involved and the momentous nature of the victory, bloodshed at Yorktown was relatively light on both sides. The British army had 156 killed, 326 wounded, and 70 missing, a total of 552. American casualties were about 30 dead and 100 wounded—an estimate because the losses among the militia were not recorded. The French had 60 killed and 193 injured. Disease cut down far more on both sides. The British had over 2,000 men in the hospital when they surrendered. The Americans and French had over 1,500 between them. One physician, Dr. Eneas Munson, declared that almost every man in the allied army had at least one "fit of ague" during the siege, because the nights were so frequently cold, with heavy dews.

In the entertainment contest following the surrender, Baron von Steuben was mortified to find himself too bankrupt to give a decent dinner for either the British or the French. He was particularly anxious to repay the French, who had feasted the Americans so often. The old soldier went to Washington and asked him if he could do anything about his back pay. Even though his $3,000 a year in Continental money was now worth only about 100 francs, he had over three years' pay coming to him. But Washington could only explain that this was outside his jurisdiction; Steuben would have to discuss the matter with Congress. He then loaned the Baron twenty guineas out of his own purse. Not satisfied with this, Steuben sold his favorite white charger to raise more cash. "I will give one grand dinner to our allies," he swore, "should I eat my soup with a wooden spoon forever after."

The Baron gave his dinner—and then, in a typically Steubenesque gesture, a few days later sold his silver forks and his watch to raise some money for one of his aides, Colonel North, who had come down with the ubiquitous fever. He left behind with North his sulky and half of all the money he had in the world, and rode off to Philadelphia to settle his accounts with Congress, no doubt goddamming all the way.

While the Americans were willing to be polite, some of them thought the French went too far in sending food into York, lending money, and all but fawning on the British. But this was merely the courtesy which the aristocracy of gentlemen and nobles which still ruled Europe always showed each other, no matter what the fortunes of war. On the twentieth, after feasting General O'Hara, Rochambeau and his staff journeyed into Yorktown, to pay a courtesy call on Cornwallis. Baron von Closen tells of the trip. "I will never forget how frightful and disturbing was the appearance of the city . . . from the fortifications on the crest to the strand below. One could not take three steps without running into some great holes made by bombs . . . with scattered white or negro arms or legs and some bits of uniforms. . . . We found Lord Cornwallis at his residence. His appearance gave the impression of nobility of soul, magnanimity and strength of character; his manner seemed to say, 'I have done nothing with which to reproach myself, I have done my duty, and I held out as long as possible.'" There was no money left in the British military chest, and Cornwallis asked Rochambeau for a loan of ten thousand pounds, which the French general immediately arranged.

On the twentieth the sloop *Bonetta* sailed, crammed to the gunwales with American loyalists who had deserted Washington's army for the British. True to their agreement, the allies let it go uninspected. But not all the endangered turncoats got aboard. At least a dozen men, most of them deserters from the Maryland regiments, were found in the British ranks by the American Commissary of Prisoners. They were tried by court-martial, and a few who were able to prove that they had never joined the American army, but had enlisted directly from civilian life, were released as prisoners of war. The others were convicted of desertion and hanged. The grim and precise justice with which the Americans distinguished between the deserter and the loyalist volunteer made a great impression on the watching French.

Washington's victory despatch to the President of Congress was utterly lacking in pyrotechnics. He let young Jonathan Trumbull, Jr., prepare it, and to his most faithful aide, Tench Tilghman, he gave the honor of bearing it to Congress. But Congress had the news two days before Tilghman arrived. On October 22, a messenger came thundering into town at 2 A.M. with the news from Governor Thomas Simms Lee of Maryland. Admiral de Grasse, corresponding with him in connection with obtaining provisions from the fleet, enclosed the news of Cornwallis' first letter, asking for a truce, on the seventeenth. Lee had made a copy of it, and ordered messengers to forward it night and day until it reached Philadelphia.

A newspaper story the following day tells how "An honest old German, a watchman of Philadelphia, having conducted the express rider to the door of his Excellency, the President of Congress . . . continued the duties of his office, calling out, 'Basht dree o'glock, und Cornal-lis isth da-ken!' "

When Tilghman arrived, two days later (the boat carrying him up the Chesapeake ran aground, and he lost a whole day), Congress had the pleasure of reading the entire story of the surrender in Washington's dispatch. Perhaps nothing symbolized the narrowness of the margin between victory and catastrophe better than what happened next. Colonel Tilghman was out of funds, like everyone else in the army, and asked Congress for a draft of money to pay for the expenses of his trip. Congress hemmed and collectively hawed. They could not do it. There was not one dollar in the national treasury. Finally, each member of Congress contributed a dollar in hard money out of his own pocket, and the messenger of victory from Yorktown was saved from arrest for debt.

At about the same time, off the capes of Virginia, a small boat containing three men came alongside the British flagship *London*. In it were a white man and two Negroes. They told Admiral Graves that they had left Yorktown on Thursday the eighteenth because the place was being surrendered. For five more days Graves and Clinton cruised off the mouth of the Chesapeake. The grim news of the first messengers was confirmed by loyalist refugees who came out to the fleet in small boats. It was over. The finest army Great Britain had in America was gone.

Admiral de Grasse made no move to come out of the Chesapeake. True to French strategy, he had no interest in fighting fleet to fleet—especially since his ulterior purpose was now triumphantly secured. To the surprise of no one, Admiral Graves had not the slightest desire to go into the bay and make him fight. So, on October 29, the English ships swung about and made for New York.

Waiting for Clinton at Sandy Hook was Cornwallis' letter reporting the surrender. With the most neutral phrasing, it could not have made very pleasant reading, but Clinton, a past master at innuendo, saw at a glance that Cornwallis was blaming the entire disaster on him:

> Sir: I have the mortification to inform your Excellency that I have been forced to give up the posts of York and Gloucester, and to surrender the troops under my command by capitulation on the 19th inst. as prisoners of war to the combined forces of America and France.
>
> I never saw this post in a favorable light but when I found I was to be attacked in it in so unprepared a state, by so powerful an army and artillery, nothing but the hopes of relief would have induced me to attempt its defence; for I

would have either have endeavoured to escape to New York by rapid marches from the Gloucester side, immediately on the arrival of General Washington's troops at Williamsburgh, or I would notwithstanding the disparity of numbers have attacked them in the open field, where it might have been just possible that fortune would have favoured the gallantry of the handful of troops under my command; but being assured by your Excellency's letters that every possible means would be tried by the navy and army to relieve us, I could not think myself at liberty to venture upon either of these two desperate attempts. . . .

The rest was a long narrative of the siege, in which Cornwallis was generous with his praise for the courage and endurance of his men. When the Earl arrived in New York on November 16, he and Sir Henry exchanged some very warm words. Soon after they both returned to England, where they opened a pamphlet war in which Sir Henry tried to prove that he had done everything right and Cornwallis had done everything wrong. He eventually wrote a 575-page book on his campaigns in America, the last part of which was devoted to proving this point all over again. But he was really wasting his time. Although the King received him graciously enough when he came home, Clinton never was given another command in the field, and Yorktown became his final military effort.

For Washington, Yorktown led directly to a personal tragedy. He left his camp headquarters on November 4 to ride to Mount Vernon, and on November 5, stopped at Eltham, where he assumed Jacky Custis was recuperating from his fever. He arrived just in time to find Martha and Jacky's wife, Eleanor, in hysterics. Dr. Craik had done everything in his power, but Jacky was dying. At dawn the following day he was dead, and Washington was left to cope with the two weeping women, the arrangements for the funeral, and the problems of the young widow and her four small children.

Eventually he adopted the two youngest, Nelly and George Washington Custis.

As for Washington the general, Yorktown was by no means the end of his war. For two more years he was to sit in his headquarters outside New York, struggling with the familiar problems of feeding the army, holding back its mutinous impulses, and otherwise keeping the Revolution alive while the diplomats dickered endlessly in Paris. Fortunately, he did not have to worry about the British army inside New York. On April 4, 1782, Sir Henry Clinton was relieved by Sir Guy Carleton, who was under orders to make no hostile moves. Once the signatures were affixed to the treaty of peace, and men had time to look back, there was no doubt that York- town was the trump card which broke the British will to win and enabled Benjamin Franklin and his fellow American ne- gotiators to insist on independence.

Aside from momentary chagrin, Yorktown did no harm whatsoever to the career of Charles Cornwallis. After this one defeat, he went on from glory to glory. He fought two vic- torious campaigns as commander in chief in India, by which he secured the power of the British raj for 150 years, and as Lord Lieutenant of Ireland he suppressed the revolt of 1798 with a ruthlessness and efficiency which undoubtedly made Americans glad he had never won the chief command in their rebellion. He went out to India again in 1805 to assume supreme command and died enroute to his troops, near Ghazipur.

As for Admiral Graves, he too never received a breath of censure from the government for his conduct of the navy dur- ing the Yorktown campaign, but he was never again given an independent command. He had the good fortune, how- ever, to be second in command under Lord Richard Howe on the glorious first of June, 1794, when the British shattered the French revolutionary fleet, and the grateful government made Graves a lord for the achievements of that day.

He was far more fortunate than the naval hero of York-town, Admiral de Grasse. De Grasse sailed immediately after the surrender to participate with the Spanish in a campaign to capture the island of Jamaica, England's major bastion in the West Indies. But before the allied troops could assemble, Sir George Rodney returned from England, his health restored, and took over command of the West Indies fleet. With Sir Samuel Hood as his fighting second in command, Rodney caught De Grasse off the Saints Islands on April 9, 1782, little more than five months after Yorktown, and utterly smashed his fleet and with it, France's reawakening dreams of power in the New World. Captain William Cornwallis had the satisfaction of commanding the battleship which was instrumental in capturing De Grasse's flagship, the *Ville de Paris*. Six other French ships were also captured and more might have been had for the taking, if Rodney had followed up his victory. De Grasse was denounced in France for the defeat, which all but annulled the advantage gained at Yorktown, as far as the French were concerned. So the man who, as much as anyone else, made Yorktown possible, lived his last years in disgrace.

Many other Frenchmen at Yorktown played dramatic roles in the Revolution which convulsed France eight years later. Lafayette and Rochambeau at one time both commanded revolutionary armies, but neither was able to control the far more complex and bloody upheaval which the French Revolution became. Rochambeau was eventually arrested by the wild-eyed politicians of the Terror, and came within a day of losing his head on the guillotine. Lafayette lasted a little longer, but eventually lost his footing on the edge of the volcano and spent almost a decade in prison. He had the consolation of outliving almost everyone, however, and returned to the United States for a triumphant tour in 1824. One of the most touching scenes was his meeting in Providence, R.I., with Captain Stephen Olney, who had led "his Americans" in the storming of redoubt number ten.

The Marquis de La Rouërie, so devoutly Republican while fighting with the Americans, chose the Royalist side in the French Revolution, and for a while led an army in northern France with considerable success. But friends betrayed him, his army was shattered, and he died of exhaustion at the château of a friend, a ruined, beaten fugitive. On the other hand, that nonpareil of nobility, the Duc de Lauzun, chose the Revolutionists (supposedly at the urging of Madame de Coigny), and for a while he fought nobly and well in their behalf. But he was accused by the politicians of being too lenient with his prisoners, and placed under arrest. His noble birth made him suspect, and he did not even attempt to defend himself. "If they want my head," he said, "let them have it." His executioners found him in his cell on the morning of his death dining on oysters and white wine. "Citizen," he said, "allow me to finish." Then, with a typical flourish he held out a glass to his murderer. "Take this wine," he said. "You must need courage in your profession."

John Laurens was another romantic hero who died unfortunately. In 1782 he was commanding American troops on the outskirts of his native Charleston. Part of his job was to prevent British foraging parties from looting the countryside. In a trifling skirmish with one of these groups only a few weeks before the British quit the city—it was almost the last hostile exchange of the war—the American Bayard was killed instantly by a bullet through the heart. Many think he would have shone brighter than Hamilton if he had been spared.

Banastre Tarleton became a Member of Parliament, and the lover of Perdita, otherwise known as Mrs. Robinson, the most beautiful English actress of her day. Ironically, she had previously enjoyed a memorable meeting with the Duc de Lauzun.

Among the French, Baron de Viomenil died at the head of the Swiss Guards defending his King against the assault of the Parisian mob. Count Axel Fersen was the originator of the daring rescue operation which almost succeeded in snatching Louis XVI and Marie Antoinette from the executioners. Comte William de Deux-Ponts won distinction fighting throughout Europe for Napoleon, and died a general in the battle of Leipzig.

Many other minor characters achieved more than a little individual fame. On the British side, Colonel Robert Abercromby won a galaxy of honors as British Commander in Chief in India, succeeding Cornwallis. Our dashing Lieutenant James died in bed, an admiral, rich on prize money from several daring voyages during the Napoleonic wars. Captain Samuel Graham became a general, and so did Lieutenant Samaurez, of the Twenty-third Regiment, who so ably defended the Fusileers redoubt.

The news of Cornwallis' surrender did not reach England until November 25. By then the city of London had already lived through nine days of agonizing suspense; on the sixteenth the frigate *Lively* had arrived with news that Cornwallis was trapped, and the fleet and army were about to sail to his relief. On the evening of the twenty-fifth, a Sunday, Captain Melcome, commander of His Majesty's sloop *Rattlesnake,* a captured American privateer, appeared outside the Admiralty office with fresh dispatches from America. They were from Admiral Graves, and had been written off the Virginia capes, reporting the melancholy information just learned from the various small boats which had reached them from shore.

The bad news was immediately sent to Lord George Germain, and on him, fittingly enough, fell the unpleasant responsibility of communicating it to the prime minister, Lord North. At ten o'clock on the morning of the twenty-sixth, Lord George drove to 10 Downing Street and made the doleful report to his superior. They both knew what it meant. Parliament was to meet the following day, and the opponents of the ministry had been hoping and praying for a setback in America to pry loose the independent country squires from their blind support of the King and his ruinous policy.

"Oh God," Lord North said, pacing up and down his apartment. "Oh God. It is all over. It is all over."

And so it was.

✪ APPENDIX

Articles of Capitulation

ARTICLE I

The garrisons of York and Gloucester, including the officers and seamen of his Britannic Majesty's ships, as well as other mariners, to surrender themselves prisoners of war to the combined forces of America and France. The land troops to remain prisoners to the United States—the navy to the naval army of his Most Christian Majesty.

"Granted."

ARTICLE II

The artillery, arms, accoutrements, military chest and public stores of every denomination, shall be delivered unimpaired to the heads of departments appointed to receive them.

"Granted."

ARTICLE III

At twelve o'clock this day the two redoubts on the left flank of York to be delivered, the one to a detachment of American infantry, the other to a detachment of French grenadiers. The garrison of York will march out to a place to be appointed in front of the posts at two o'clock precisely with shouldered arms, colours cased and drums beating a British or German march. They are then to ground their arms and return to their encampments, where they will remain until they are dispatched to the places of their destination. Two works on the Gloucester side will be delivered at one o'clock to a detachment of French and American troops appointed to possess them. The garrisons will march out at three o'clock in the afternoon, the cavalry with their swords drawn, trumpets sounding and the infantry in the manner prescribed for the garrison of York. They are likewise to return to their encampments until they can be finally marched off.

"Granted."

ARTICLE IV

Officers are to retain their side-arms. Both officers and soldiers to keep their private property of every kind; and no part of their baggage or papers be at any time subject to search or inspection. The baggage and papers of officers and soldiers taken during the siege to be likewise preserved for them.

"Granted." To this Washington added: "It is understood that property obviously belonging to the inhabitants of these States in the possession of the garrison shall be subject to be reclaimed."

ARTICLE V

The soldiers to be kept in Virginia, Maryland or Pennsylvania, and as much by regiments as possible and supplied with the same rations of provisions as are allowed to soldiers in the service of America. A field officer from each nation, to wit, British, Anspach and Hessian, and other officers on parole, in the proportion of one to fifty men, to be allowed to reside near their respective regiments, to visit them frequently and be witnesses of their treatment and that their officers may receive and deliver cloathing and other necessaries for them, for which passports are to be granted when applied for.

"Granted."

ARTICLE VI

The General, Staff, and other officers not employed as mentioned in the above articles, and who choose it, to be permitted to go on parole to Europe, to New York, and to any other American maritime ports at present in the possession of the British forces, at their own option, and proper vessels to be granted by the Count de Grasse to carry them under flags of truce to New York within ten days from this date, if possible, and they to reside in a district to be agreed upon hereafter, until they embark. The officers of the civil department of the army and navy to be included in this article. Passports to go by land to be granted to those to whom vessels cannot be furnished.

"Granted."

ARTICLE VII

Officers to be allowed to keep soldiers as servants according to the common practice of the service. Servants not soldiers are not to be considered prisoners, and are to be allowed to attend their masters.

"Granted."

ARTICLE VIII

The Bonetta sloop of war to be equipped and navigated by its present Captain and crew, and left entirely at the disposal of Lord Cornwallis from the hour that the capitulation is signed, to receive an Aid de Camp to carry dispatches to Sir Henry Clinton; and such soldiers as he may think proper to send to New-York, to be permitted to sail without examination. When his dispatches are ready, his Lordship engages on his part that the ship shall be delivered to the order of the Count de Grasse, if she escapes the dangers of the sea. That she shall not carry off any public stores. Any part of the crew that may be deficient on her return and the soldiers passengers to be accounted for on her delivery.

"Granted."

ARTICLE IX

The traders are to preserve their property and to be allowed three months to dispose of or remove them. And those traders are not to be considered as prisoners of war.

"The traders," Washington wrote, "will be allowed to dispose of their effects. The allied army having the right of pre-emption. The traders to be considered as prisoners of war upon parole."

ARTICLE X

Natives or inhabitants of different parts of this country at present in York or Gloucester are not to be punished on account of having joined the British army.

"This article cannot be assented to," Washington wrote, "being altogether of civil resort."

ARTICLE XI

Proper hospitals to be furnished for the sick and wounded. They are to be attended by their own surgeons on parole; and they are to be furnished with medicines and stores from the American hospitals.

"The hospital stores now in York and Gloucester shall be delivered for the use of the British sick and wounded. Passports will be granted for procuring them further supplies from New-York as occasion may require; and proper hospitals will be furnished for the reception of the sick and wounded of the two garrisons."

ARTICLE XII

Waggons to be furnished to carry the baggage of the officers attending the soldiers, and to surgeons when travelling on account of the sick attending the hospitals at public expence.

"They are to be furnished if possible."

ARTICLE XIII

The shipping and boats in the two harbours, with all their stores, guns, tackling and apparel, shall be delivered up in their present state to an officer of the navy appointed to take possession of them, previously unloading the private property, part of which had been put on board for security during the siege.

"Granted."

ARTICLE XIV

No article of capitulation to be infringed on pretence of reprisals; and if there be any doubtful expressions in it, they are to be interpreted according to the common meaning and acceptation of the words.

"Granted."

✪ SOURCES AND METHODS

In my previous book, *Now We Are Enemies,* I invented a very small amount of dialogue to augment the realism. That has not been necessary for the story of Yorktown, which has far richer source material and is illuminated by so many strong personalities. Otherwise I have followed the basic technique evolved in *Now We Are Enemies*—treating British and Americans as equally interesting and equally in need of explanation and understanding. To eliminate the necessity for cumbersome notes, I have woven into the text itself a fairly comprehensive indication of my primary sources. However, for those who are stimulated to read further, the following comments on the sources for individual chapters may be of assistance and interest.

CHAPTER I

The story of the second mutiny of the Pennsylvania Line is based on Wayne's letter (to an unknown correspondent) which is in the

Bancroft transcripts at the New York Public Library. There has been some dispute about the date of the event. Wayne, writing three weeks later, referred to it as the day before the Line marched to Virginia. But other sources, such as the court martial records, indicate it may have happened a few days earlier. The number of men executed is also uncertain; some witnesses say six, others count as many as eleven. This much is certain: there was an attempted mutiny, and Wayne put it down with the ruthless severity described. In the section on Laurens, his exchange with Vergennes is the recollection of William Jackson when he was an old man, and may be somewhat over-dramatized. The remainder of the chapter will undoubtedly startle those who have accepted the myth that it was Lafayette who maneuvered Cornwallis into the trap at Yorktown. The Marquis gives us this impression in his memoirs, written almost fifty years later. But his contemporaneous letters, and the accounts of others, including British eyewitnesses, tell a different story.

CHAPTER II

The acrimony between Cornwallis and Clinton is drawn largely from Benjamin F. Stevens' compilation, *The Campaign in Virginia in 1781,* which is perhaps the most thoroughly cross-referenced history book ever published. All the correspondence between the two generals, as well as Clinton's notes on the correspondence (made when it was published in England), and the pamphlet war conducted by Clinton and Cornwallis partisans after Yorktown, with Clinton's notes again appended, are contained in these two volumes. Also helpful is the *Correspondence of Charles Cornwallis,* edited by Charles Ross, son of his old aide. Cornwallis' letters give a far different view of his personality than the traditional one most Americans have obtained from tracts (and TV programs) denouncing him as an arrogant monster. Lafayette added to the portrait in his memoirs by reporting that Cornwallis said: "The boy cannot escape me," while he pursued the Marquis around Virginia. There is no evidence that Cornwallis ever made such a statement. In his several letters to Lafayette, in regard to such matters as flags of truce, Cornwallis was the model of politeness. For insights into Clinton's personality I am indebted to William Wilcox, Professor of History at the University of Michigan, whose introduction to Clinton's narrative, *The American Rebellion,* is a masterful estimate of this strange commander. Clinton's book is also strongly recommended to those who would like a deeper insight into the British side of the Revolution.

CHAPTER III

The portrait of Rochambeau may perhaps need a small reservation. His generosity and tact in dealing with the Americans were genuine and remarkable, but those on his staff often complained of his bad temper. Commissary Blanchard, in particular, had a number of collisions with Rochambeau, and Chastellux seems to have actively disliked him. Rochambeau's paternalism won the loyalty and enthusiasm of the enlisted men, but seems to have galled his officers. Information on the French Royal Army, a comparatively neglected subject in English historical writing, is from an article by General Tyrell in the *United Service Magazine,* London, 1898. Most of the quotations from French officers about Washington and the American army are from journals, and can be found in the bibliography under the individual's name. Almost every French officer kept a journal; at least it seemed that way at times to the weary researcher. Militarily, the two best are those by Baron von Closen and William de Deux-Ponts. Abbé Robin's and Commissary Blanchard's are also excellent, and give many details and sidelights of the French stay in America which I was forced to omit.

CHAPTER IV

I have tried to strike a balance between the views of Douglas Southall Freeman on the decision to march to Yorktown, and those of other writers, such as Rupert Hughes, who suggest Washington was all but carried south a protesting captive. Freeman seems to place too much dependence on plans Washington made to move troops south before the news of De Grasse's arrival. An examination of the orders indicates, to me, that these were to be no more than a detachment, to bolster Lafayette. Desandrouins' journal is not the best historical document; there is not much internal evidence that he actually wrote it on the spot; it was found years later. But the strong assertion in the journal of Rochambeau's son that it was necessary to "fool" Washington is significant. However, the Vicomte's choice of words is certainly too strong. Once Washington decided to march, he was in masterful command of the situation. Nor does young Rochambeau's reasoning on Washington's reluctance stand up: "General Washington had his reason for attacking New York—he was to be in command of this attack himself, while he disliked the march on the South because he feared that General Rochambeau would want to attribute to himself alone the glory of a victory which the French general could win without Washington." Washington had demonstrated a hundred times that he was far more interested in winning the war than he was in furthering his personal reputation. Witness his treatment of difficult officers, such as Hamilton.

CHAPTER V

Hood's letters are the invaluable basic source for the sea battle of September 9. The Graves Papers are also useful, as well as *Naval Researches* by Captain Thomas White, another eyewitness. Some writers have attempted to picture Graves as a victim of the general British inadequacy in the signaling department. But it is hard to accept this as the explanation for the timid, inconclusive battle he fought. White's book is interesting for the insight it gives into the purely naval mind. He maintained that Graves might have blundered with the signals, but neither he nor the fleet could be blamed for failing to beat De Grasse back to the Chesapeake and rescue Cornwallis, since this was not their responsibility. Only Hood seemed capable of thinking of the war as a united effort.

CHAPTER VI

Most of the sources for this chapter are indicated in the text. The compilation of Washington's correspondence with De Grasse, published under the title *Correspondence of General Washington and Comte de Grasse,* gives a compact glimpse of the diplomatic problems Washington faced in dealing with the impatient Provençal. It includes a transcript of the vital interview aboard the *Ville de Paris.* The story of De Grasse calling Washington *"petit"* is from George Washington Parke Custis' reminiscences of his famous step-grandfather, admittedly not the most reliable source. If any laughing was done, it surely must have been much later. The adventures of Joseph Plumb Martin, the GI Joe of the Revolution, have been republished recently under the title, *Private Yankee Doodle,* with helpful notes and an introduction by George F. Scheer.

CHAPTER VII

Again, the letters of Cornwallis and Stevens' book tell us much about Yorktown during September. Tarleton is the one authority for the proposed attack on Williamsburg. Clinton in one of his innumerable notes also says Tarleton told him of the weakness of the French West Indian troops in private conversation, after they both were back in London. The journal of Bartholomew James, probably the most engaging British memoir of the Revolution, has some internal indications of being compiled after Yorktown, probably from jottings made at the time. James has a tendency to exaggerate, as all good story tellers do, but the records show that he was at Yorktown, and if we subtract a few embellishments, he undoubtedly had the adventures he recounts.

CHAPTER VIII

For the description of the cavalry fight between Lauzun and Tarleton, I have relied largely on the version given by Light Horse Harry Lee, who was at Yorktown at the time and may have been an eyewitness. As I indicate in the text, Lauzun's memoirs are not reliable. They were edited by a ghost writer after his death, and no one knows how many words were put into his mouth.

CHAPTER IX

William Smith's unpublished diary, in the New York Public Library, is an invaluable source for the situation in New York during the Yorktown crisis. Likewise the diary of Captain Frederick MacKenzie, of the Royal Welsh Fusileers, on detached duty as deputy adjutant general. The minutes of the various councils of war are from the *Clinton Papers*, at the William L. Clements Library, University of Michigan. I would like to acknowledge the generous cooperation of Howard H. Peckham, director of the library, in supplying me with photostats of this material.

CHAPTER X

Again, most of the source material is from individual journals and diaries, indicated in the text, and easily found in the bibliography. The anecdote of Steuben's exchange with General de Viomenil is from a letter written by the Baron, and quoted in *Kapp's Steuben*, 457-8, and in Freeman's *George Washington*. The anecdote of Lafayette's exchange with Governor Thomas Nelson about firing on his house is from Custis' memoirs of Washington. It is so much in the character of Nelson, who bankrupted himself by signing notes on his own credit to provide supplies for the Revolutionary army during the Yorktown campaign, that I have let it stand. No one agrees on the precise number of allied guns firing at any one time. Freeman, in *George Washington*, frankly gives up trying to get an exact figure, and I have done likewise. Every diary differs.

CHAPTER XI

The story of the dinner ruined by a cannon ball is from the memoirs of Captain Samuel Graham, of the Seventy-sixth Regiment. The Americans vowed it was the first ball fired, by Washington himself, but this is not certain. The anecdote of the two officers killed by the American night fighters is from Bartholomew James, but he puts the officers in the Forty-third Regiment. According to the British returns, this regiment did not lose two lieutenants. I have let the story stand, on the supposition that James, a naval man, was not likely to be too clear about regimental connections. Several lieutenants from other regiments do appear in the British casualty lists. James also seems to have exaggerated the casualties of his gunners during his heroic tour of duty at the battery, if the British report on over-all naval casualties is accurate. However, some of his men may have been recruits from the merchant seamen, and hence not counted in the final official reckoning.

CHAPTER XII

The main sources for the assaults on redoubts nine and ten are Deux-Ponts' journal, Joseph Plumb Martin's narrative, and Olney's account, which is contained in Stone's *Our French Allies.* This rather odd and disorganized book has some original material on Yorktown not available elsewhere. The amusing anecdote about Hamilton and Knox and their impromptu wrestling match is from an eyewitness account by Dr. Eneas Munson of Connecticut.

CHAPTER XIII

The description of the storm which upset the British sailing schedule in New York is from MacKenzie's diary. Tarleton is the best authority for the last gasp attempt to break out of the Yorktown trap, although Cornwallis' long dispatch to Clinton (in *Correspondence of Charles Cornwallis*) reporting on the siege after the surrender, adds a few helpful details. British narratives of their sortie two nights before the final surrender are scanty and confusing. I have had to reconstruct the action from their point of view. The amazing laxity of the French and American guards has seldom received any comment, in the over-all glow of the Yorktown victory.

CHAPTER XIV

The sources for most of this chapter are obvious and indicated. The exchange between Laurens and Ross over the "harsh article" refusing to permit the honors of war is from Thomas Balch's *Letters and Papers Relating Chiefly to the Provincial History of Pennsylvania.*

CHAPTER XV

Just what the British band played at the surrender ceremony is a matter of considerable dispute. Alexander Garden's *Anecdotes of the Revolution,* published in 1828, is the first to make the specific claim for "The World Turned Upside Down." But we do know from eyewitness letters that the music came from full regimental bands, and not merely from drums. One letter refers to the music as "Not military marches, but of certain airs, which had in them so peculiar a strain of melancholy." Johann Doehla specifically refers to a "band" playing. "The World Turned Upside Down" is one version of an old folk tune, which had many other verses written to it, one being called "When the King Enjoys His Own Again." Various authorities on the music of the Revolution have identified the tune as being quite popular at the time—and it is a very melancholy air. It is not necessary to believe the British were abasing themselves by playing it. There may have been many other sets of words to the music, now lost. But Americans seized on the "Upside Down" version because it so exactly fitted their view of the event. The story of Admiral Barras' sinking horse is from Von Closen's diary. I have omitted the story of O'Hara proffering his sword to Washington, and the latter refusing it, saying "Not from so good a hand." Comte Mathieu Dumas' memoirs are the only authority for this attempt to give up a weapon which the articles of surrender had specifically stated the British general could keep. No American eyewitness mentions it. Elias Budinot is the authority for Congress dredging up a dollar each to pay for Tilghman's victory dispatch expenses. The story of Lord North's reaction to the news of York-town is from Nathaniel W. Wraxhall's *Memoirs*. It was not, of course, immediately "all over." The opposition took another four months to bring the ministry down. On March 5, 1782, Parlia-ment passed a bill authorizing the government to make peace with America. North resigned on March 20.

✪ SELECT BIBLIOGRAPHY

PRIMARY SOURCES

d'Acteville, Chevalier; *Campagne de la Chesapeake* (*Journal of the Chesapeake Campaign*); Archives Nationales. Transcript copy Colonial National Historical Park; 1931

Anonymous; "Siege of York and Gloucester, Virginia"; *Magazine of American History,* VII, No. 3 (September, 1881)

Beatty, Joseph M., Jr., contributor; "Letters from Continental Officers to Doctor Reading Beatty, 1781-1788"; *Pennsylvania Magazine of History and Biography,* LIV, No. 1 (April, 1930)

Blanchard, Claude; *Journal of;* Thomas Balch, editor; Albany, 1876

Boudinot, Elias; *Historical Recollections of;* Philadelphia, 1894

Burnham, Major John; "Personal Recollections of the Revolutionary War"; *Magazine of History,* XIX (1917)

Butler, Colonel Richard; "Continental Line. Fifth Pennsylvania,

Jan. 1, 1777-Jan. 1, 1783"; *Pennsylvania Archives,* Fifth Series, III (1906)

Chastellux (François Jean) Marquis de; *Travels in North America;* London, 1787 (also later editions)

Clinton, Sir Henry; *The American Rebellion;* edited by William B. Willcox; New Haven, 1954

Closen, Baron Ludwig von; *The Revolutionary Journal of Baron Ludwig von Closen;* translated and edited by Evelyn M. Acomb. Chapel Hill, N. C., 1958

Cobb, Lieutenant-Colonel David; "Before York-Town, Virginia, October 1-November 30, 1781"; *Proceedings of the Massachusetts Historical Society,* XIX, (1881-1882)

Cochrane, Charles; Memorial; *Massachusetts Historical Society Proceedings,* Ser. 2, Vol. 6, 1890-1

Cornwallis, Charles, First Marquis; *Correspondence of;* Charles Ross, editor; London, 1859

Cromot du Bourg, Marie François Joseph Maxime, Baron; "Diary of a French Officer 1781 (Presumed to be that of Baron Cromot du Bourg, Aid to Rochambeau)"; *Magazine of American History,* IV, Nos. 3-6 (March-June, 1880), VII, No. 4 (October, 1881)

Davis, Captain John; "The Yorktown Campaign"; *Pennsylvania Magazine of History and Biography,* V, (1881)

Dearborn, Henry; *Journals of;* Lloyd A. Brown and Howard H. Peckham, editors; Chicago, 1939

Denny, Major Ebenezer; *A Military Journal;* Philadelphia, 1860

de Deux-Ponts, Count William; *My Campaigns in America;* Boston, 1868

Doehla, Johann Conrad; *Tagebuch eines Bayreuther Soldaten, des Johann Conrad Dohla aus dem Nordamerikanischen Freiheitskrieg von 1777 bis 1783;* Bayreuth, 1913. Translation of Yorktown section by Robert J. Tilden, 1941

Dumas, Mathieu, Lieut.-Gen. Count; *Memoirs of his own Time;* London, 1839

Duncan, Captain James; "Diary of Captain James Duncan, of Colonel Moses Hazen's Regiment, in the Yorktown Campaign, 1781"; *Pennsylvania Archives,* Second Series, XV, (1890)

Evans, Chaplain; "Journal of the Siege of York in Virginia by a Chaplain of the American Army"; *Collections of the Massachusetts Historical Society,* First Series, IX, (1804)

Feltman, Lieutenant Williams; "The Journal of Lieut. William Feltman, of the First Pennsylvania Regiment, from May 26, 1781 to April 25, 1782, embracing the Siege of Yorktown and the Southern Campaign"; *Pennsylvania Historical Society Collections,* I, No. 5 (May, 1853)

Fersen, Count Axel de; "Letters of de Fersen Aid-de-Camp to Rochambeau, Written to His Father in Sweden, 1781-1782"; *Magazine of American History,* III (May-July, 1879)

French Engineers: "Journal of the Siege of York in Virginia (Engineers)"; *Magazine of American History,* IV, No. 6 (June, 1880)

de Gallatin, Gaspard; *Journal of;* Washington, 1931

Graham, Samuel; *Memoirs of;* Edinburgh, 1862

de Grasse, Count; *The Operations of the French Fleet under Count de Grasse in 1781-2;* Two contemporaneous journals; New York, 1864

Graves, Thomas; *The Graves Papers and other Documents relating to the Naval Operations of the Yorktown Campaign;* French E. Chadwick, editor; New York, 1916

Graves, William; *Two Letters from W. Graves, Esq., Respecting the Conduct of Rear Admiral Graves in North America;* London, 1783 (Reprint: New York, 1865)

Hamilton, Alexander; *The Papers of;* Vol. II, 1179-1780, Harold C. Syrett, editor; New York, 1961

Harper, Lillie DuPuy; *Colonial Men and Times, Containing the Journal of Colonel Daniel Trabue;* Philadelphia, 1916

Hood, Sir Samuel; *Letters of;* David Hannay, editor; London, 1895

Huntington, Ebenezer; *Letters of;* New York, 1915

Irvine, General William; Papers of; MS Philadelphia

James, Rear Admiral Bartholemew; *Journal of;* London, 1896

Krafft, J. C. P. von; "Journal of Lieutenant J. C. P. von Krafft, 1778-1784"; *New York Historical Society Collections,* XV, (1882)

Lafayette, Marquis de; *The Memoirs, Correspondence and Manu-*

scripts of; Published by his family; London and New York, 1837

Lafayette, Marquis de; *Letters of Lafayette to Washington;* Louis Gottschalk, editor; New York

Lamb, R.; *Journal and Occurrences of the late American War;* Dublin, 1809

Laurens, John; "The Diary of Col. John Laurens (Yorktown)"; *Collector,* XV, (1902)

Lauzun, Armand Louis de Gontaut, Duc de; *Memoirs of;* New York, 1928

Lee, Henry; *Memoirs of;* New York, 1870

MacKenzie, Frederick; *Diary of;* Vol. II; Cambridge, 1930

Martin, Joseph Plumb; *Private Yankee Doodle;* George E. Scheer, editor; Boston, 1962

McClellan, Captain Joseph; *Journals of Captain Joseph McClellan and Lt. William Feltman; Pennsylvania Archives,* Second Series, Vol. XI

McDowell, William; "Journal of Lieut. William McDowell"; *Pennsylvania Archives,* Second Series, XV, (1893)

Moore, Frank; *Diary of the American Revolution;* New York, 1860

Munson, Dr. Eneas; "Siege of Yorktown, 1781" in Benson J. Lossing, *Hours with Living Men and Women of the Revolution;* New York, 1889

Ogden, Aaron; "Autobiography of Col. Aaron Ogden"; *New Jersey Historical Proceedings,* Second Series, XII (1892-1893)

Pennsylvania Line; "Diary of the Pennsylvania Line, May 25, 1781-April 25, 1782"; *Pennsylvania in the War of the Revolution, Battalion and Line, 1775-1783;* Vol. 2; Harrisburg, 1880

Pontgibaud, Chevalier de; *A French Volunteer of the War of Independence;* New York, 1898

Popp, Stephan; *Diary of;* Philadelphia, 1902; Privately Printed, 1953

Queen's Rangers; "A Letter Regarding the Queen's Rangers"; *Virginia Magazine of History and Biography,* XXX, No. 4 (October, 1922)

Robin, Claude C.; *New Travels through North America;* Philadelphia, 1783

Rochambeau, Count de; *Memoirs of the Marshal Count de Rochambeau Relative to the War of Independence of the United States;* Paris, 1838

Simcoe, Lt. Col. J. G.; *Military Journal;* New York and Welford, 1844

Stevens, B. F. The Clinton Cornwallis Controversy: Two Vols. London, 1888

Thacher, James, M.D.; *A Military Journal during the American Revolutionary War;* Boston, 1827

Tilden, John Bell; "Extracts from the Journal of Lieutenant John Bell Tilden"; *Pennsylvania Magazine of History and Biography,* XIX, No. 1 (April, 1895)

Tornquist, Karl Gustaf; *The Naval Campaigns of Count de Grasse;* Philadelphia, 1942

Trumbull, Jonathan; "Yorktown, Virginia, Aug. 12-Nov. 5, 1781"; *Proceedings of the Massachusetts Historical Society,* XIV, (1875-1876)

Tucker, St. George; "Journal of the Siege of Yorktown"; *William & Mary Quarterly,* 3rd Series, 5, 1948

Van Cortlandt, Colonel Philip; "Autobiography of Philip Van Cortlandt, Brigadier-General in the Continental Army"; *Magazine of American History,* II, No. 5 (May, 1878)

Washington, George; *The Diaries of;* Vol. II, John C. Fitzpatrick, editor; Boston, 1925

Washington, George; *The Writings of;* Vol. 23, John C. Fitzpatrick, editor; Washington, 1937

Washington-de Grasse; *Correspondence of General Washington and Comte de Grasse, August 17-November 4, 1781;* Washington, 1931

Weelen, Jean-Edmond; *Rochambeau, Father and Son;* New York, 1936 (contains Journal of Vicomte de Rochambeau)

White, Captain Thomas; *Naval Researches or a Candid Inquiry into the Conduct of Admirals Bryon, Graves, Hood and Rodney;* London, 1830

Wild, Ebenezer; "Journal of Ebenezer Wild"; *Proceedings of the*

Massachusetts Historical Society, Second Series, VI (1800-1801)

SECONDARY SOURCES

Augur, Helen; *The Secret War of Independence;* New York, 1955

Balch, Thomas; *The French in America during the War of Independence of the United States;* Philadelphia, 1891-1895

Bates-Batcheller, Tryphosa; "Le Marquis de La Rouërie"; *Légion d'Honneur,* II, No. 2, Yorktown Number (October, 1931)

Bolton, Charles Knowles; *The Private Soldier Under Washington;* New York, 1902

Bowman, Allen; "The Morale of the American Revolutionary Army"; *American Council on Public Affairs;* Washington, 1943

Broughton Mainwairing, Major Rowland: Historical Record of the Royal Welch Fusileers; London, 1889

Callahan, North; *Henry Knox: General Washington's General;* New York, 1958

Chamberlain, Mellen; *Memorial of Captain Charles Cochrane, a British Officer in the Revolutionary War;* Cambridge, 1891

Chinard, Gilbert, editor; *George Washington as the French Knew Him;* Princeton, 1940

Christie, Ian R.; *The End of North's Ministry;* London, 1958

Claudel, Paul; "Yorktown et De Grasse"; *Légion d'Honneur,* II, No. 2, Yorktown Number (October, 1931)

Cobb, Samuel Crocker; *A Brief Memoir of General David Cobb, of the Revolutionary Army;* Privately printed, 1873

Coffin, Charles; *The Lives and Services of Major-General John Thomas, Colonel Thomas Knowlton, Colonel Alexander Scammell, Major-General Henry Dearborn;* New York, 1845

Coleman, Mary Haldane; *St. George Tucker, Citizen of No Mean City;* Richmond, 1938

Corwin, Edward S.; *French Policy and the American Alliance of 1778;* Princeton, 1916

Craik, Dr. James; "The Story of a Great Patriot, Dr. James Craik, Chief Physician and Surgeon of the Continental Army"; *Minute Man*, XXIII, No. 3 (January, 1929)

Curtis, Edward E.; *Organization of the British Army in the American Revolution;* New Haven, 1926

Dillon, Count; "All the Brothers Were Valiant"; *Légion d'Honneur*, IV, (1933)

Freeman, Douglas Southall; *George Washington*, Vol. 5: *Victory with the Help of France;* New York, 1952

Gay de Vernon, Simon Francois Baron; *A Treatise on the Science of War and Fortification;* New York, 1817

Guttridge, George H.; "Lord George Germain in Office, 1775-1782"; *American Historical Review*, XXXIII, No. 1 (October, 1927)

Harrell, Isaac S.; *Loyalism in Virginia;* Philadelphia, 1926

Hughes, R.; *George Washington;* New York, 1930

James, Rear-Admiral W. M., C.B., R.N.; *The British Navy in Adversity;* London and New York, 1933

Johnston, Henry P.; *The Yorktown Campaign and the Surrender of Cornwallis;* New York, 1881

Kimball, Leroy Elwood; "Fleury in the American Revolution"; *Légion d'Honneur*, VI, No. 1 (July, 1935)

Kite, Elizabeth S.; *Brigadier-General Louis Lebègue Duportail, Commandant of Engineers in the Continental Army, 1777-1783;* Baltimore, 1933

Knox, Dudley W.; *The Naval Genius of George Washington;* Boston, 1932

Lallemand, General H.; *A Treatise on Artillery;* New York, 1820

Landers, Colonel H. L.; *The Virginia Campaign and the Blockade and Siege of Yorktown;* Washington, 1931

Lewis, Charles Lee; *Admiral de Grasse and American Independence;* Annapolis, 1945

Lord, Arthur; "Alexander Scammell"; *Proceedings of the Massachusetts Historical Society*, LII (1919)

Lowell, Edward J.; *The Hessians and the other German Auxiliaries of Great Britain in the Revolutionary War;* New York, 1884

Lynah, Mary-Elizabeth; "John Laurens—Carolina's Romantic Contribution to the Revolutionary Ranks"; *Americana*, XXX (1936)

Mahan, Alfred T.; *The Major Operations of the Navies in the War of American Independence;* Boston, 1913

Marcus, G. J.; *A Naval History of England;* Boston, 1961

Palmer, John McCauley; *General von Steuben;* New Haven, 1937

Stille, Charles J.; *Major General Wayne and the Pennsylvania Line;* Philadelphia, 1893

Stone, Edward Martin; *Our French Allies;* Providence, 1884

Townsend, Sara B.; *An American Soldier—the Life of John Laurens;* Raleigh, N. C., 1958

Tyrrel, Lt. General; "French Army in the 18th Century"; *United Service Magazine,* April-Sept., 1898

Wilcox, William B.; "The British Road to Yorktown—A Study in Divided Command"; *The American Historical Review,* October, 1946

✪ INDEX

✪ ABOUT THE AUTHOR

Thomas J. Fleming is the author of *Now We Are Enemies,* a book on the battle of Bunker Hill which was chosen as a Literary Guild selection, and two novels, *All Good Men* and *The God of Love.* He has worked as a reporter on the *Yonkers Herald Statesman,* as assistant to the late Fulton Oursler of *The Reader's Digest,* and executive editor of *Cosmopolitan* magazine.

Mr. Fleming, who now devotes himself full-time to writing, lives with his wife and four children in New York City.

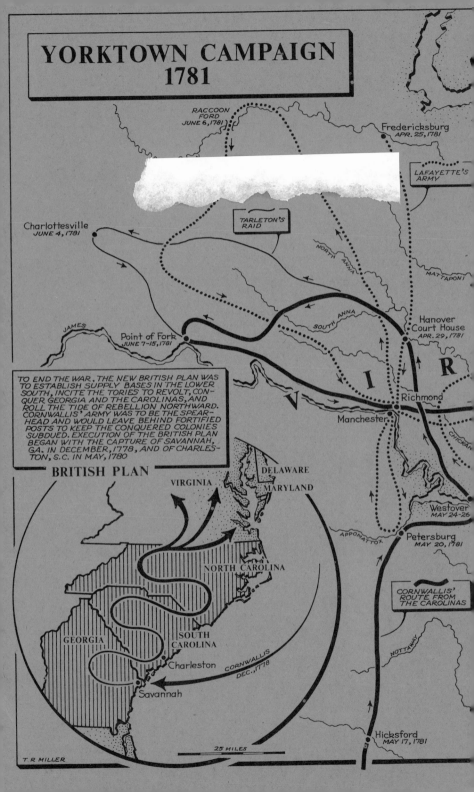

YORKTOWN CAMPAIGN 1781

RACCOON FORD
JUNE 6, 1781

Fredericksburg
APR. 25, 1781

LAFAYETTE'S ARMY

Charlottesville
JUNE 4, 1781

TARLETON'S RAID

NORTH ANNA

MATTAPONI

JAMES

Point of Fork
JUNE 7-15, 1781

SOUTH ANNA

Hanover Court House
APR. 29, 1781

I   R

TO END THE WAR, THE NEW BRITISH PLAN WAS TO ESTABLISH SUPPLY BASES IN THE LOWER SOUTH, INCITE THE TORIES TO REVOLT, CONQUER GEORGIA AND THE CAROLINAS, AND ROLL THE TIDE OF REBELLION NORTHWARD. CORNWALLIS' ARMY WAS TO BE THE SPEARHEAD AND WOULD LEAVE BEHIND FORTIFIED POSTS TO KEEP THE CONQUERED COLONIES SUBDUED. EXECUTION OF THE BRITISH PLAN BEGAN WITH THE CAPTURE OF SAVANNAH, GA. IN DECEMBER, 1778, AND OF CHARLESTON, S.C. IN MAY, 1780

Richmond

Manchester

CHICKA

BRITISH PLAN

VIRGINIA

DELAWARE

MARYLAND

NORTH CAROLINA

Westover
MAY 24-26

APPOMATTOX

Petersburg
MAY 20, 1781

CORNWALLIS' ROUTE FROM THE CAROLINAS

GEORGIA

SOUTH CAROLINA

Charleston

CORNWALLIS DEC., 1778

NOTTAWAY

Savannah

Hicksford
MAY 17, 1781

25 MILES

T. R. MILLER